# NATURALLY BAD MANNERS

A Comedy of Manners – Mostly Bad

By
Richard B. Carter

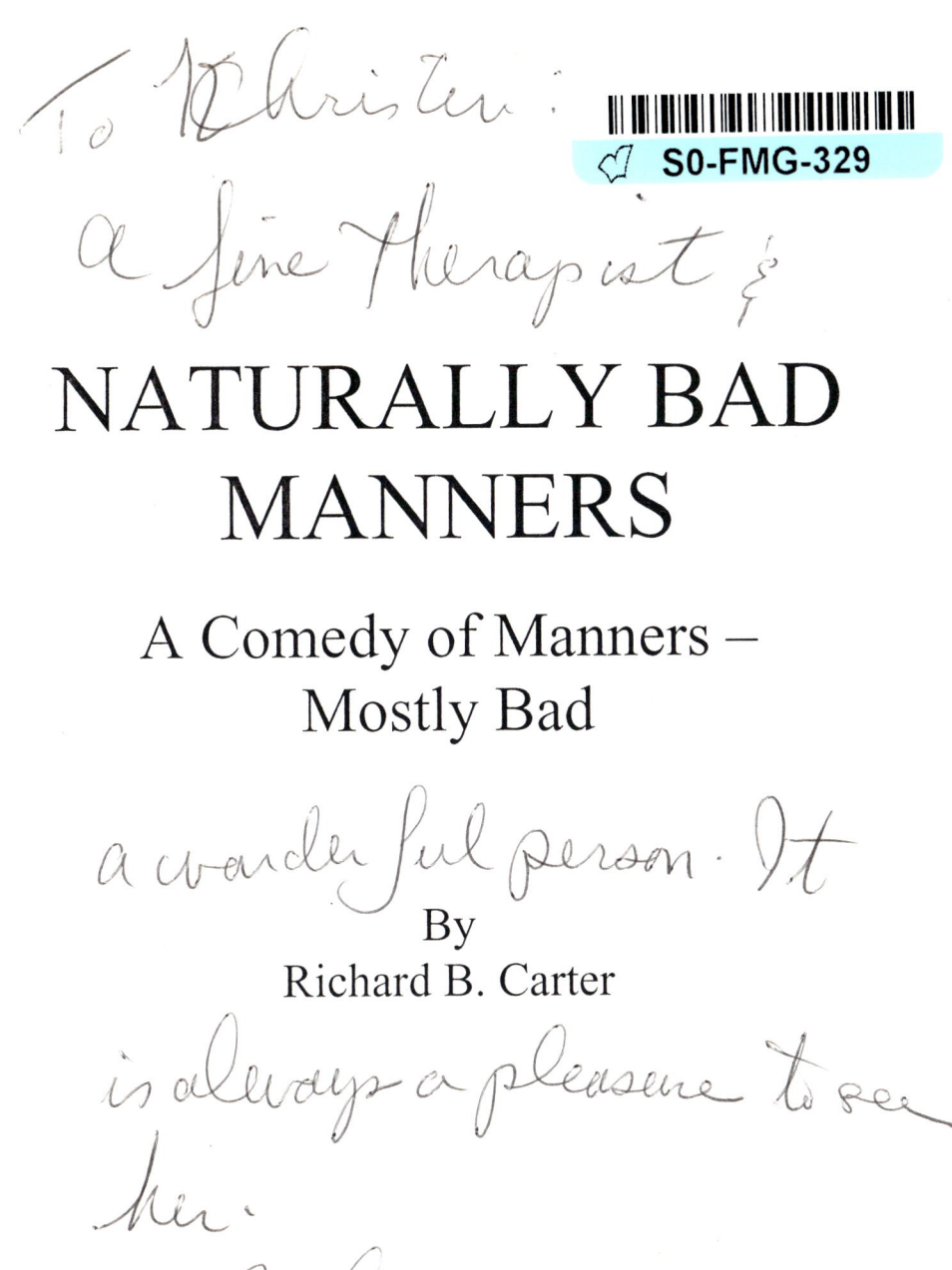

AmErica House
Baltimore

© 1993 by Richard B. Carter.
All rights reserved. No part of this book may be reproduced in any form without written permission from the publishers, except by a reviewer who may quote brief passages in a review to be printed in a newspaper or magazine.

First printing

ISBN: 1-58851-209-6
PUBLISHED BY AMERICA HOUSE BOOK PUBLISHERS
www.publishamerica.com
Baltimore

Printed in the United States of America

# DEDICATION

*To MacKensie, whose natural sweetness makes her naturally good mannered, against all odds.*
  *—Richard Carter*

# PROLOGUE

## The Story of Ptah and Baalor

Somewhere around 1400 B.C., in a part of Africa, which if it weren't Carthage already, would later become Carthage, there lived two merchants who prospered greatly from trade. One was named Ptah, and he was an Egyptian. The other was named Baalor, a Phoenician, and he was a large, red, and hairy man.

Ptah and Baalor were the best of friends. When Ptah was not sitting in the cool courtyard of the tavern sipping beer with Baalor the Phoenician – for these events took place so long ago that wine, according to some, had not yet been given to mortals by Dionysus to help them forget their griefs, to make women burn with desire, and men unable to satisfy those desires – then Baalor was to be seen brawling and drinking beer with Ptah, the Egyptian. Now this very Ptah was a plump and merry man who had a plump and merry wife, and six, or seven (or perhaps even eight), plump and merry children scattered noisily around the cool, palm-shaded, courtyard of their spotlessly clean house. Whereas Baalor, as was well known, boasted of a very tall, raw-boned wife with blazing eyes, and an unnumbered brood of quarrelsome children who lived in a pig-sty of a house which was filled with cries, shouts, braying, squealing, and such-like din, from very early morning until the sun set. But, still, these two men, Ptah the placid, fat, and merry Egyptian, and Baalor, the large, hairy, red Phoenician, were the best of inseparable friends – except, that is, for one very little, but very dark cloud in the otherwise sunny, serene, and joyful heaven which smiled down upon their business ventures and their friendship. This cloud was that Baalor was forever after Ptah to leave the religion of his fathers and his fathers' fathers, and to join him in the worship of mighty Baal-Murdak, Lord of Hosts, Slayer of the Weak, Supporter of the Strong, etc., etc.

Time and time again, Baalor, the large, red, and hairy Phoenician, would wait for Ptah, the plump and merry Egyptian, to get tipsy and, when all the world seemed so agreeable to Ptah that he fairly shook like a waterskin on the back of a trotting camel, Baalor would begin to pull a long face – resulting in an expression which often took a long time to get through his enormous red beard and, once free of its russet entanglements, to come to the attention of the tipsy, deeply contented Ptah.

Indeed, as often as not, Baalor would fail in his attempt to appear sad to Ptah, and he then had to feign tears – again, no little feat in the case of so large and hairy a face. When he got finally got through to Ptah, however, the joyful expression on the Egyptian's plump face fell as if it were a freshly risen lump of dough which had just been punched by his plump, merry wife.

"By Ammon-Ra! My dearest friend, why do you weep?" Ptah asked Baalor the Phoenician.

"Ah, dear Ptah, I do love thee as I love the white bitch camel, Baalbek, apple of my eye though she be; I love thee even as I love the great brindled bitch-dog, Baalbeka, whose puppies are my heart's delight; and, indeed, were it proper for a man to love his friend as he loves his wife, I should love you as I love my own wife, Baalbelah, whose man-whelps are the comfort of my old age."

By now, of course, Baalor was weeping in truth and in torrents.

"Dear friend, Baalor, why do you weep as you say these things which touch my heart so?"

"I fear for your soul, my dearest Ptah."

"My soul?" cried a thoroughly alarmed Ptah, his everywhere rounded frame aquiver. "My soul? What, pray tell, is the matter with my soul? Have I not paid in full my yearly dues to Rimmon-ta, the priest? Have I not nightly recited verses from the hymns to the particular deity who rules and regulates the affairs of the following day? Do I not..." Baalor tried to interrupt the eloquent Ptah, but all the hippopotamuses in Upper Egypt could not have silenced this litany of observances. "Did I not," Ptah continued, "embalm that disgusting cat, who habitually left headless mice, and even wads of vomit containing their hair, on my pillow? Did I not, at the feast of the Autumn Solstice, have every hair of my body – yes, dear Baalor, EVERY hair! – plucked from my body as the custom prescribes? And, this, by that disgusting temple assistant, Ammon-Rim, who, after yanking out a handful, asks

## Naturally Bad Manners

me so sweetly, 'Does it hurt, Ptah?' Ah! My best of friends, my soul is, I think, not in such bad shape! Why, then, do you fear for it?"

Deeply calmed by this recitation of his own virtues, Ptah regained his happy composure, and his merry countenance with it. He took a very large gulp of beer – he had become parched in the course of his breathless recitation – and belched loudly, cracked his knuckles, put his elbows on the table and his chin on his hands, and waited for an answer.

"Embalm a cat, embalm a gnat!" thundered Baalor.

"Our particular creed does not require the eternal preservation of gnats," Ptah explained condescendingly to Baalor, as if to a feeble-minded child.

"Why not? If you embalm a cat, why not other vermin?" Baalor asked haughtily. "Do you really think, my dear friend of Egypt, that the high gods care what happens to the rotten carcasses of vermin?"

"I never thought about it. I am a merchant, not a priest. My business is to make money, pay my yearly tribute, and observe the prescribed rites of my forefathers," explained Ptah, again as if he were talking to a feeble-minded child.

"Oh, my dear Egyptian friend. The commands of your gods are the commands of a chambermaid to the man who empties out the slop-buckets. I, as did my fathers, serve the Lord of Lords, the Leader of the Hosts, the Slayer of thousands, Baal-Murdak!"

Now, so little did Ptah the merry, plump Egyptian trouble his brain about who was who in heaven – feeling, quite correctly, that his business-affairs were about all he could keep straight in an average working day (he reserved nights for drinking with Baalor and, somewhat infrequently, for his family) – that Baalor's claim troubled him not a bit. But, he was troubled by Baalor's obvious distress.

"Oh, Baalor, my Phoenician friend. I care not for cats, gnats, chambermaids, the man who empties out the slop-buckets..." and here he started to say, "or who is sitting on the throne of heaven," but thought better of it. "What, oh Baalor, is shattering the tranquility of this lovely evening for you? Your wife and children are well; you are rich; your bitch-camel is pregnant. You are Baalor the Phoenician! What may I, your good friend from Egypt, do to complete your happiness? Tell me, and I shall try to do it at once."

"Ah. My dear Egyptian friend, Ptah. Do but this for me. A ship of mine sails next month for Phoenicia. Take it, and be my agent. Then, while you are in Baalopolis, the metropolis of Phoenicia, observe closely the court of the Great King, the living personification of Baal-Murdak, and see with your own eyes the greatness of my god. Then, when you return, Oh, Ptah, best of friends, then do you decide which gods you and your descendants shall serve and worship!"

"Well, now. I have never been to Baalopolis, the metropolis of Phoenicia, and, as a matter of fact, I do have interests there which I would rather not trust to the hands of any agent. I'll do it!" Ptah said, and leaned back beaming once more.

"Wonderful, Oh, Ptah. Go, and you will see what a real god looks like...here, among mere humans."

The appointed time to sail, and a favorable wind arrived together, and Ptah, armed with letters of introduction to very exalted persons at Baalopolis, the metropolis of Phoenicia, sailed, and was gone for six months.

When he returned, Baalor had gone south into the interior to trade gold for ivory, and did not arrive back for two months after Ptah. When he returned, Baalor fed, watered, and groomed his white bitch-camel and her colt, kissed his wife and those of his children in the immediate vicinity, petted his bitch greyhound, stroked his falcon's neck-feathers, and then set off to see Ptah, the Egyptian, who lived nearby.

Upon reaching Ptah's house, Baalor was both surprised and overjoyed to see that a bas-relief stele of Baal-Murdak had replaced the great Eye of Ra, which, earlier, had hung so prominently over the entrance gate. Opening the gate, after knocking loudly, he was yet more surprised to see that the mummy-portraits of Ptah's ancestors had been painted over, and a number of idols of Istar had been set up in their place. As he opened the inner door, he entered the reception room, which was afloat in the smoke of Baal's sacred incense. The small household altar at the rear wall had been stripped of all its polished stone falcons and manikins, and was now crammed full of the idols of Phoenicia. He was stunned.

"What happened, friend Ptah?" he asked Ptah, as he approached him with open arms to embrace him.

Over the wailing of his formerly happy children and the raucous

## Naturally Bad Manners

scolding of Ptah's formerly placid wife, Baalor heard Ptah say, "Oh dearest, and best, and wisest, of friends, worshipper of Him who is, indeed, and beyond any possible human doubt, the greatest, most powerful, most subtle…"

Here Baalor said to himself, "Most subtle? I've never heard that title bestowed on the Lord of Hosts before," and then, he heard Ptah continue.

"I arrived in Baalopolis, the metropolis of Phoenicia, safe and sound, blessed be the provident care of the great and…"

"Most commendable, Oh Ptah. But, your great piety, otherwise most exemplary and salutary, as I have no doubt, keeps you from your story. Pray, tell me your story, and thank the merciful…" Here he was interrupted by his friend Ptah's recitation of Baal-Murdak's infinite virtue, until Baalor's great red beard began to bristle dangerously, and his nose began to turn bright blue – both of which signs signaled great anger in the breast of Baalor, the red and hairy Phoenician. Ptah saw this, and returned to the main thread of his story.

"Armed, as I was, with your letters of introduction to various highly placed functionaries and dignitaries, priests, acolytes…"

"Oh, get on with your story. I know to whom I sent letters of introduction!"

"Well, I was singularly blessed to see the inner workings of the court of the monarch who is the living personification of…"

Here Baalor put up a threatening ham of a fist to direct the story back into its appointed path.

"…Baal-Murdak. I saw the Living One," and here Ptah made a low obeisance, touching his hands to his lips reverently, while Baalor only nodded and made a smacking sound with his lips, "and, reflecting on the greatness of the metropolis, the extent of the Empire, the wealth of its nobles, the prosperity of its Lord's worshippers, and the might of its fleet…" and here Ptah paused for a long moment, while his previously merry and contented children filled the air with their wails, and the raucous screaming of his formerly placid wife completed the cacophony celebrating the introduction of a new set of gods into the household. Continuing, as if deaf to these sounds of pandemonium, Ptah proceeded. "I then reflected on the meanness of the metropolitan officials, on the narrowness of imperial policy, on the misery of the slaves, the perversity of its young men, the willingness of all the officials, from the monarch on down to the most humble acolyte, to extort, cheat, even kill for gold to spend on luxuries beyond what were hitherto my wildest dreams..." and Ptah again fell silent for a long moment, which was again occupied by wailing and teeth-gnashing on the part of his previously happy family, "...And, so, I reflected that so mean a body of officials, so perverse a gentry, so greedy and dishonest a monarch, so miserable a crowd of slaves, and so wicked a body of priests had never before supported so great and powerful an empire. Only a very great god indeed, for whatever subtle end He envisages, could be behind this imperial greatness. And, so I made my decision."

# PART I:
## NATURALLY STRANGE THINGS

# CHAPTER 1

## J.J. Rufus

It was only natural for the citizens of West Athens, Vermont, to gossip when a Swiss company, the Société Suisse-Française, paid an arm and a leg for a long-unused parcel of woodland, then cut down all the sugar maples on it, and built a Suisse chalet-style hotel on it – complete with plaster deer and ducks on the spacious front lawn, and plaster cats climbing the simulated oak beams framing the entrance door. Real, live, deer were as plentiful as rats in the area, and live cats were to be had for the asking at the local ASPCA, so, this expenditure on plaster imitations of creatures which were both free and bountiful in the immediate area seemed downright profligate to the thrifty townspeople.

The Lions, Optimists, and Rotary Clubs of West Athens met on Tuesday, Wednesday, and Thursday, respectively, and included among the membership of these clubs was the group which, by universal agreement, comprised the cream of the crop of the movers and shakers in the locality (including an Episcopal minister, who insisted on being called Father Lyons). The members of these civic clubs were so sure of their own importance that, when numerous invitations to the noon-day luncheons put on by The Lions, The Optimists, and The Rotary Club, were not even answered by the folks at The Geneva Inn, the result was simple puzzlement. As Charlie Shay, the Allstate Insurance man, concluded, "Those people got their lights on, but nobody's home, that's for sure."

Discreet inquiries at the State's Attorney's office in the state capital, Montpelier, revealed that, according to the U.S. Chamber of Commerce's admittedly loose standards, The Geneva Inn, and its corporate owner, the Société Suisse-Française, was duly chartered and legally blameless. These same sources revealed that the inn's owner-manager was one Mr. Jean-J. Rufus, a citizen of Geneva, Switzerland.

This Mr. Jean-J. Rufus, who called himself, 'J.J.,' and insisted that everyone else do so, loved to talk about himself. After lunch, before the afternoon's business session began at The Geneva Inn, he would often sip brandy, and talk about himself, and his meteoric rise to vast riches. His accent was that of a Swiss-Frenchman who had learned to speak American English from watching afternoon talk shows shot in New York, and an endless number of late-night reruns of grade B Hollywood Westerns.

"So," he one day asked a group of newly arrived, shy, polite businessmen from Taiwan, "you think I was born with a silver dollar up my nose? Well, I wasn't. I begged, borrowed without paying back, and when I couldn't beg or borrow, I stole my way to the top. You know...?"

A Taiwanese guest, whose English was rather formal, was puzzled by J.J.'s expression, "You know?" He asked, "Excuse, please, but what exactly is it you mean when you say, 'You know?'"

"Money, *mes enfants*, MONEY. When I was just a kid, back in the old country, I used to get guys to bet in the schoolyard when I started fights between friends. I knew that the other guys knew who would win, and I would bet that the guy who everyone knew was the loser wouldn't lose. Get it? I didn't bet he'd win. I'd only bet he wouldn't lose! And then, just as my guy was getting the you-know-what beat out of him, I'd sneak indoors, and tell a teacher that a hellofa fight was going on, and he'd come charging out, and break it up. My guy didn't lose, and their guy didn't win. I did. You know...?"

Here, J.J. looked reflectively over the heads of his largely uncomprehending audience around the table as he meditatively picked at a pimple on his chin. Continuing his sketch of how he did it, he said, "One way and another, I made a few bucks, and when I had enough, I bought my ticket to America. I knew what greedy pigs we all are, and here I was, in A-mer-ri-ka! with a little capital. Well gents, I found my first real mark, oh, some twenty/thirty years ago. I found this drunken Irishman, who owned an advertising agency that was on the skids. I didn't have a lot of dough, but what I did have let me work for a very small salary when I finally met what I was looking for, this fifty-year-old drunk on the skids, who was sure that, if he boozed enough, it'd be okay again, and the firm would pick up and make money like it did when his father died fifteen years before. So, this one," here, J.J. jabbed an angry thumb into the watch-pocket of the vest of his ill-fitting, years-out-of-date, double-breasted business-suit, "got new accounts for 'the boss,' Tom Harris, and I made damned sure that any upturn in business was always followed by long drinking parties which included his daughter, Mary. I didn't mention her before, did I?"

Here, J.J. fell silent for a moment, and then, with a sly grin at the stony-faced men facing him, asked, "Would you believe it? I am a father! Well, I am. I don't give a diddly-damn if you do, or you don't. But, I'll get to that. At any rate, if I wasn't pushing drinks on the boss, I was tut-tuting with this Mary over her father's drinking problem. Of course, the silly drunken bastard just got sicker, and little Miss Mary got this weird idea, which I put into her head, that she was in love with me. Well, when the doctor guaranteed the boss's death within the year, I asked the hair-ress, Miss Mary, to marry me. She jumped at it, like a duck on a June bug, and I got the old sot to leave me the business, without any strings attached. This was easy, because the jerk assured me that Mary was a woman, and 'Women have no heads for business.' Ain't that a stitch?"

J.J. grinned at his embarrassed fellow-businessmen.

"Nothing complicated. My plan was slick as soap on a doorknob. You see, as soon as Tom, the ex-boss, was safely in the hospital dying, I planned to kiss off the little lady, and tell her that I finally realized she married me because she wanted me to run the business, and suck me for the earnings. Well, lemme tell you, I didn't like to be exploited in this way. Not even a little bit. So, I had to throw her out, and sell the business, and go on to other things, which would open up capital for other ventures. Nice, eh? But, then, just when I planned to tell her to scram, the woman told me she was pregnant! Now, I don't get mad easy, but this did it. The woman was pregnant! This female had tried to bilk me! That drunken Tom Harris had tried to bilk me! Well, I'd still get her! At any rate," he continued, while scratching his belly under his tight-fitting vest, "Tom – the Mick who used to own the company – died within two weeks of the time the brat was born. I was a daddy! Now I ask you," J.J. asked his incredulous audience conspiratorially, "for a man of business, a daughter's worthless as nipples on a boar hog, eh?"

Here J.J. wiped his mouth with his sleeve, and asked no one in particular, "Any of you know anything about insurance?"

Several men at the table nodded.

"Well, then you will really like this next move. You guys are thieves too, only I'm better at it than you."

The angry titter from the members of the group was met with J.J.'s utter indifference. The angry tittering soon subsided, and he continued. "The old man's son – I don't remember his...Mike! That was his name, Mike. This Mike was in construction and hated business, so he wouldn't work for his Pa, and so his old man left the whole business to me. I was supposed to take care of his daughter with the money I made off it. Do you believe it? Well, I threw Mom and her daughter out, alright, and this Mike character raised hell, and I told him, 'Look, Mike. Cut the crap. I got you by the short hairs, and there is nada, zip, zilch, you can do about it. Your drunken old man left the business to me.' So, you know what I told the silly son-of-a-bitch? I told him, 'since you are my brother-in-law, I'm gonna buy a big whole-life insurance policy on me, and make your sister's brat the beneficiary. She's newborn, and I'll pay up the policy for a million dollars – it's cheap for a healthy man under thirty – and when I croak, in maybe sixty years, she'll get some dough from her Daddy.' Now, ain't that a kick in the head? And you know, folks, the dumb bastard fell for it. I paid for that policy from the sale of his father's business and still had a pile left over! Ain't that a joke?"

An embarrassed silence met this question. J.J. looked over his audience, rubbed his hairy belly, which, by then, was peeking out from his shirt, and continued. "Now, gentlemen, you might wonder at the ethics of this next move, but if you do, that's why I'm rich as all hell, and you jerks are only rich. Well, at any rate, Mary next gets this cancer, and dies in a year, and that idiot Mike adopts – can you believe it...adopts! – the brat, and that was the end of it. He was so unpleased with me that he renamed the brat, and dropped my name – a whole hell of a lot of good that did him! Did I cry buckets? Don't you bet on it. I made nearly a hundred and fifty thou' out of that caper, after paying for the insurance policy, and the rest is history. Pretty damned edifying, eh? You guys should invite me home, and I'll tell the young guys how it's done."

With a wave of his hand, J.J. indicated to his guests that it was time to get down to business in the conference rooms.

\* \* \*

After selling the ad agency and ditching his newborn daughter, J.J. Rufus moved on and, within a few years, was filthy rich because of his unerring eye for promoting stocks in companies which sold such snake-oil remedies as cures for aging skin, falling hair, sex rejuvenators, and the like. (And these were the more respectable ventures he dealt in.)

His genius was that he could divine exactly what pitch for each particular kind of pies in the sky masquerading as heavenly manna would catch investors' fancies. And so it was that J.J. Rufus made his millions in Europe and America, simply by interpreting brochures describing stock offerings – all of which were legal in the country in which they were sold. He was what might be called a "meta-fraud," in that he never misrepresented anything to anybody. Rather, like the side betters at the billiard and pool tournaments, who never play themselves, but only wager on the success or failure of the principals, all his bets were placed according to his judgment of which fraudulent misrepresentation of this or that product would bilk the public most, before it crashed. His success was amazing.

He always bought for pennies and sold for pounds, francs, dollars, yen, or whatever. This selling, what is more, almost always took place just before the stock crashed. How he did it, no one knew, but he did it. Sometimes, a sensational account of a ghastly death induced by one of the products manufactured by a company, whose stock he had just unloaded, brought the stock tumbling; sometimes, a previously remiss regulatory agency blew a whistle; and sometimes, an enterprising young reporter discovered what was in "Beau-Derm: An Elixir For Rejuvenating Tired Skin. He Wants You to Be Forever Young. Don't You?" and blew the scam wide open. But, by then – indeed, usually just before then – J.J. Rufus had sold his stock in the company. This happened so often that the more impressionable among his fellow speculators swore up and down that his selling caused the collapses. He was called, "The buzzard of the bourse."

Bilking no one directly, he continued to build his fortune merely by side-betting the bilkers as they made their own preparations to bilk. He provided capital to fledgling would-be bilkers who, when they had money to begin their scams in earnest, attracted other investors in earnest. It was this latter group whose greed had made J.J. very rich.

His pursuit of money took up all of J.J.'s time and energy, and so, he never gave a thought to his daughter. So, throughout all these years, Claudia, whom her uncle Mike had adopted, and then given her his own last name, had never heard one word from or about her "natural" father, and therefore, had no reason to imagine that there ever existed a "natural" father, other than Mike. She was nurtured, not by her natural father, but by Mike, and his wife, Celeste – by a legal, conventional father and mother, whose love for her naturalized Claudia into their own family, along with four other, natural children. All these adored Claudia, from the youngest, Tony, to Megan, who was only fourteen months younger than Claudia. None of these brothers and sisters knew anything about the deal Mike had made with J.J., and thus, when after nearly thirty years, the beautiful economist, Dr. Claudia R. Harris – the R was for "Rufus, the name of a distant relative" – decided to marry a successful poet named Stafford Wyatt, Mike and Celeste gave her away, with many tears and much love. They paid for her wedding without stinting, and her brothers and sisters were all attendants and maids of honor. Only legally a Harris, and only legally her natural uncle's "child" through love's naturalizing power, she legally took Stafford Wyatt to have and to hold, and thereby got her third name, which she added to "Harris," to make "Harris-Wyatt." But, her heart, seconding the law of adoption, had made her natural uncle, Mike, her real father, and his heart had transformed a natural niece into a real daughter, and, now, her heart took an unrelated man, Stafford Wyatt, and made him legally the other half of her natural world, the world of those well-married couples whose major sources of friction were things such as flavors of tooth-paste, and living within a quite-generous budget – Claudia's sensitive teeth requiring her to use a foul-tasting brand of tooth-paste, which Stafford wouldn't touch, and Stafford, coming from a family of two physicians, being somewhat spendthrift.

While all this was happening to his daughter, Claudia, her natural father, J.J. Rufus, had gone on to become very rich. What Freud was as a theoretician of a frail and childish humanity's naughty dreams, so was

J.J. to frail humanity's greedy dreams. So, transforming his shameful dealings with his business competitors into glorious victories over them, he steadily progressed in his apparently inexorable meta-fraudulent journey toward vast riches. Considering all business contracts – and the laws which were shaped to ensure their performance – as mere bagatelle that small-fry clutched to themselves in order to try to protect themselves against the likes of him, J.J. made up his rules as he went along, and, since he was smart enough only to work with associates whose venality made them easy marks, he almost always managed to succeed in his efforts to out-swindle the pikers.

But, J.J. only dealt with his own kind, and, as so often happens in such cases, he was firmly convinced that everyone, without exception, was, "deep down," one of his own kind. The so-called "decent" men and women of this world were all dismissed, out-of-hand, as being merely too scared to play his dangerous game, and so, rather than act to satisfy their true desires, they hid them and pretended to be the good guys. His daughter, and the man she was to marry, the poet, Stafford Wyatt, were two of those kind and decent "good guys."

But, this Stafford Wyatt was something more than a mere goodie-goodie. His poems neither proved how empathetic he was by moaning about the horror of the human condition, nor were they written to be sold as messages in "Sympathy" cards. Not that he couldn't write whatever he needed to. Indeed, to prove to some drunken friends at a party that he could write both moaning/groaning, and feeling-good trifles with the worst of them, he had sat down, taken a deep slug of Chianti, and penned:

> *THE HUMAN CONDITION*
> *Pus. Piss.*
> *Running sores!*
> *The injustice of it all!*
> *OUTRAGE!*

Next, to prove that he could write the touchy-feely tripe with the worst of them, he took yet another slug of Chianti, and penned:

*HAPPINESS*
*When clouds and rain do visit,*
*Remember this, my friend.*
*It's not so bad, now is it?*
*For this is not the end.*

His own preference in poetry was shown in his dedication, which he wrote, when he was sixteen, on the fly-leaf of a book on sea birds. The book was a birthday present to his first lover.

*ON WALKING WITH YOU BY THE SEA*
*Oh rise!*
*Rise up, and up, and up, and up yet higher – out of sight and sense,*
*and out of all but Phoenix-recollection.*
*Then, spread wide your thin, long, wings of ageless awe,*
*And be gone!*
*Be gone, Oh, Closest Love,*
*Be gone to our ancestral place,*
*Where we were, are, and will be, always.*

(She had been so offended by, "Then, spread wide your thin, long, wings," thinking that it was entirely too graphic, that she sent it back and never spoke to him again.)

Although he became a published professional writer before he was thirty, Claudia's Stafford had studied to prepare for medical school through most of college. But, the poet in him became more and more dominant in guiding his interests, until that element in his fabric demanded his full attention. So, he gave up medicine and began seriously to work on his writing.

Now, just as it had been a foregone conclusion in the Harris household that Claudia, who had done so well in languages in Saint Thomas Aquinas High School, would pursue graduate work in comparative literature, so it had been a foregone conclusion in the Wyatt household that Stafford, the only child of two physicians, would either be a doctor or a medical researcher of some sort. But, J.J.'s contribution to his daughter's genetic make-up began to make itself manifest during her senior year of college, leading her, naturally enough, to major in Economics in graduate school.

For his part, Stafford was a descendent of the great English poet, Thomas Wyatt the Elder, and his ancestor's demands on him at last overwhelmed his parents' ambitions for him. Also, he had found organic chemistry at Williams College nowhere near as much fun as general chemistry had been in the American School in Switzerland, where the chemistry lab had been universally viewed by the students as the place where forgetful professors stored all manner of substances that, when ignited, or, in some cases, merely mixed with extremely small amounts of water, produced prodigious stinks or terrific explosions. The Williams College view of chemistry, especially of organic chemistry, was considerably less indulgent of such giddy antics and, although Stafford Wyatt tried with all his might, he could not bring himself to do more than was required to get A's in his pre-med courses; but he could not bring himself to enjoy any of them – except for comparative anatomy and human development. So, at the end of three years, he decided that he was just not cut out for the study of medicine.

Stafford approached his physician-parents with the news. They were mildly disappointed, but Stafford had always been a very good student, and a pleasantly mischievous and witty son at home. So, since they had no real complaints, they did not complain, but only insisted that he keep them posted as to the progress of his life's work.

But, this change is career-plans demanded nowhere near so much of an educational re-tooling for Stafford as is usually the case. He was hardly educationally disadvantaged in areas other than medicine. When he was only eleven years old, his mother had spent five years as a Fellow at the Pasteur Institute in Paris, while her husband was working with the World Health Organization in particularly remote and pestilential parts of Africa and Asia. At the advice of several of their medical friends who also traveled a great deal, Stafford's parents enrolled him in The American School in Switzerland. There he learned to read, write, and speak French, German, and Italian. Also, he read Latin quite well, and even managed to write yards of wretched Latin doggerel, specifying in it parts of the bodies of his least-favorite teachers, and he had written them, what is more, with an awful attention to particulars, which included shocking, medically sound, attributions of clinically-recognized deformities, caused by the obscure vices he had hit upon in reading martial and other libelous Roman satirists. So, at an early age, Stafford had both learned languages, as well as how to take a remote, cool, and literary view of human vices—especially of those vices with clinically identifiable consequences.

Thus, at the beginning of his fourth year at Williams, Stafford became the editor of the student literary magazine, to which he had contributed so many near-libelous, scurrilous commentaries on his fellow students and teachers during his first three years. Then, since his command of his languages and their literatures was already far in excess of what was expected of college seniors in America, he was given, and easily passed, the comprehensive examination in comparative literature, and thus had a full year to play in as he wished.

He wished to take developmental anatomy and Hebrew. His interest in anatomy, however, was not, primarily, a consequence of his being the son of two physicians. Rather, it dated back to his Sunday excursions to the wonderful Swiss Tierfilme, "Wildlife Films," shown to edify those Swiss who were not Sunday churchgoers. He took Hebrew because he did not know any, and he had heard that a visiting teacher of Hebrew language and literature, Professor Avram Bonapoggio, was a marvel, and that he would give him private tutorials.

This odd pairing of electives echoed something that had happened to Stafford years before, as a student in Switzerland. The school's protestant chaplain had, after a long life dedicated to church and choir-boys, finally mellowed into a sentimental old pederast who supplemented his all-too meager retirement-stipend by acting as the school's chaplain. The boys did not like him a bit and missed compulsory chapel as often as they could manage to. Stafford disliked him so much that he simply refused chapel and told the headmaster that he was not going to have his fledgling sexuality—he was a precocious thirteen at the time—molded by an old sod like the chaplain.

Now, the headmaster knew who the Doctors Wyatt were and that Stafford's mother was likely to be nominated for a Nobel Prize during the next year or two. Headmasters make it their business to know these things, even if they are ignorant of the sexual tastes of their counseling staff. A Nobel Laureate's brat at his school could but add luster to the crown of The Head, and so an arrangement was made. Stafford Wyatt was called into the headmaster's book-and-leather-lined study and informed that, if he wished to attend the wildlife films, which the local Kino showed on Sunday mornings for the town's enlightened agnostics, he was free to do so. The Head justified this by telling Stafford that, "Pondering the oddities of the Lord's creations, while you are yet a child, might well lead you to a mature appreciation of the gospel's message!"

Stafford thought that the idea was a good one and opted at once to go to a nature film each Sunday morning, in place of chapel.

And with what instances of natural folly hath the Lord, in His unsearchable wisdom, seen fit to stock the particular corner of His creation called Earth. For example, while Stafford's less fortunate schoolmates were listening to the chaplain's thunderings concerning the sin of Onan (i.e., "spilling one's seed upon the ground"), Stafford was only a few blocks away, observing the antics of all manner of water-dwelling creations of the wise Creator, as they spilled their seed merely in the general direction of females. On another Sunday, while his friends were listening, first to the story of Cain slaying Abel, always a great favorite of those boys whose little brothers went to school with them, and then listening to the chaplain accuse, all too accurately, these elder brothers of harboring less than perfectly charitable feelings for their younger brothers, Stafford was at the movies watching the first newly-hatched chick of a brood of birds butcher all his siblings, using a special hook on its beak which was apparently designed to do just that. The film narrator intoned that this was all part of nature's wonderful and inspiring design, since the chick's mother and father could care for only one chick. Stafford, an only child himself, had a bad moment or two over this, but, on returning to school, he vastly delighted the unfortunate boys who had younger brothers, by telling them exactly why it was that other students did not have brothers or sisters!

Another Sunday, although there was not a boy in the chapel who had ever had thoughts of anything so sophisticated as adultery, the sentimental old pederast chose to thunder out threats of perdition at the older of the school's students, after first detailing the divine sanctions against violating the vows of marriage. The boys' understanding of the relations between the sexes was much more transient, and even fantastic, than marriage— which is what their parents had! Much-puzzled confabulation concerning adultery—"God a 'mighty! Two girlfriends? At the same time? I should be so lucky!"—was to be heard during the early part of the afternoon, before, that is, Stafford returned with tales of how he spent his morning hours.

For, precisely during that time when his fellow students were being uplifted by the story of the marriage at Canaan, Stafford Wyatt was being entertained by film-yardage taken at the Gombe Game Preserve in Kenya, where Jane Goodall had filmed the results of the chimp, Flo, coming into estrus. The wondering (teenage) Stafford was treated to the spectacle of the whole male population of the chimp group lining up, as if for popcorn, and, in a completely orderly and unhurried fashion, taking their turns breeding Flo. One can imagine what an impression this account had on the lads who, that very morning, had been informed that monogamy of the most severe and total kind, a monogamy which even precluded lusting after another woman in your heart, was the natural order of things, and that any little deviation from the straight path of holy matrimony—which, of course, the literal-minded old priest had never entered into—was a crime both against God and against that nature which had been so providentially ordained by its Creator.

At any rate, the more or less uninspired sermons of the padre were, if in a very inverted manner, often strikingly echoed in the offerings of the nearby Kino, and Stafford was not altogether unprepared to use the experience gained through his study of comparative anatomy to understand Hebrew literature. According to that literature, what is more, the Creator of the individuals who provided the subjects studied by comparative anatomy, also gave the moral law to Israel at Mt. Sinai.

Furthermore, Stafford was his parents' own child, and so, the world manifested in the Wildlife Films made a deep and lasting impression on him. At home, medicine had always been presented as mankind's own way of dealing with the exotic misbehavior of one of the more confusing examples of Deity's handiwork, the human body, and so Stafford grew into early adulthood weighing Catullus' naughtily exquisite, "Odes to Lesbia," against Romer's weighty "The Vertebrate Body." And now a senior at Williams College, Stafford embarked on a two-fold course of studies which was to lead him to the ensouled body of a human being—surely one of the oddest of the Deity's creations.

But, even before this, Stafford had begun to wonder if perhaps medicine were not too mild a regimen and too insipid an elixir to soothe the spiritual birth-traumas of his fellow human beings, let alone to cure various spiritual agonies brought about merely by living to a naturally preordained maturity. He came to see doctoring as a sort of veterinary art of soothing that crudely obvious and relatively gentle, simple, predictable, and merely animal part of humans, and he began to think that the Enlightenment's replacement of prophecy by medicine might have unchained the wild souls of humans and turned them into raging Avatars which totally lacked, and endlessly sought, kith and kinship. And so, along with his classes in comparative anatomy, Stafford studied Hebrew with Avram Bonapoggio.

Although Hebrew is part of a language system, which is distinct from the French, Latin, German, Italian, and English that Stafford had previously cultivated, he made good progress in his studies with it. Bonapoggio never told him what to do, and Stafford never received criticism for not doing this or that. By April, Stafford had learned both a great deal of Hebrew, as well as many choice bits from the lore of its texts, along with a taste for a dark German beer Bonapoggio served at the end of every lesson. They became very good friends and spent as much time as either could afford in the company of the other. The term came to an end, and Stafford graduated and left Williams for Europe, while Bonapoggio was offered, and accepted, a chair in Semitic Literature and Thought at Chaldes College in upstate New York. Then, while his teacher was writing learned papers on exceedingly obscure medieval Jewish and Moslem thinkers, Stafford spent several years doing what so many good writers before him had done to learn their craft: He translated, turning Latin into German, and German into French, and all these into Latin, and so on and on.

In this way, Stafford learned to write and to make a name for himself as a translator of verse. His Hölderlin and Stefan George translations were razor-sharp, and his Baudelaire was like the evening sun finally bursting through a cloudbank after a week of rain. Then he wrote original farces and masques that had the flair of the Restoration comedies, but in a sort of jagged diction that his critics said was deeply Chaucerian in its feel for English. When Stafford completed a translation out of any one of his languages, Bonapoggio helped to get it published.

After he had been working in Paris for several years, both Stafford's parents were killed in the crash of a small commuter plane, and he went into a poet's mourning for a year. In his retirement, he did as his namesake, Thomas Wyatt, had done so long before: He versified a number of The Psalms of David, only he did this after he had first translated them out of Hebrew. Bonapoggio then felt that he had a dossier on Stafford that was heavy enough to justify inviting him to Chaldes for several lectures, and a series of master classes, with an eye to the possibility of a permanent position as a writer-in-residence the following fall. Bonapoggio next pulled strings with his rich friends who, he thought, had endowed enough artistique atrocities, and so got an endowment for a writing chair at Chaldes. So, on a clear, warm, Friday morning nearly ten years after Stafford had left Bonapoggio as a student, Bonapoggio picked him up at the Elmira-Corning Airport for his first lecture— and to meet Doctor Claudia Harris.

When Stafford met him at the airport, Bonapoggio was accompanied by a tall, soft-spoken African-American, who was introduced as Detective Captain Jim Dixon. Turning to Stafford, Bonapoggio told him, "Jim's family has been here at Chaldes since the mid 1860's. He can tell you the history of the town."

"I look forward to hearing about it," Stafford answered.

Jim drove them to Bonapoggio's house and, having to refuse his offer of a drink or a snack, left them with the remark, "Monkey-business calls, Rabbi. You are of the prophets, and I am of the law. Prophets are, when not being thrown into cisterns or lion's dens, rather more often at their leisure than are we."

"True, true, Detective Dixon. But, when the reckoning comes, it truly comes. Whatever else He is, the Lord is a stringent accountant, and we of the prophets are His officers of the court. But you will hear from me soon. I would like you to come to a reception for Stafford. I'll be arranging something in the near future. Thank you again for your help."

Stafford seconded this thanks and accompanied Bonapoggio into his house, lugging the first of several suitcases.

After all his suitcases had been brought in, and he had been shown his room, he joined Bonapoggio in his study, and the two of them drank dark German beer while they reminisced over old times. After they had brought one another up-to-date, Bonapoggio, with a sly smile on his long, narrow, face, informed Stafford that he was soon to meet a very interesting single woman. Claudia Harris.

"Rabbi Avram moonlights as Uncle Pandarus, it seems," Stafford answered. "I can hardly wait to meet this Cresida of yours."

"Speak words of good omen, Stafford! Claudia's no Cresida, and the true story of Pandarus is only presently beginning to unfold."

With that, the two friends began to wrangle with one another concerning certain of Stafford's choices in his translation of the psalms he had sent to his mentor.

# CHAPTER 2

## Angelina and Mamman

That same sun, whose bright early April light had fired Rabbi Bonapoggio's dark and bitter beer to gladden Stafford's eyes before it stung his lips and warmed his heart, also shone elsewhere. And, during one of those hours when Stafford Wyatt and Avram Bonapoggio were so agreeably disagreeing about God and Nature in the Old Testament, J.J. Rufus sent an urgent message to Lotario, a young man from St. Lucia, and told him that he was badly needed in Miami Beach.

J.J. had no scruples about how he made money. Not too long before he built The Geneva Inn, he saw that he would have to lay hands on a large sum of money for a very chancy investment that interested him, but not enough to lead him to liquidate any of his holdings to invest in it. So, a yacht, a cigarette boat, and several natives from a French-speaking Caribbean Island, and he was in a position to raise a large amount of capital, quietly and quickly. His employees took all the risks and he took most of the profit. And, foremost among his dependable employees was an incredibly handsome daredevil, Lotario Ursina, who, J.J. said, was needed immediately. He had no time to get a U.S. passport, but was to meet a small seaplane on a beach not far from Castries, the capital of St. Lucia. It would deposit him at a location on the Florida coast, where there would be a car waiting for him.

Lotario did what he was told–and more. The seaplane pilot landed, taxied up to the beach and was greeted, not only by Lotario, but by him and his newly-wedded wife, Angelina, together with her mother, a tiny, wizened black lady, who Angelina and everyone else addressed as Mamman. Since his orders had been to pick up "one male passenger, by name of 'Lotario," he told the two women that they were not permitted to board the plane.

But, there was something about Lotario which neither J.J. nor the pilot knew. For instance, neither knew that Lotario's mother-in-law, Mamman, was also La Videnta (The Woman Who Sees Far), who knew charms, spells, medicines and, so some said, the future. Nor did they know that she could cluck rabbits out of their holes. Or, that she could whistle birds out of the trees. Or, that she could lisp poisonous serpents out of their lairs. Or, that those serpents never bit her as she handled them. When this unknowing, unsuspecting pilot, also a native of the islands, informed Mamman and her daughter that they were not permitted to accompany their newly-acquired family member, Lotario, to Miami, Mamman became La Videnta and forecast storms and death at sea for the pilot – after he had been horribly savaged by sharks. This pilot was a prudent islander and so he took them all to the Florida coast. Soon, the three of them were snugly aboard J.J.'s trim yacht, *Les Lumieres*–The Enlightenment – at the Miami Beach Marina.

During the ensuing weeks, Angelina spent long and idle days lounging around the piers and making friends with the wives of the islanders who worked as crews on the boats. Mamman, however, soon became La Videnta again and sold quantities of charms and philters, told large numbers of fortunes and, for a very small price, healed minor ailments. When business was slack, the old woman either chartered a boat to take her to outlying islands, where she could replenish her herbal stocks, or she made friends with the local sea gulls – who were already half tame from being fed so much by the crews of the boats. One of these birds, a very large male of unlimited appetite and foul temper, took to Angelina and Mamman. His harsh cry of *"aiiee! aiiee!"* was quite unmistakable and soon he came to be known in Mamman's Saint Lucian patois as *"L'Aiieee,"* which soon became *"Larry"* to everyone else.

But, this idyll was to be short-lived. Lotario, illegally in America, and thus without any health insurance, got into a terrible automobile accident and was taken, near death, to the emergency room of a local hospital, where his status of illegal alien was soon figured out. Without a U.S. citizen as a co-signer, the hospital staff refused to do more than keep him from bleeding to death. As soon as she was told this, Angelina called J.J. and told him that she needed his help desperately. "Lotario is one of your workers, Mr. Rufus, and he is here at your request. You must help us. Please!" Angelina pleaded with him. "All our money is deposited, illegally, in a Puerto Rican bank in his name, and I can't even write a check to cover medical care. Can you co-sign the hospital's financial responsibility form, so that he can get admitted? We'll pay you back, as soon as we can get to San Juan."

J.J. told her to meet him at his yacht in twenty minutes and that he would see what he could do. He also told her that Mamman made him nervous and that she must not be there for the meeting. He hung up and immediately called a physician who was deeply in debt to him for stock tips and told him to find out at once what Lotario Ursina's chances of survival were. The doctor made his call and then called J.J. again in a few minutes. This Lotario was as good as dead. It was only a matter of a few hours, at most.

At four o'clock sharp, J.J. arrived on board his yacht and he soon saw Angelina running down the boardwalk toward his slip. J.J. had to admit to himself that she was not unattractive, although he was certainly no great admirer of feminine beauty. They cast off, with J.J. taking the helm, and the powerful motor had them some twenty-five miles offshore in a very short time. They were now deep in international waters and hence under the jurisdiction of no particular country.

Once J.J.'s yacht was deep within those international waters, he stopped the motor, cast out a dragline and the two of them sat down in the yacht's spacious lounge. J.J. was much too self-absorbed to be a lover of women, but he could not help but stare at Angelina as she sat in front of him. He gave her a drink and offered her some sandwiches from a large plate piled high with them. Angelina gladly took the drink, but was in no shape to eat. He questioned her very carefully as to the amount of money she thought Lotario had in Puerto Rico and then asked her a number of questions about what would happen if thus and so were to happen. After some twenty minutes of this, Angelina was a little tipsy and extremely distressed.

"Please. For God's sake, Mister Rufus, help us."

J.J. answered, "Tell me, Angelina, do you know where we are right now?"

She answered "No," looking around her in alarm, but, then, seeing nothing except the sea, with its flying fish and a nearby cloudless sky, she felt reassured. "Where are we, Mister Rufus? Aren't we just at sea?"

"No, no, my dear Mrs. Ursina. Not at all. You are presently in J.J.

Rufus' yacht, some twenty-five or so nautical miles off the coast of Miami Beach, U.S.A. Do you know what that means, Mrs. Lotario Ursina?"

"Good God! What are you going to do to me?"

"'Good God?' No, dear Angelina," J.J. intoned, "God is not good. At least not outside the twenty-mile limit, in international waters."

"This man is crazy!" Angelina thought to herself. As J.J. continued, his speech was punctuated by the screams of a recently arrived sea gull. It soon dawned on Angelina that those screams were the normal *"aiee's"* of her pet sea gull, Larry, who was equally at home both in God's own international waters, where law was not always enforceable, and flying around mankind's floating hotels at Miami Beach.

J.J., unaware of Larry's presence, continued looking meditatively, now at her, and now at the sea outside one of the cabin's windows. He continued, "God is indeed here. We have now left the world of *les meurs*–of 'mores', as the sociologists call customs. Now, out here, Mrs. Lotario Ursina, there is only a world of sharks and flying fish–think of it! Flying fish!" J.J. shouted, his hands making the gesture of flying. "Oh yes. And, dolphins that breathe air and love human beings. And, of course, there is God," he ended in a throaty whisper.

As if on cue, the circling Larry–who had long-since learned, at the Miami Beach Marina, that it was better to beg for food from humans than to hunt for it out in the waters of Miami Bay – landed on the railing, just outside an open porthole and let out a blood-curdling squawk. Angelina laughed and J.J nearly jumped out of his skin.

"Where did that damned thing come from?" he demanded.

"Oh, I don't know. God sent him, I guess," Angelina said and, following an inspiration of truly divine origin, she threw Larry a piece of J.J.'s uneaten sandwich, which he had left on the table near her. Now, at last, Larry knew for sure he was among his friends and, gobbling the piece of sandwich down, stuck his head in even further, and squawked even louder for more. J.J slammed the porthole shut, nearly breaking the glass on the retreating bill of the gull, and, whirling around to face Angelina, continued, gathering momentum as he went on.

"Yes. God!" yelled J.J, as if the whole episode with the bird had not occurred. "God, you, and me, Mrs. Lotario Ursina. God is nature!

## Naturally Bad Manners

Human life is only pus in the abscesses of nature's vast, immoral body. Most humans are terrified pygmies, hiding under their stupid little laws, cheating when they can and suing whoever they can't cheat back. You, Mrs. Ursina, you go to church to ask permission to have sex with Lotario. They say 'yes,' charge you fifty dollars and you go home thinking that you are safe from nature. Well, out here you aren't!"

As if to punctuate these last words of J.J.'s, Larry smashed against the recently closed porthole so violently that both Angelina and J.J. wondered whether he would break it out. But, J.J. continued, as if he had heard nothing.

"God, Mrs. Ursina, is the storm that kills thousands with its tidal waves. He is the shrieking mother holding the body of her mutilated child in her lap! He is the lust of the rapist who..." Angelina turned white and sank back deeper into a corner of the large chair in which she was sitting. Smirking at this, J.J. continued, "...God is the joy of the rapist, who rapes because there is nothing to stop him!" Then, pausing dramatically, J.J. added in a throaty whisper, "...and not because he is mad at his mother, or some such garbage."

Now Angelina forgot all laughter. She was frightened. "What do you want, Mister Rufus?"

"God is the defiler of convention, Mrs. Ursina," J.J. now intoned.

"Just exactly what do you want from me?" Angelina asked, coolly and beyond fear, and, if need be, prepared to die by jumping overboard.

"Oh, no, my dear lady. I never rape or defile. That is not the way to God. No. Those rapists you read so much about in the papers are merely bad boys, who want a strong father figure to punish them and tell them that, in prison, they are safe from nature – what you call God! I am a lover of truth!" he screamed. "I am natural man. I live with God on Earth. But, He is invisible here, because here, on this planet Earth, He is hidden and surrounded by law and convention and by the laws of the ants who run their little human ant-farms according to law and convention."

"What do you want, then?" Angelina asked.

"My dear Angelina...uh, that is, Mrs. Ursina. You know that your husband will die – unless, of course, I co-sign for the hospital bill. You know, illegal aliens...?"

Angelina looked up at him from where she sat. "Yes," she said slowly, "It is certain."

"And, you understand, don't you, Mrs. Ursina, that if I co-sign the note and your husband dies, I will have to pay, and you cannot get at his money in Puerto Rico? It is a U.S. possession, after all, and you are as much an illegal alien there, as here."

"Yes. I know that. But, for the love of God..."

J.J. reached out, with a rapidity that amazed her, and slapped her face. "Listen and stop babbling on about God. You know nothing about God. God strips bare. He does not love!"

"What do you want me to do, so that you will co-sign?"

"Well, Mrs. Ursina, if you want to save your husband's life, you will beg me, here, now, to join you in doing certain acts which are popularly known as unnatural acts, but which are, in point of truth, only unconventional and thus very much natural acts. It is this, or your Lotario dies!" he ended with a stage flourish.

Angelina looked at him dumbly as he began to take his clothes off. Just as he was down to his shirt and socks, she saw Larry walk in the opposite door, which, he had just discovered, was open. Angelina quickly reached out and swept the whole plate of sandwiches on the floor between her and J.J., who was, by then, almost entirely naked. Larry let out a shriek of delight, which made J.J. whirl around, to find the bird charging in his general direction, with his six-inch beak snapping open and shut in anticipation of a feast. Then, for reasons that no one will ever know, J.J. stood between the bird and the sandwiches, waving his outstretched arms and his legs wide open, to keep the bird from the food on the floor. Larry's violent temper asserted itself. His head darted out and he cut a long gash on the inside of J.J.'s right leg. Howling with pain and fury, J.J. grabbed the huge gull at the base of his long neck, leaving his head and most of his neck mobile and, so, Larry bit his penis. J.J. doubled up in agony and, somewhat aided by Angelina's strong push from behind, fell on top of the bird. Larry squawked bloody murder, bit J.J. again and, while it could, grabbed as many sandwiches as its beak would hold, and then beat a hasty retreat to a corner of the room. J.J. was rolling on the floor, vomiting and yelling, "I'm bleeding to death. The pain! Oh, Christ! For the love of God, help me!"

Angelina darted out the open door through which Larry had entered

*Naturally Bad Manners*

and, looking wildly around, saw a boat hook neatly stowed away. She grabbed it and ran back in to confront a J.J. who, covered with blood and vomit, was madly crawling around to get as far from the bird as possible. That beautiful creature, as Angelina thought of Larry, was leisurely waddling around, snapping up scraps of food and paying no attention to J.J.

Then, Angelina gently poked J.J. in his exposed rump with the boat hook and told him to lie down on his stomach on the floor, with his arms behind him. He hesitated and she poked him again. He obeyed at once. Then, disconnecting the removable strap to her purse, she used it to tie his hands firmly behind his back and then prodded him up onto his feet.

At the far end of the cabin, there was a raised platform with two swivel chairs facing an enormous array of radios, nautical wheels, radar screens, ship-to-shore phones and the like. Angelina prodded J.J. into one of these two chairs and then tied him into it securely with his belt, which he had somewhat overly dramatically discarded in his haste to celebrate his urge to commit truly natural acts with his "consenting" guest. Sitting down in the other swivel chair, boat hook held to the ready, Angelina asked sweetly, "How do you work this ship-to-shore phone?"

A sharp prod halfway between J.J.'s navel and his genitals managed to help him collect himself sufficiently to tell her. She called the hospital and at once learned that her husband was dead. Putting down the phone, she asked J.J. if he had known this. Her question was met with a very superior smile and silence. Angelina placed the point of the boat hook to his left ear and said that she would scramble his brains if he did not answer her question.

"My dear Angelina. I know people. I, myself, am one who never does anything myself. I only skim the cream off other fools' folly. And, you are certainly not a murderer."

Angelina lowered the point of the boat hook and thought for a moment. Then the odd cooing of the sea gull caught her attention. She swiveled her chair around and saw it dancing in a tight circle a few feet behind her.

"The blessed thing is in love with me," she thought out loud. And, indeed, as Larry saw her look at him, he doubled the tempo of his love-dance. A little fearfully, to be sure, she held out her open palm. Angelina's feathered "natural" lover pranced, bobbed and spun on one flat foot, with the other tucked up against his breast and then, just as he reached her feet, he whirled around with astonishing speed and ended up sitting on them, looking up at her and cooing.

Although Angelina did not consider herself a witch, Mamman, with whom she had grown up, viewed such liaisons between widely separated biological classes of animals, birds, and reptiles as day-to-day stuff. Angelina put out her hand and stroked Larry's enormous head. The bird responded like a tomcat and arched its neck for further scratching. Then, Angelina picked him up and, pointing him in the direction of J.J., hissed, "Bad J.J.! Bad! Bad! Bad!" Larry reacted, as any lover should. He hissed and spread out his six-foot wings to their utmost extent and prepared to do battle.

Now, J.J., as is the case with most worshippers of "Nature," had a deep and unalterable terror of anything natural – that is, of anything he could not talk to, lie to, and, hence, manipulate. He not only could not talk to Larry, but he viewed him as the very essence of the unexpected, the wildly other. Thus, as Angelina brought the furiously hissing bird slowly toward his face, J.J. caved in completely.

"For the love of God, Angelina..."

"Mrs. Lotario Ursina, if you please."

"For Christ's sake, Ms.. ah..."

"No, not Mizzz, Misses Lotario Ursina!" she yelled, as she brought Larry even closer – and the bird responded like the best of the Hollywood props. He hissed more and more fiercely and struck out more and more frequently at J.J.'s face.

"Now, then, tell me, before Larry here gouges out your eye-balls, did you know that Lotario was dead?"

J.J. had completely lost his composure. "Yes! I...I...oh Christ! Don't let that damned bird get at me!"

"Are we talking about Larry, the only support the recently widowed Angelina Ursina has for her old age?"

"Who the hell is Larry?" J.J. asked, wildly looking around the cabin.

"Larry? Why Larry is my new lover, now that Lotario is dead. A widow needs a gentleman to protect her, Mister Rufus, what with so many cads around."

This kind of talk horrified J.J. beyond all measure. He was not afraid of almost anything else. But, talk that he considered genuinely weird was deeply unsettling to him and Angelina sensed this. She had seen heavily armed bullies dissolve into terrified little boys in the face of La Videnta's familiarity with goats, pigs, pigeons, and, when the going got rough, with lizards and enormous anacondas. Thus, J.J. could not have chosen a less auspicious victim than La Videnta's much beloved daughter, Angelina. Was she not "Angelina" – La Videnta's own angel?

The upshot of all this was that J.J. told her how to get the boat back to Miami Beach. Once they pulled into the slip, Angelina ran off breathlessly to the Coast Guard station and told them that she had captured a rapist and that he was on the yacht, Les Lumieres. The very excited young man who was on duty at the time ran to the boat and there discovered the bloody, vomit-smeared, nearly naked J.J., strapped into the co-pilot's swivel-chair – but no rapist and no Larry. A serious infection from the gash on J.J.'s thigh developed into blood poisoning. He would get over that, but not over his terror of large birds and, when he recovered, he sold his yacht and never sailed aboard a ship again.

But charity and forgiveness were not major components of J.J.'s character, if it may be called that. So, using his wide-flung network, he had it broadcast that one Angelina Ursina had taken illegal advantage of his generous offer of help and that she should be viewed as a very dangerous scam-artist. So, the name Ursina was soon well-known to U.S. immigration and Angelina, after retrieving Lotario's money from an illegal account in San Juan, remembered that the name of the old woman whose social security number Lotario had used to deposit his money at the bank in San Juan was Laura Miller. Angelina chose her name and social security number under which to emigrate and, with a quarter of a million dollars and a British/Jamaican accent, this very beautiful woman had no trouble at all with exit visas. She came to America with Mamman and Larry and settled down in Lake Placid, New York. Once there, she looked around for a profitable investment opportunity and soon heard that a highly respected travel agency, Windward Tours, was up for sale due to its owner's decision to retire. She bought it and was soon doing very well as its owner-manager, catering primarily to rich locals who fled upstate New York's brutally cold winters by vacationing on various islands in the Caribbean.

* * *

Several years after Laura Miller, as Angelina had christened herself, bought this business, she received a telephone call from Ted Simms, a newly-hired professor at Chaldes College, which was located a little under an hour's drive south of Lake Placid. Ted wanted to know if Windward Tours was interested in having the customers of a local bank be referred to her, in return for her guarantees that she would provide dependable service to them. She assured Ted Simms that Windward Tours was very interested, and she made an appointment to meet Ted to discuss the matter.

# CHAPTER 3

## Conventions of Love

Ted Simms and Laura Miller reached upstate New York by very different routes. Laura's odyssey began on St. Lucia, in the Caribbean and Ted's at a Roman Catholic orphanage for boys located in Cairo, Illinois.

During his fifteenth spring, his twelfth spent at St. Paul's School, Ted Simms had shot up so fast that he constantly barked his shins as he slid in and out of the steel classroom desks at St. Paul's Orphanage School. This made him very clumsy and so, when he heard Sister Angelica call his name from the back of the classroom one day, soon before his eighteenth birthday, he nearly turned the desk over in his attempt to get up without disturbing the rest of the class. Sister Angelica hissed at him to make less noise and motioned him to follow her outside the door and into the hall. Once they had moved down the hall, out of earshot of the other students, the nun's face softened, but kept a pinched, worried look. She was obviously very upset about something.

"Ted, I'm afraid that Father Feeney is very ill. He wants to talk to you. Now, Ted," she continued in a very strained voice, "he is very old and very sick. Don't upset him, whatever you do. Please try hard, okay? And, Ted, don't cry, please."

"Yes, Sister Angelica, I'll try," Ted answered in a small, hollow voice. After they crossed the open schoolyard, they entered the rectory of Saint Paul's Orphanage. Mrs. Healy, Father Feeney's housekeeper and cook, joined them and whispered something to Sister Angelica that Ted caught as, "This is it, I'm afraid."

They climbed the stairs to a hall lined with statues, religious pictures and spindly sword-plants. At the far end of the hallway was a grimy window, which doled out the late February light that had lost most of its power to illuminate and cheer during its transit through the smog of Cicero to the windows of the orphanage. The last door on the right was open a crack. Mrs. Healy, asserting her secular ascendancy in matters of domesticity over Sister Angelica's otherworldly prerogatives, stepped in front of them and opened the door for Ted. He tiptoed in.

Ted had spent many happy hours in this room. Its windows were always clean and its whitewashed walls glowed in the room's soft, clear, southern light. A large sixteenth-century Spanish crucifix was hung opposite the plain iron cot the priest slept on. There, he could see it first thing in the morning and the last thing at night, before he turned off his light. When visiting priests had commented that the crucifix was not over his bed, Father Feeney would answer, "I do not wish to enter my Lord's presence in the after-life with a thorough knowledge of the divine toenails."

Under the crucifix, there was a small prayer stool, and in front of that, there was a thin cushion that the old priest had begun to use only a few years earlier. A small sofa took up the space between the two southern-exposure windows. There were several flowerpots hanging from ceiling hooks and a small finch sang merrily in its bamboo cage by one of the windows.

But, now, for the first time, Ted found this room repellent. The sickly, sweet odor of illness frightened him. The sight of Father Feeney, lying still and pale on the iron cot, terrified him. That cot had been their overflow library table when they had covered the sofa with open books. And, now, Father Feeney, who had always been the liveliest man Ted had ever known, was silent and unmoving on it.

The invalid slowly opened his eyes and, seeing Ted, beckoned him over to the cot. He waved Mrs. Healy and Sister Angelica away. They left the doorway, shaking their heads.

Ted didn't have any idea what to do, so he knelt by the bed, as straight as a poker. Father Feeney smiled and reached out for his hand. Ted felt the clammy, sticky sickness on the hand that now grasped his, and he felt he would be sick.

"No, Ted, here, next to me...Sit beside me, here. I am not a dying God...not even a plaster saint. Don't kneel."

After a moment's pause, the old priest began to cough. This cough began deep in his stomach, and it gained strength as it fought its way up to his mouth. Wide-eyed with panic, Ted slowly rose while Father Feeney hacked and coughed, until he was limp with the effort. Ted was completely panicked. Seeing his terrified eyes, the dying priest tried to comfort his young friend.

"Ted, I'm over ninety years old. I was a medical missionary for thirty years before I came to St. Paul's and I know what I am dying of...Renal failure weakened me until pneumonia set in. Ah, Ted. Pneumonia. The old folks' friend. Ted, God is so subtle in His mercy. To kill me with quiet, tranquil pneumonia, rather than swamp me with the agonies of urine's nitrogen-poisoning. God is merciful."

Ted's young and ardent love was too strong for such mercy. His grief swamped him with an agony that made him want to howl. Only the eloquence of his inmost heart, which had been trained in the graces of rhetoric by this same Father Feeney, had the power to save him from the further agony of being ashamed of crying in front of his friend. Eloquence saved him, as pneumonia was soon to save his teacher. Bound together by what they saw as the *suavity* of their common Lord, the gentleness of the priest's pneumonia was echoed by the good manners of his young charge's love and concern.

"Ted. You are now seventeen. You came here when you were three. Many boys came to me who left St. Paul's as men. You came to me as an orphan, and you will leave me as a son."

Here his coughing began its insistent call to death. Ted saw the tears of effort run down Father Feeney's deeply lined cheeks as the old man tried to stop. He smiled at Ted, but the young man's misery was beyond soothing.

"Ted, my death is a sweet, gentle one. Be comforted. I have something to tell you."

He closed his eyes and his breath came fast and shallow. Ted ran to the door and beckoned to Sister Angelica. She stood in the doorway and looked at the old man with the practiced eye of nearly fifty years of nursing and patted Ted's head.

"He's just resting. He insisted that he tell you what he recently learned. I tried..." She trailed off and smiled at the old man. "He wanted to tell you himself. Go back and sit next to him. He has hours, well, some time before..."

She stopped, for pity of the boy.

Ted crept quietly back to the bedside so as not to disturb his sick friend. He knelt down again when he reached it. How could he stand up when Father Feeney was laid so low? He prayed softly, but audibly. He didn't want to keep his hopes and his fears to himself. He vowed to go into the priesthood, "If only Father Feeney gets well again."

Father Feeney heard that prayer and, turning his eyes from the crucifix over the little table opposite his bed, said softly, "No, Ted. Men who become priests as part of a deal make very bad ones. A man should become a priest only if he is truly and completely enamored of Mother Church."

He held out his right hand and pointed to the wedding ring he had worn since his ordination.

He began to cough again, but Ted had heard the old elegance in Father Feeney's speech and he was comforted by it. He felt better and, after the coughing fit had subsided, asked in his normal tone of voice, "Why is it Mother Church, Father Feeney?"

The old man's face relaxed for a moment as death's presence retreated into another corner of the room. Turning his head in the direction of the orphan kneeling at his bedside, he answered, "We are father and son, you and I. But, what a thing a mother is, Ted. No sooner do we leave the wet darkness of her womb, than we are dried off and laid on her breast. What we leave behind, we return to at once. What has fed us, we seek again. The body of the mother is eternity's promise to the newborn. The mother's body feeding us and her voice crooning in our ear, dispelling...Ted?"

"Yes, Father," the weeping boy answered, feeling motherless as never before.

"Ted, remember that we translated some Rilke?"

"I remember. 'Every angel is terrifying.'"

"Yes. '*Jeder einer Engel ist schrecklich.*' Well, I think what he means to tell us is that a mother doesn't know what it is her terrified child has seen when it cries out in the night and she comes to comfort it."

Here, Father Feeney lapsed into an old man's reflections. He started as he remembered Ted and continued, "You know? Perhaps, just perhaps, Ted, the child is right to cry out. Perhaps that child has seen something that its mother cannot remember...and her comforting makes the child forget something memorable. That's what Rilke says. But, just perhaps, Ted, she, I mean her warmth, her mother's body, perhaps they are all that stand between the young child and those very terrible forms which people the eternity the young child has just left so short a time before. If so, perhaps the mother is wise in her insistence that there is nothing there...and so, nothing is there to fear."

"I think I see, Father," Ted said, knowing he would see some day. "But, why can't I be a priest?" he insisted, choking up again.

The old man shut his eyes. His end, he knew, sat nearby, miraculously ignoring him for a few moments more, displaying a courtesy he had never before realized it could boast of. The old man then reflected on the terrible pride and grace behind the very human demands that would be laid on God's mercy in the funeral service his fellow priests would be holding for him in a few days: "Oh Lord," the imperative would ring out, "This alone I will require of Thee. To see the goodness of the Lord in the land of the living."

"God is merciful," the old priest breathed to all the sensed but unseen presences in the room. He continued, "Well, Ted, Mother Church is Heaven's gift, given to locate us here, outside eternity. But, Heaven gave us other mothers and fathers, who stand between us and certain very terrible powers, which the ancients personified as gods. They were not so far off, Ted. Not so far off as we like to think...and, as I, fibbing somewhat, in obedience to my mother, the church, have taught very many young men."

The old man patted Ted's head as a gesture of peace between them. Then, realizing that Death's courtesies were not to be tempted too far, he resumed, but with a faint voice and great effort, "Be a warden of those lesser personages of eternity, Ted, and I shall rest quietly."

He looked up, saw the terrible panic on Ted's face and he groaned out loud in his pity for the young man.

"God bless you, my son. Now you must go. Sister Angelica has something to tell you."

He touched the bell on the table by his cot and Sister Angelica came in and led Ted out, stepping aside for Mrs. Healy, who came in as they left.

"Did he tell you?" she asked Ted gently.

"Tell me? Tell me what?" Ted asked, dazed and sick with grief, love, and fear.

"Your real, natural mother...I mean your biological mother, she died last week and your half-brother is coming to take you home with him."

"Oh God, no. I hate them. Christ! I hate them!" Ted cried out, and Sister Angelica knew his oaths were not blasphemy and that Ted had caught sight of the creatures that peopled eternity.

The nun took his limp hand into hers and led him, like a child, until they came to the orphanage church and its side chapel, with its old statue of the Virgin Mother. Mary's statue was placed so that it permitted her to look over the heads of the worshippers kneeling at the altar at her feet. Her outspread arms supported a fine cloak of a deep blue, embroidered with golden stars. A small brilliant was sewn into the center of each star. As the votive candles at her feet trembled in their red glass containers, the stars shimmered on her deep blue cloak like the winter sky.

"Take comfort, Ted Simms. Your love for that good man will strengthen you...even on the edge of despair...even in the pit of it."

Ted looked blankly at her and, then, focusing his eyes on her face, asked her, in a low and trembling voice, "Have you ever had a broken heart, Sister?"

"Ah, Brother Ted," she answered with a smile that echoed her lovely name, "this withered face and body have not always been so...not always."

They knelt together and Sister Angelica continued, "The cloak you like so much, I made that for her statue, Ted. Each star, each brilliant. I did that."

"You did?" Ted asked, for a moment distracted from his sorrow.

"Yes, many years ago, when I was only a girl four years younger than you are now. This statue of the Blessed Mother was the pride of an Alsatian church. My family was very rich and we traveled every summer to Strasbourg. Being good Catholics, we went to Mass in the local church. She was there."

As she was telling her story, the choir began its rehearsals for the great Easter festival, now only a few weeks away. The imperative Te Deum, the soaring Jubilate and Gloria washed over Ted like the strong, soft hands of a mother examining her lost child for injuries when it is returned to her. Sister Angelica continued her story in a low voice, and Ted listened as he watched the Virgin's stars dancing in their sparkling light that they had borrowed from the votive candles.

"One summer, oh, I was fourteen, the little church was packed for a christening. Among the godparents' party was the most beautiful creature of God I had ever seen. In my enchantment, I thought I saw the Blessed Virgin herself, this very statue here before you, smile at him. He was very fair-skinned, with jet-black hair in tight ringlets. His brow was magnificent, and it was set over eyes of the deepest blue I've ever seen."

Here the old nun caught her breath, crossed herself and shut her eyes for a moment. Then, she continued, "My mother was a famous Philadelphia beauty, and, Ted, as hard as it is to imagine now, I took after her. Jean-Yves – that was his name, 'Jean-Yves' – graciously bestowed his smile on me, and I was nearly struck dead with joy. Such grace, Ted, such grace. Looking into his eyes, oh, dear Ted, I saw, as I then thought, and as I still believe now, so long after..."

Sister Angelica paused, frowned, and shook her head, "...well, to say it, the infinite fullness of God's own Heaven. But, I was a good daughter of the church, even then and I also saw in Jean-Yves' eyes that flaming sword that a merciful Heaven places before us, to keep us from paradise this side of the grave."

Sister Angelica was quiet for a long time. Then, she continued, after heaving a sigh that made her shudder so that Ted could see it, even under her thick robes, "That summer was truly terrible for me. I could see paradise clearly over Jean-Yves' shoulder when he rode by our house, but all institutions, sacred and civil, forbade me paradise and I was not, nor am I now, one to take Heaven's gifts to humans lightly. And, don't you, Ted," she added, looking at him sharply. In another moment, her face softened and she continued, "On the night before I was to return to America from that terrible summer...No," she corrected herself, "it was early in the morning we were leaving..."

Sister Angelica was again quiet. Then, with a start, she continued, "Yes...the last waxen, yellow phase of an old moon was just rising in the east. It was the final moment of an old man's faded glory, before the young sun rose behind it. I was sitting at my window looking over the park around our house and weeping for joy."

"For joy, Sister? Weren't you sad you were going home, away from..."

Ted could not bring himself to name Sister Angelica's suitor. His own loss lay too heavily on him.

"Oh, Ted Simms," the old nun said in a gay whisper Ted had never heard before from a nun, "Jean-Yves was never mine. How could I lose him? No," she continued meditatively, "no, my love for him, my joy in his beauty and manly grace, these were mine, Ted, and so I wept for joy."

She continued, after another long pause, "Well, I heard a noise and there, with his head level with mine, was Jean-Yves on the back of his hunter. He leaned into the window, and softly brushed my lips with his, and, then, without a word, rode off."

"And?" Ted asked softly, when she had been silent for a long time. "What then, Sister?"

"I was broken hearted," she whispered.

"Broken hearted? Not happy?" Ted whispered back.

"But, Ted! Jean-Yves, whom I loved dearly, had taken from me what was not his to take...and that without even asking me! At that moment, I vowed myself to the life-long service of the Church, and I have never regretted it for a moment."

"But, he only kissed you, Sister, and you loved him," Ted objected.

"Yes, and, at that moment, I knew I was born to gaze at paradise, but not enter it in this life. I have spent my life and it has been a long one, Ted, comforting other outcasts and foundlings. I was born, it seems, into exile."

Just then, the great base bell of the church carillon began booming its death-knell. Father Feeney had died.

"Oh, dear Mother of God!" Ted cried to the statue, glorious in its blazing cloak. "Oh, Sister, my father is dead," he cried out, turning to the old nun, groping clumsily for her arm.

Then, Sister Angelica, for the first time in her long life, held a young man in her arms and she kissed the top of the head she clasped to her bosom. Her plain black robe enfolded the boy and comforted him as the Virgin's robe had bedazzled him. But, this was not done in pity, for what was there to pity in such loving grief? And, it was not an act of mercy, for that same grief asked for no mercy and gave no quarter. Sister Angelica has ceased to be a nun to Ted and had become his sister.

Ted lived the next few days until the funeral in slow motion. He attended to each and every task, no matter how small or trivial, with an infinite care for detail. And, time flew. Nothing followed anything; nothing caused anything; nothing was the consequence of anything. Each and every single thing in his world jostled and shoved its way into importance, only to be replaced by another jostling and shoving something. And, then it was time for the funeral to take place in the packed orphanage church.

No funeral is pleasant, no matter how hated the deceased. But, in the orphanage, funerals had a terrible immediacy that made them particularly horrible to the mourners. Sitting packed together, the children were a sea of despondency and loss in a world that had denied them their status as the welcome consequence of the natural human act of love that results in generation. Their adoptive fathers were celibate priests who loved them in the name of a long since dead, long since risen, God-Man, and their mother was something called Mother Church, a vast organization whose body covered the planet and whose head, in Rome in Italy – so far from Cicero, Illinois – was a man known to them as The Holy Father. Thus, they were doubly motherless, since a human Holy Father dominated even this mystical mother, Mother Church. So, the death of the man who had been a friend and teacher to so many of them unleashed the specter of the loss of human life itself. If Mother Church taught that Christ, in dying, killed death, these terrified orphans saw Father Feeney's death as killing life. And so, they clung to one another and wept tears as a single boy.

Ted learned two things that dismal day, things that he carefully remembered, thought about and never forgot.

First, his thirteen years as the rector's particular favorite at a Roman Catholic orphanage had involved a great deal of exposure to real discussions about the supernatural. But, it was Father Feeney's death that gave Ted his first true experience of the supernatural. His dear friend, Father, teacher and almost daily companion, was now dead and, looking like a wax doll, lay motionless in his simple, box-like casket. It seemed to Ted that only a great power could have done this to so great and vital a friend. The first lesson Ted learned that day, even in the face of the terrible power that hurt him so by killing Father Feeney, was that no hurt is so great or private that fellow-mourners could not lift off some of it and make it more bearable. So, if the same power that killed Father Feeney was the power that caused him such pain, his fellow mourners had a power to comfort that was somehow comparable to the other's power to kill and hurt.

The second, allied thing Ted learned at Father Feeney's funeral was that human institutions of burial and interment were human institutions, no matter who said they were divinely commanded. As he watched the officiating priests go through the carefully prescribed funeral rite, he saw living men, who were like what the dead Father Feeney had been, doing what living humans do in the face of death's mindless intrusion into human affairs. Death's sting was delivered by death, but these living humans who had survived it felt it. The comfort living humans gave to each other when they mourned the death of a friend, that seemed to Ted to be the way live humans face off against that immense power that so terribly disturbs the human orders of love, friendship, and learning, by killing us.

As an echo of this second lesson, Ted learned to love and revere human institutions and to fear what he saw as those supernatural powers from which they were designed to protect us.

# CHAPTER 4

## Natural Affection

Father Feeney had died on Thursday. The funeral had been on the following Monday and, at nine-thirty sharp on the Monday morning following that, Ted and his new-found half-brother met in what had been Father Feeney's office. Sister Angelica introduced Ted to his only living blood relative.

"Ted, this is your half-brother, David Serles. Mister Serles, your half-brother, Ted Simms."

She had seated Ted in a large chair facing David Serles, and she had taken a third chair between them, but somewhat to the side. She sat up very straight, as did David. Ted slumped.

"Hello, Ted," David said. He was around thirty years old, and he sported a blue-black five o'clock shadow, even at nine-thirty in the morning.

"Hi," Ted said flatly, looking at the floor at his feet.

"I've come to take you home with me, Ted."

"This is my home. The only home I've ever had. It's good enough for me. It's always been good enough before," Ted answered, without looking up.

"Well, I know how you must feel."

Still, without looking up, Ted answered, "No, you don't. You couldn't." Then, finally looking up, he said, "Please, it's nearly Easter. If you have money for me, put it into an account, and let me finish school here in," and, looking at Sister Angelica, he finished, "twelve weeks?"

"About that, Ted," Sister Angelica answered.

"I'll pay room and board here. But, if they'll let me, I'll stay here until I graduate, and then I'll go to college. Father Feeney, my real father, wanted it that way."

Sister Angelica nodded her consent to this proposal.

"Okay, Ted, if that's what you want."

"That's what I want, and ... how much money do I have, anyway?" Ted asked, looking at David with an expression of icy indifference on his face. "And, where is it?" he asked, as an afterthought.

"Your father, who was named Martin Parker, died several years ago. 'Simms' is your mother's maiden name. Your father left you the beneficiary of his insurance. One hundred thousand dollars."

"Why didn't you tell me right away?"

"My...our mother was named as co-owner of the policy, and she didn't tell anyone. It was in her will that we first discovered it."

Ted did not move a muscle. "Where is it?" he asked after a moment.

"I'm a banker. It's in my bank. It's safe."

"Thank you."

Ted got up and walked out the door, without looking back. Sick with fury, he sat in the hall outside. "That bastard. Now he comes. I hate him!"

After what seemed a long time to Ted, the door opened, and David came out. He walked up to where Ted was sitting and said, "I didn't know about you until two weeks ago, Ted. I'm sorry. I hope someday we can be better friends."

Ted had just been through such storms of pain and grief from his own loss that he was unable to turn down any pleas for kindness. He looked up at David's stricken face and held out his hand.

"I'll try. But, it'll take time...okay?"

"Thank you, Ted." He turned around and slowly went down the stairs. When Ted heard the front door close behind David, he turned to Sister Angelica and slowly asked, as much to himself as to her, "Christ! Won't it ever stop, Sister?"

"Be patient, Ted. Your heart is wounded, again. Only people with real hearts can be wounded more than once. Trust your good heart and be patient. It will stop. But, trust your heart, Ted, trust your heart."

She was right. A few weeks of hard schoolwork, with his life-long friends' spontaneous care and special shows of affection, brought Ted to where he could again laugh and play pranks. His dreams were terrifying, but his waking hours were sweet. Saint Paul's had been a kind and gentle home to him, and he loved it.

And, then, one day very close to graduation, and the time for leaving Saint Paul's permanently, it struck him: "One hundred thousand dollars. All mine to do with as I want!" He grinned to himself and, then, his face became blank. He began to think about his responsibility to that bequest. He thought long and hard and, several days later, he casually waylaid Mrs. Healy at the rectory.

"How's yerself, Ma Healy?" Ted asked, with an impish grin.

"Ah, Ted, you've bounced back nicely. You look much fitter," she said, carrying a pail of water and mop into her kitchen.

"Here now, let me do that for yer," Ted said, taking the pail from her hands.

"It's a pleasure. I'm getting on, and my rheumatics is a trial to me and no joking about it, I'll tell ya," she answered with a smile.

"No, you old thing, you! Why, Mrs. Healy, I was just going to ask ya to marry me," Ted said, shaking his head in disappointment.

"It's Elizabeth Anne Healy yer talkin' ta, not to Abraham's wife, Sarah, you scamp. And, what would I be doing with another man, after Ar-ther? And, me goin' on sixty-three," she said, beaming.

"Ah, then, if I cannot have you, its Sister Angelica I'll be courting now. I'll write the Pope himself in Rome and ask His Holiness to release her, so we can get hitched. What do you think? Will she have me?"

"Oh, Ted, listen to yer run on! It's the hot place for ya, if ya go on this way."

"Well, how old is Sister Angelica, Ma?" Ted asked idly, as he helped her by filling the pail with hot water out of the tap.

"Oh, Sister Angelica would be sixty-eight, or maybe even sixty-nine."

"Why doesn't she retire?" Ted asked, as he brought the pail over to where Mrs. Healy was standing with her mop.

"She's a saint, that one, and no two ways about it, Ted Simms. Her people was old Philadelphia money, and her the only child. She was rich when her own family died years ago. She gave it all to the poor, just as our own dear Savior counseled us to do, if we would enter the Kingdom of Heaven. A living saint, that one, Ted Simms."

"So? Why doesn't she retire?"

"She'd have to go to one of them homes for the poor religious, and that would break her. No...she'll not rust. She'll wear out in harness and drop in the traces. A living saint, that one."

"She's old enough to retire? Really?"

"Lord, yes. She could've retired years ago."

"Bless ya, Mither Healy. I'll dance at your wedding, I will," Ted said, and amazed her with a peck on the cheek.

"That's my wake you'd be dancing at, you scamp."

Ten days before he graduated, Ted, an orphan with one hundred thousand dollars with which to enter the world, turned eighteen. During those ten days, Ted was constantly humming, whistling, and full of pranks and laughter. Everyone was glad to see him so well. During the morning of the last day of classes, he was called out of Algebra to sign for a registered letter. He opened it and found three gold credit cards, in his name.

"Ha!" is all that he said, as he shuffled them back and forth in his hands. After lunch that day, he gently knocked on the door of Sister Angelica's office and told her secretary, Miss Blake, that he was there for his appointment. He was shown right in and stayed for a long time. After an hour, Miss Blake's intercom began to buzz with requests for surprising phone numbers: the German Embassy; the passport bureau; Chase Manhattan Bank – foreign deposits; The First National Bank of Lake Placid, New York; the bishop.

"Jesus, Joseph, and Mary! What is going on?" Miss Blake asked herself.

Inside the office, Ted had come straight to the point as soon as he sat down. "This unknown mother and father of mine have left me a lot of guilt money, Sister. I want to go to Europe, to study *Stattswissenschaft*, or whatever they call Political Science. I think that's what they call it. Father Feeney tells me...told me...they are less provincial than most American departments."

"Wonderful! I have some family friends left in Strasbourg. Could they help?"

"They sure could. That part of Europe is pretty much bilingual, and I understand they like Americans, and that a lot of them study at the university there. But, Sister," Ted continued with an anxious look and a strain in his voice, "I have an idea. I want you to hear me out without interruption. Will you, please?"

Sister Angelica had been around boys for too long to want to do anything of the sort, but the expression of supplication on Ted's face

*Naturally Bad Manners*

softened her heart. She nodded "Yes."

"Well, I'm just eighteen and a babe in the woods. No! I've never even been in the woods! I don't want to live with David and his family. It would be too hard now and, besides, I want to study in Europe. I have nowhere to call home back here, and I'm a little afraid that I'll have a lot of trouble making it, if I don't have some help."

"Yes?" Sister Angelica asked, completely aware of the truth of what he was saying.

"Well, I'm an heir, and what with your Social Security and pension, we two could live cheaper than one."

Sister Angelica gasped out loud, and her right hand clutched at her chest in surprise. Her left hand felt for her rosary.

Ted continued evenly, "With your pension and your Social Security, you would have an income of around a thousand a month."

"How could you know all about that, Ted Simms?" Sister Angelica asked, wide-eyed with astonishment.

"Oh. I cozied up to some people," Ted answered, with a very self-satisfied grin.

"Ted Simms, you were born a Jesuit!" the old nun said, in spite of herself.

"No, Sister, Father Feeney warned me away from that path. So I'm practicing Machiavellianism on my own. At any rate, Sister Angelica, I need a Dutch Aunt. Will you help me? I'll be a good Dutch nephew, if you'll agree. Will you?" Ted finished with a strong tremor in his voice. They were both silent for a moment and then, Ted continued, with a mischievous grin, "I'm tired of being adopted. I want to adopt for a change. I want to claim you for my own aunt."

Sister Angelica reached over and patted Ted on the cheek.

"Ted, I'll speak to the Mother, to my confessor, to the bishop, and I'll pray on it. I'll let you know within two weeks, at most. And, Ted, I like the idea of being adopted." Pointing to the thin gold band on the ring finger of her right hand, she continued, "I've been married to the church since I was eighteen. I am now..." and she interrupted herself, with a smile.

"You know how old I am, don't you, Ted?"

"Sixty eight?"

"No. I'm seventy-two. So, I've been married to the church for fifty-four years. I think that my Lord would not mind so much if I were also adopted as an aunt, at this late date. I am very complimented. Thank you, Ted. Thank you for asking me."

The old nun's eyes misted up and Ted looked away.

Sister Angelica conferred with her confessor, with her Mother Superior, with her bishop, and, only when they had agreed enthusiastically, did she, through her prayers, ask her Lord and Savior to ratify or veto the idea. Her spiritual exercises all pointed in the direction of an unequivocal seconding of her earthly motion by the Divine Senate, and so she retired on July 15, after fifty-four years of service, first as a medical missionary, and then as a teacher of Biology and Latin to homeless, unwanted boys.

Ted was delighted when she told him. He took her out to dinner to celebrate, and scandalized her by insisting that he call her Aunt Angelica. But she soon came to like it. They flew to Strasbourg in late September, where they took up a comfortable apartment near the university. The old lady, her robes and enormous white wings of her headdress flapping in the breeze delighted the locals, talked loudly to the handsome, gray-eyed student. Ted found her unendingly good natured, and never suspected for a moment that, since she had been dealing with boys for over forty years, she could read his moods even before he even had any sense he was in one of them.

And so, Ted's first real activity as a legal man was to establish a sort of family for himself. He and Aunt Angelica argued as any very old maiden aunt might argue with her young, handsome nephew. And, just as was the case with any true nephew, Ted had to abide by his aunt's final decisions on matters of faith and morals. Ted argued his points loudly and at length, but if he could not persuade her, he gave in. And, by no means always gracefully. The power and soundness of their mutual love and respect was nowhere so clearly revealed as in those cases where Ted thought that Aunt Angelica was being a pig-headed old dinosaur. For, although he often gave in with very bad grace, he never just pretended to give in to soothe her – only to do later whatever it was that he had wanted to do. He might moan and groan, but he never cheated when she stood firm. She knew this, and particularly loved him for it.

After three years of this life together, Ted woke one morning to discover that the coffee had not been made and the croissants had not been laid out on the little table set by the bay window. He knew at once that he had lost his adopted aunt to death during the night. But, by now, Ted was on his own. He had been twice elected – first by the orphanage and then by his dead father's will – and he had twice elected to love in his twenty-one years – the first time, Father Feeney, the second time, Aunt Angelica. Ted had overcome his lifelong feeling that he was nothing but someone's scandal. Ted now knew that the Father Feeneys of this world did not love, teach and nurture scandals. Likewise, Sister Angelica would never have permitted a true mistake to adopt her as his own. Ted was somebody. He had loved and he had been loved. He had been adopted and he had adopted.

\* \* \*

Ted took his time and took three more years to finish his college studies. He went to Paris to work on Rousseau for his Ph.D. dissertation. He finished this in four years and it was published, simultaneously, in a French and in an English translation. He spent another year traveling around Europe and only began seriously to job-hunt when a letter from David Serles informed him that life in Paris had been very expensive, and that he had better start earning money. He was not broke, but it was time to begin work. He began to apply for teaching jobs and was soon offered a position at Chaldes College, in Chaldes, New York. He accepted.

During the time he was studying in Europe, Ted had his friends at St. Paul's forward his mail. David Serles wrote once or twice a year, and Ted dutifully sent him a polite progress report at Christmas. He wrote David and told him that he had a job at Chaldes, not far from Lake Placid. David wrote him a warm letter asking him to let him know when he settled in. After he found an apartment in Chaldes' Left Bank, Ted sent David his address and, in a short time, received an invitation to spend a few days with him and his family.

"My daughters, your nieces, will vamp you unmercifully, but, at ten and twelve, that's what girls do to houseguests – and, of course, to the postman, when the spell's on them."

Ted accepted, with a sense of anticipation that surprised him. "I must be getting over something," he thought to himself, as he wrote his letter telling David that he would like to meet his family.

The visit was a delight. David was intelligent and genuinely kind. His wife, Sue, was both warm and a little shy, a combination Ted found made him feel very much at home right away. His two half-nieces, Anne and Margaret, amazed and charmed him with their constant indecision as to whether they were little girls or young vamps.

David had done well in banking. He and Sue spent little and did not plan to have more children. An account for the girls, fully funded by insurance, was enough to guarantee them educations at good colleges and a year or two of traveling after that. So, at thirty-seven, David and Sue enjoyed a quiet security that Ted found very pleasant.

On the evening before he was to return to Chaldes, David waited until after Sue had disappeared with the girls; then, he asked Ted to come with him to the den.

"Before you go, I'd like to ask if there is anything I can do, money wise or otherwise, to give you a little help in getting started, now that you have a position at Chaldes."

"Well, you know...? I don't really make enough. Europe, at least Paris, was damned expensive and I..." here Ted hesitated. David sat quietly and waited.

Ted continued, "Well, I make enough at Chaldes to make ends meet, but I couldn't marry on what I am making. And, David, I want someone to call my own. I don't like being lonely...so I'll take you up on your question."

"Shoot," David answered, sitting back comfortably.

"Would it be legal for your bank to pay me a consultant's fee, if I figured out a way for you to get a set of accounts you probably wouldn't have otherwise?" Ted asked slowly.

"Possibly. What's your idea?"

"I don't want really big money. But, I would like to make around three to five thousand a year more than my teacher's salary will give me for the next few years. My idea for your bank is a sort of steal from Sears. They have all those home and personal services, like window-replacement, vinyl siding, and that sort of thing. Those services sell Sears products, but private contractors that Sears locates and pays up front do the actual installation. The customer charges it on their Sears

## Naturally Bad Manners

credit card and Sears in turn charges their own interest on the loan, plus what it costs them to borrow the up-front money they paid the service contractors. Am I on target?"

"Yes, very much on target. But, where did you get your business savvy?"

"It just occurred to me one day as I read the papers, and they had an ad for Sears services. I asked myself the fundamental question of Political Science: '*Cui Bono*?' – 'Who Benefits?' – and this came to mind. At any rate, I imagine that your mid-sized business loans are to small home improvement companies, appliance stores and that sort of thing."

"Exactly."

"Am I right in thinking that most of your smaller personal loans are to people who want big appliances or home improvement loans?"

"Well, except for second mortgages and car loans, sure."

"Well, my bright idea is to do like Sears does...or better. Your bank could computer-date goods and services. Mr. and Mrs. Jones come in for a home- improvement loan. You have ready a stable full of home-improvement companies who owe your bank money. You match up the customer with the company, and the customer pays you back, after you have paid the company. Only you get a lock on the loan and the interest. I have a feeling this banking service would get you a lot of small businesses you don't now have. And, if you did a sort of Dun and Bradstreet rating to check their reliability and the worth of their warranties, you could give good advice on prospective personal loans."

"A very interesting idea, Ted. How do you see yourself as fitting into the picture? Just how could I approach my trustees to get them to pay you a consultant's fee? Any ideas?"

"Sure. Tell them I'd interview all your business accounts within the area you do most of your business in. I'd get each of them to design a brochure – or even do it myself – listing their services. By the way, do you have either an advertising account or a printer among your clients?"

"Sure, both."

"Well, have these accounts pay for their own brochures, and then file the services of the other companies, according to what type of loan would pay for their services. As Mr. and Mrs. Borrower come in, you match 'em up."

"Ted, that's interesting. I think it might fly with my trustees. I'll certainly give it a try."

They drank to the idea and to the possibility of a friendly and mutually profitable business relationship in the future – and to the as-yet unknown wife Ted could entice with the money such a relationship would realize. As they were toasting the future, the girls came bouncing into the room, demanding to sit on Uncle Ted's lap and, when they had been cuddled and put to bed, Ted, Sue, and David sat up and drank until their own bedtime.

Ted returned to Chaldes the next day. Anne and Margaret were in their Sarah Bernhart phase that day, and they wept to see Ted off in his classic Volvo convertible, the top down, as if he were leaving them on the back of the executioner's cart. He returned to his classes, and David returned to his bank. Since David was known to be a careful and prudent banker, his proposals were always considered carefully, and the board gave its approval to an initial three-year, nine thousand dollar contract. The only qualification they added to the proposal David had presented was, if the bank's stable of borrowers did not happen to include some particular business that was needed by a particular loan applicant, then Mr. Simms was expected to seek out and close with a reasonable addition. Also, the first year's fee of three thousand dollars was to cover his initial review of the bank's clients and a general statement of strengths and weaknesses in his own area – for example, was the bank's portfolio of small businesses essentially lacking in some area?

Ted received a long letter spelling out the conditions of his consultantship. He sent his unqualified agreement with their terms in the next mail, with his own proviso that his first check would be paid to him no later than May 31st.

Ted began working on the project after Christmas. He immediately discovered that he liked American small-businessmen. They were intelligent, resourceful, and very hard working. He also discovered that many small businesses involved a wife in a central capacity, acting as secretary-treasurer-office-manager, with a brood of children at home being cared for by a grandma. These wives kept the books, bought insurance, and paid premiums and taxes, on time, filled out workmen's compensation forms, social security records, and so on. However glamorous and amusing the famous European wife might be, her American counterpart could work, manage, mother, and smile. Ted liked this work.

His pleasure in meeting these businessmen, together with the obvious advantages of his idea, made Ted successful. He soon found a printer who was willing to be the in-house jobber, and the list of brochures of businesses ready to serve prospective borrowers at the bank was soon impressively long. By April 15th, the bank's accountant reported that, since the first of the year, business had picked up impressively and that the three thousand dollars to be paid to Mister Simms was a sound investment for the bank. David was complimented by his board of trustees and immediately wrote to congratulate Ted and to thank him. They had both profited because of Ted's efforts. David ended his April 16th congratulatory letter to Ted with what would be a fateful question:

"You've certainly earned your fee many times over by establishing an excellent working relationship with these clients. We are also getting a lot of requests from our big personal depositors for a really trustworthy travel agent, but we don't have one on the books, as yet. Any ideas? Best from Sue, Anne, and Margaret. Sincerely, David. P.S. Your check will be arriving on or about June 1. We are paying your withholding taxes ourselves, as a sort of bonus. The check will be all gravy! Congratulations again. D."

Ted's years at St. Paul's, together with his years spent in Europe under the watchful eye of Sister Angelica, had made business second nature to him. He smiled at the last line of the letter and then immediately re-read David's request for the name of a good travel agent whom Ted was to contact and vouch for. He picked up a pencil and began to tap it as he collected his thoughts.

"A travel agent. Someone in this area who has real connections with a foreign country, preferably England or France...and who is thoroughly dependable. Large order."

Ted looked through the business directory for the triangle whose three apexes were Lake Placid, Corning, and Chaldes. A lot of rich people lived in that area and many of them banked at David's bank. The directory listed a number of travel agencies, but a little investigation revealed that most of them did their business selling tours to senior citizens' groups and high schools. He was looking for personalized service. Then, he saw a half-page ad that read: "Feeling Wayward? Call Windward Island Tours. Lake Placid, New York." Ted liked the ad, but was puzzled as to where these Windward Islands were. So, surveying the bookshelves that occupied every square inch of wall space not already taken up by doors and windows, Ted located his atlas. Taking it down, he found that the Windward Islands were in the Caribbean. They included French-speaking islands like Martinique and St. Vincent, together with St. Lucia. Still pretty much in the dark, Ted next called the college librarian, who knew everything about everything, whether or not it mattered to anyone. He was told at once that St. Vincent spoke a mixture of French and English, and St. Lucia spoke a sort of compote of French and God-knows-what, which they called "patois." When Ted asked about the dominant culture there, he was told it was deeply French, with a British overlay. Ted thanked him and hung up.

"So," he thought to himself, "this is interesting...British and French. Good. David's rich vacationers should go for that."

He called the number listed in the ad, and a voice answered, "Yes? This is Laura Miller, the proprietress of Windward Island Tours. May I be of help?"

Ted had never heard a female voice like this one. It was very deep, rather British, and very lilting – almost singsong. Ted told her who he was and then gave her a quick sketch of what he did for David's bank. Laura Miller sounded interested and said she would very much like to pursue the matter further. A date was named and, after a few minutes' polite wrangling as to who would travel to see whom to discuss the matter face-to-face, Ted persuaded her to let him come to Lake Placid, where both his brother and the bank were located. She agreed and Ted hung up.

"What a voice," he mused to himself. "I wonder what Laura Miller looks like. Well, I'll soon find out."

Laying down his pencil, Ted sat back in his chair and thought about his imagination. He had been alone too long to be sentimental about it. It was almost always stupid and depressing, showing him commodities that he was either too bankrupt or too decent to buy. He thought out loud to himself, "But I am about ready to marry. This money from David's bank would make it possible. What a voice."

Since he taught on a Monday-Wednesday-Friday schedule, Ted was free on Tuesdays and Thursdays. His appointment with Laura Miller was at noon on the following Tuesday. Since the sixty-mile drive to Lake Placid usually required a little over an hour and a half to drive, he planned to leave at ten o'clock.

The day arrived with a late-spring intensity that made the prospect of driving unpleasant. One minute, the white-gray clouds framed a Mediterranean blue sky, and the next minute, a black-black blanket of cold rain that made it next to impossible to see out the windshield swallowed up that blue.

Ted drove into the Lake Placid Inn parking lot twenty minutes late for his appointment. His jaws hurt from clenching them and his neck hurt from hunching over the steering wheel. The rain was skimming the blacktop of the parking lot as it fled April's furious attempt to keep winter nearby. When he reached the lobby, he was damp, cold, and tense. As he entered, he scanned the deep armchairs scattered around the lobby, and his eyes stopped at the third chair. He knew this was Laura Miller. Even sitting down, she seemed tall. Her skin was *café au lait* creamy-brown. Her hair was chestnut-red, with flecks of bronze highlighting, and her eyes were green. She sat with her ankles crossed. Ted felt sure that no one else in the lobby could possibly have had the voice he had heard on the phone.

"Good Lord!" Ted breathed out loud to himself when he saw her. Laura heard this and smiled. Ted realized that he was breathing like a beached catfish, and he tried to hide the fact by attempting to breathe with his mouth closed. This only made his nostrils flare like a bull in heat. Laura saw this, too. She smiled, again.

"You must be Ted Simms." She stood up and indeed, she was tall. She reminded Ted of a whirlwind, of a living tornado that touched the ground with feet domesticated in stylish Italian leather shoes. As he took in her bronze-red hair and dusky skin, with her flame-green eyes, Ted thought of the storm he had just driven through to get there. But, this graceful tempest facing him in the lobby was no flighty April. Laura's colors were very carefully welded together by her short, v-neck dress of a wet tree-bark brown, overlaid with a pattern of russet maple leaves, and deep green slashes. Her shoes were the same green, and her stockings were cream-colored. She wore heavy earrings of twisted gold, and no other jewelry. Ted glanced at her left hand, and he saw, with a relief that Laura saw, that there was no wedding ring. Ted sighed, and they went into the dining room, where Laura had reserved a table by the large bay window that even good inns insist on in their dining rooms – usually overlooking the parking lot.

The business part of their meeting was a disaster. Each time they came to some crucial question of facts and figures, the whirling clouds took their shadows and their rain elsewhere and a brilliant sun shone on them. Ted and Laura were dazzled into talking about this. And, then, they looked at each another and nibbled on the tips of bread-sticks or chewed on the plastic straws that had been set into their largely untouched drinks.

By two o'clock, Laura had told Ted about Lotario and Mamman, and how and why she had shed "Angelina Ursina" in favor of "Laura Miller." By three o'clock, Ted had told Laura about St. Paul's orphanage, about Father Feeney and about Sister Angelica and Europe. They touched sympathetic fingers at particularly pathetic moments in their narrations of their personal dramas, and by four o'clock, they were told to please go out into the lobby, so that the waiters could set up the dining room for dinner.

As they waited for their check, Ted told Laura that he would very much like to have her come down to Chaldes for a social visit. Laura answered, "I would very much like to do this, Ted. Would you then like to meet Mamman?"

At the moment the word "Mamman" left Laura's lips, a tree just outside the lobby-door responded to a particularly powerful blast of wind by snapping off a few feet above the ground and crashing into both of their cars. As it fell, its branches tore down the wires leading into the inn and tore out a number of panes of glass from the bay window. Everything was in pitch black darkness for a moment, and then the emergency lights came on and showed Ted and Laura, locked together as if they had been carved from a single block of granite. The transformer on the utility pole just outside the broken windows then exploded, and a geyser of sparks and blue-green flames shot into the air, illuminating the couple in its flashes. Waitresses ran screaming

*Naturally Bad Manners*

through the room, while bus boys and managers filled the kitchens and lobby with their curses and directions. The heavens ignored their curses and the help ignored their directions. A downed high-voltage wire in the parking lot whipped back and forth and, touching a car, set it on fire. Laura and Ted moved closer to the bay window, and were immediately drenched by torrents of wind-driven rain coming through the openings left when the tree branches broke out most of its panes. The blue-green flashes of the transformer's flames picked out the green of Laura's eyes and the slashes on her wet, clinging dress. The orange flames of the burning car picked up the russet of the maple leaves on her dress and highlighted her fashionably upswept hair, with its tiny points of brilliant red-bronze. Ted looked at her in this light and whispered into her ear, "What a storm you are, Laura. What a raging calm. It stills me."

Laura smiled and held him lightly. Then, placing her lips to his left ear, she whispered back, "I like your style, Ted Simms. It suits me."

That April's storm subsided, and a sullen sun shone orange-red beneath the clouds, as it sank slowly in the south. Washed in that somber red, Ted and Laura walked around until they found an empty bar. They made themselves drinks and filled some bowls with olives and peanuts. They then wandered around until they found a comfortable sofa, where they sat, drank, ate, and talked, knowing that, sooner or later, someone or other would come and take them wherever it was they wanted to go – something neither of them knew nor cared about. But, after a while, they heard the sirens, which announced that the utility and fire companies were coming and, at six o'clock, Ted and Laura were standing on the front steps of her large home in an expensive suburb of Lake Placid. Just as Laura was about to ring the bell, she explained to Ted, "Marie only speaks the patois of St. Lucia. It is not the French you spoke at the university in Paris. Her husband, Charles, the chef and man-of-all-trades around the house, knows English. Mamman does not like to use English."

She was about to respond to Ted's quizzical look, when Marie opened the door, a very fat, short, black woman with the most contagious smile Ted had ever seen. She smiled, and Ted smiled back, and then she bowed them in. As they entered a wide hall lighted by a large chandelier, Laura explained to Ted that there was a separate apartment in the house – "Mamman sometimes has visitors." Ted was asked to follow Marie to it and told to take a shower to warm up, while Marie dried out and ironed his damp clothing.

"I'll see you at seven thirty for dinner, Ted. *Au revoir.* Ah, if you need anything at all, touch the buzzer by your bed...no matter what the hour. We do not keep especially regular hours in this house," she explained, with a vague wave of her hand.

Marie took Ted upstairs into a large living room off the hall. Ted saw that it was part of a separate apartment, which had a kitchen, bath, and bedroom. The living room even had a sizable library. Ted stood and looked around, while Marie hovered just behind him. He turned and addressed her in his very good Parisian French. Marie broke into gales of laughter, which shook her like a waterbed. After her laughter had subsided somewhat, she told him, in the worst French he had ever heard, that his French was the worst she had ever heard. They both laughed and then spoke very slowly to each other. They thought they could make out what the other said. Marie told him to strip, so she could prepare his bath. She brought him a number of robes from the bedroom closet, and one of these fit him very well. He proceeded to undress under Marie's coolly appraising gaze – he felt sure that she would give Laura a preliminary report – and then he gave her his damp, wrinkled clothes. She left and Ted had no sooner finished showering and shaving than Marie was back with his clothes, dry and beautifully pressed.

"Merci," Ted said.

"Pooh! Day roan – presumably, *de rien.*"

As he followed Marie down the front hall stairs, Ted took a better look at the house. Its walls were hung with authentic eighteenth-century French engravings and the furniture was good Empire. The rugs were deep and richly colored. Marie led him into a large living room, which had an ornate crystal chandelier and a fireplace, with a small fire burning in it. Laura stood in front of it, with a very small black lady at her right side. The old lady's left hand, no bigger than a child's, rested on Laura's right forearm.

Laura was dressed in a fashionable, electric blue silk cocktail dress, obviously Italian, and the old lady was dressed in a floor-length, bright orange tube of raw silk, with a black vest. On her head, she wore a

*Naturally Bad Manners*

deep blue turban.

"This is Mamman?" Ted asked, walking up to the old lady and extending his hand.

"Yes, this is Mamman," Laura answered. The old lady extended her hand slowly and, when she shook it, Ted felt its strength. She looked keenly at him and then acknowledged his presence with a slight nod and a faint smile. Ted felt as if he were being presented to the queen.

They had drinks, and Ted thanked Laura for the accommodations, and complimented her on Marie.

"Oh...Marie...yes. She goes with the place. Mamman delivered the first of her many children after the local M.D. had given both her and the baby up for lost. She had quite a few more after that, and Mamman delivered them all. She and Charles adopted Mamman and, when we came to North America, they all came with us. They go with the house."

Ted was delighted. There were many ways in which the orphanage was a terrible and cold place to grow up, but it was never lonely, and Ted had a taste for large families. He thus heard this last piece of information about the size of Laura's entourage with glee.

"I like a large family," he said with an open smile. Laura looked at him and raised a speculative eyebrow. Mamman permitted herself a slight smile. She had never really been close to a white skinned, blonde haired, gray-eyed male before. And, this Ted seemed to know how to behave himself.

Dinner was announced by Marie, and they went into the adjacent room, where a large sideboard was loaded with fish, roasts, vegetables, and fruits – many of which Ted had never seen before.

"Are we expecting anyone else?" Ted asked.

"No, why?"

"There's enough here to feed an army."

"Marie and Charles have a large family, and Marie herself is not a light eater," Laura answered as they sat down. Marie brought dish after dish, from which they chose their dinners. When she had served them, Marie opened bottles both of red and white wine, from French châteaux Ted had never heard of before, and poured whichever each of them asked for. They were delicious.

Soon after dinner, Mamman looked at her watch and got up.

"Mamman gets up early, Ted. Will you excuse us for a few moments? I like to chat with her a little before we part for the evening."

"Of course. And, thank you, Madame, for your hospitality," Ted said bowing to Mamman. She smiled and went out with Laura.

Ted sat for the half hour Laura was gone and reflected that he could not remember a more pleasant evening. Then, looking around him at the rich furniture and rugs, Ted found himself thinking ruefully that it was not likely a rich widow was going to become seriously interested in a political scientist at a small liberal arts college in upstate New York. By the time Laura returned, Ted was in a very bad mood.

"Good heavens, Ted. What is the matter?" Laura asked, as soon as she saw his face.

Ted had been Aunt Angelica's nephew for too long for him to beat around the bush when asked a direct question. He told her simply that he had never found a family as pleasant as hers and that he had begun to think he would like to be a part of it. But, he was only a semi-poor nobody at a small college. What chance did he have?

"Ted, dear, I am neither American nor British. In the islands, a woman is expected to bring a good dowry with her to her husband – especially if he is a professional, as are you. But, if even things go that way," and she here held up a cautionary hand as Ted began to sputter his embarrassment, "although Mamman has taken to you more than I dreamed – your combination of gray eyes and being a college professor has impressed her very much, and she thoroughly approves of your courtesies toward her...still, she is old, and she is afraid that if I were to marry a North American, he would treat her badly. She made me promise just now that I would marry no one who is not an islander until after her death."

"An islander?" Ted asked, more surprised than disappointed.

"Ah! Mamman knows that no island male would dare ignore her wishes..." Laura shrugged and her voice trailed off.

"But, she would not mind your living with one of the fair skinned barbarians?"

"Oh, yes. I am a widow, a rich widow, and I can do pretty well as I please in matters of love and money. Indeed, Mamman rather approves of my loves."

"Loves?" Ted asked, and then quickly corrected himself. "Sorry...Well, I'm a little disoriented from the day's excitement and the evening's good food, wines, and company. Perhaps I should be quiet and we can talk later?"

"I think that is a very good idea."

Laura got up, went to a large console and put on a tape of slow dance music. Holding out her arms to Ted, he went to her and, for the next hour, they slowly danced throughout the halls and rooms of the first floor. They even glided into the kitchen – much to the delight of Marie, Charles, and their brood of children. Laura was obviously pleased with her new conquest.

But, this, like all other good things, came to an end, and Marie led Ted back up the stairs, with Laura bringing up the rear. As Marie went into the bathroom to lie out Ted's necessities, he and Laura bade one another *au revoir*. She kissed him promisingly gently and went out, soon to be followed by Marie.

After getting ready for bed, Ted began to do what every school teacher does in a room with books in it. He looked them over. They were mostly old, leather-bound French and Spanish editions of voyages to the New World. Among these, however, was a sprinkling of more modern French and German anthropological texts, whose titles announced that they dealt with Voodoo and, in several cases, with something Ted knew nothing about, Obeah. He took several of these down, spread them over a reading table, and began to look for an explanation of the term. Leafing through them, he soon found it referred to a uniquely island form of Voodoo.

"What's this all about? It's obviously some sort of medicine. I wonder how it works," Ted's deeply skeptical Roman Catholic self asked his scholarly self. "If Christ, the Man-God, died to kill death for all who believe in him, then there's at least one belief that can heal sicknesses and even conquer death."

He frowned and looked closely at some color plates of the ceremonies associated with the Obeah rites.

"Clinical death...You die when some muscle, artery, or whatever, gives out. We conquer death, we humans, only if we keep these from giving out. But, these people believe that, too," he said to himself in a subdued voice, as he carefully looked at the illustrations and read their captions, "If that's true, then somehow belief keeps an artery from rupturing and heart muscle from giving out." He flipped over a color plate, and the next one showed, in vivid colors, a naked woman, smeared with blood, gesturing over the body of a naked, pregnant woman.

"They certainly seem to believe. Does belief repair weakened arteries? I suppose their medicine works. Does any really strong belief conquer illness or nature? Or must there be a belief in Christ, who died to kill death? What a thing that is to believe!"

He frowned and continued flipping through the pages of the text. Other plates showed women holding the severed heads of goats and the headless bodies of freshly killed chickens, whose necks spouted geysers of blood over the faces and shoulders of patients lying on the dirt floors of small huts. One picture showed a woman biting off the head of a large snake, which was writhing in such agony that the camera shot was blurred.

"We take bread and wine. Jews take bread, salt, and bitter herbs. We're lucky!"

As curious as his professorial self was, Ted's weariness finally overcame his interest. He returned the books and sat back in his chair.

"What a day," he said softly to himself. "I wonder what Father Feeney would say about all this Obeah."

Ted felt himself slumping into his chair, and he suddenly became aware of how really tired he was. Just as he got up to get into bed, however, he heard a slight tapping on his door.

Without thinking, he called out, "Come on in." The door opened and Laura stood there, framed in the doorway.

"Come in, please!" he corrected himself.

Laura came in and shut the door behind her. A glance showed Ted that Laura's decision to visit him was not spur-of-the-moment. Her hair was held back from her forehead by a gold headband decorated with a number of chip-diamonds set into tiny engraved stars. Her earrings were made of green enamel that exactly matched her eyes. She wore a floor length peignoir, the color of burnt umber, around her shoulders; it seemed to melt into her café-au-lait skin. As he took this in, Ted heard himself catch his breath. Laura heard him, too.

"Laura. You are wonderfully beautiful," Ted said out loud to himself. He was struck with that sense we have when we are at a crossroad in our lives. A slight rustling made him look up from her feet, which, he noticed, were particularly well shaped, and he saw that, under her outer robe, Laura wore a tight gown of a thin, almost translucent, gauze. Its own color was so delicate and its fabric so fine that it merely qualified, rather than hid, the rich tones of her skin. She was shapely and this gauze clung to her figure so that it picked up highlights and cast shadows. Ted was jolted by his realization that this robe was precisely the troubled dark of the storm-racked sky he had seen earlier that day as he drove to the Lake Placid Inn to meet this same Laura. Those clouds had been ripped open here and there by the turbulence of the storm, and that outer robe was just the color of the edging of those rents and tears in the storm-tossed clouds. Laura's inner robe overlaid her skin with a wash that very nearly matched the patches of clouds that promised a break in the weather the day had not delivered. Her skin was the color of the dry, rain- washed remnants of last fall's roadside flowers, which still stood to cast their shadows on the late spring snow.

"Laura, you rage in my heart like today's storm," Ted said in a low, deliberate voice. As Laura opened her arms to him, her outer robe fluttered to the side and hung quietly on her forearms stretched out to him. As he looked at her face, his eyes re-focused and, centered directly behind and above her, he saw a squat, bloodstained cult-statue of wood. He had not noticed it before. Its eyes squinted through little cowry-shells, and its slit of a mouth was hung with lips, under which gleamed rows of shark's teeth. Focusing back on Laura's face, he saw her own lovely head and, for the first time, he noticed that she wore a very small silver cross, hung from a necklace of jet beads.

"Oh, Laura," he whispered into her ear, as he held her, "be there, between me and those wild, bloody hearts that so soon throw away what they have captivated. I'll do that for you too. Can I be between you and them, and you be between them and me? I need you."

\* \* \*

Hours later, at about six-fifteen, when the April sun rises in northern New York State, Ted opened his eyes to Laura's lazy gaze at his face and chest. Her head was on his belly and her knees were drawn up comfortably under her chin.

"Let me tell you something about me, Ted, something I didn't say this afternoon...well, yesterday afternoon," she said, moving her head to kiss his navel.

"Anything...I want to hear," Ted answered. Then he corrected himself. "If I can stand it."

Laura spoke quietly, but disjointedly. "Please try, Ted. You have offered me strength in return for strength. Be strong. I want you to know something about me, so that I don't perplex you too much. My ménage is confusing enough. I don't want you to become confused and tired. History kills anyone but a lover. Did you know that, Ted?"

"Oh, God, yes," Ted said, running his index finger around her earlobe.

"You told me what Father Feeney's death meant to you. You must know that my Lotario's death will stand between us for a long time. You must try to understand this, Ted. He was so alive to me. Then, in a moment, he was dead and crushed. He was not even 'beautiful in death,' as they say some are. He was bruised and horrible. But, Oh, Ted, Lotario's smile before he was dead...He's been dead for ten years now, ten years..."

The following silence was broken by her quiet, deep sighs. Ted gently reached over and touched her hand with the tips of his fingers. But, he said nothing.

After a long pause, Laura continued, her voice deep and low, "Oh, Ted, what that crushed and bruised corpse had been. Lotario's mouth was sculpted like butter. His lips were full and dark as longing, and when Lotario Ursina smiled...oh, God...his teeth were the sharp, keen edge of all desire. And, all that, in a moment, only a nasty, bruised doll in a wooden box. Lotario was my love. He died. My love for him has not died. But, Ted, if I come to love you, as I think I can, will my love for Lotario die too?"

"You'll have to cold-bloodedly adopt me for your own, Laura. I can't stand between you and the living Lotario. Only between you and his..." Ted could not finish.

Laura lay her head back down on his belly and smiled herself to sleep. Ted's misery was a darkness that only created light could shatter.

But, he was happy, too. The light created by us when we adopt a lover casts brilliant shadows. As he sank back into sleep, Ted dreamily thought to himself, "To love is to kill death...But, perhaps, not by dying."

During the next six months, Ted spent every moment he could beg, borrow, or steal, either on the road to and from Lake Placid or at Laura's house during breaks and vacations. Mamman began to become very fond of this French-speaking Nord Americain, and one fall weekend, when he could not make the trip because of Parents' Weekend, Mamman was as cross as Laura had ever seen her. That Sunday evening, Laura called Ted, and told him that she had plenty of money, and that Mamman missed him. What is more, she pointed out, the drive to and from Lake Placid would be both difficult and dangerous during the depth of winter and, so, if Ted agreed, she and Mamman would sell the house in Lake Placid, and perhaps they could all buy one together in Chaldes?

Ted was beyond joy. His whoop of delight nearly deafened Laura. Mamman, who was listening to the phone conversation, heard it and smiled broadly: Laura's Nord Americain was all right. And, so, Laura found a buyer for her very profitable travel agency, but kept herself on as a well-paid consultant – it was she who knew everyone worth knowing in the French-speaking islands. She and Ted shopped around for real estate during the Thanksgiving break and, finally, found an old frame house that was on a good-sized piece of land. It sported two small wings and seemed ideal for division into three apartments. So, they were set. The contractors were all bank customers and, in record time, with a minimal outlay of cash, the house was ready by New Year's. The house-warming was their New Year's Eve party, and those members of the faculty who were in Chaldes over the holiday all came and warmed the house with their good wishes. Ted lived in one small apartment, Laura and Mamman in another, and the largest part of the house was filled to overflowing by Marie, Charles, and their brood. Ted saw the goodness of the Lord in the land of the living.

# PART II:
## NATURAL ARTIFICE

# CHAPTER 5
## The Facts of Life

J.J.'s long-forgotten daughter, Claudia, had grown up in a very happy family. In the twenty years she had known them as her mother and father, Claudia had never seen Mike and Celeste in a nasty fight. Disagreements and spats were never more than that.

In college, she had experimented with several affairs, as much because everyone did as because she wanted to or thought it was a good idea, and those affairs were catastrophes. Her men were all very good-looking, as was she, and they were smart, as was she. They were all very conceited, which she was not, and they were entirely unable even to imagine that any woman they had possessed in bed, as the saying goes, could be as intelligent as they were, let alone a better student. As if Claudia's superiority were not enough to distress her lovers, she insisted on the same thoughtfulness, tone and attention to civility after they had become lovers as before.

Two or three carbon-copy repetitions of this behavior in men who, otherwise, seemed rather distinct and different from one another, made Claudia sour. She stopped serious dating for a long time. Her schoolwork was extremely interesting to her, and she very much enjoyed the fast-paced, witty, no-holds-barred company of the militantly anti-male contingents at her school. The fact that she paid no attention to their rhetorical excesses misled them into thinking that, just perhaps, she was permanently off men and thinking about "alternative sexual orientations."

She wasn't, and her friends were puzzled. Her large single dorm room was almost always filled with a group discussing everything from Plato, Marx, and Darwin to some of the more exotic of the widely current theories of female sexuality. Then, in her senior year, during a raucous mid-semester party attended by a number of unusually good-looking Villanova athletes, Claudia found herself very attracted to a football and rugby star named George Strauss. It was a whirlwind evening and it ended in a posh motel some forty miles away. When she awoke in George's arms the next morning, Claudia wondered seriously whether she might not really enjoy being the wife of a George Strauss, writing and editing as she raised beautiful children and went to club meetings. They met for several weekends after that, but Claudia soon realized that this beautiful man was also a spoiled brat. Any disagreement, no matter over what triviality, led to a sulk that made Claudia laugh and point her finger at him in disbelief. The affair soon ended and Claudia, puzzled and humiliated by his nasty cracks about the kind of female she really was – "Otherwise, you wouldn't be putting me down all the time. Don't I treat you good enough in bed?" – was left seriously angry with the whole tribe of young men.

A holiday at home, however, reminded her of her true inclinations in these matters, and she finished her final year at college and then the first two years at graduate school, looking for a mature male friend with whom she could be a student-friend and, if it seemed a good idea to them both, a lover. But, above all, she now knew that she had to forget about marriage for the foreseeable future. She also knew that love affairs would probably be at the expense of acting somewhat feebleminded around her lovers. As the truth of this began to dawn on her, Claudia felt a deep revulsion at having to pay such a price and thought out loud to herself, "Damn, damn, damn. I'm a human; humans are rational animals and rational human females find some rational human males very attractive. Why can't those rational human males find rational human females attractive? They don't have to desire me for my mind, but why can't they desire me even if I have a mind? Minds don't bite. I like beautiful, smart men. Beauty and brains! What an aphrodisiac! But, not for them. Brains in women are warts and hairy moles. Damn!"

During the first semester of her third, and last, year of graduate school, Claudia spent most of her time in the library and took almost no classes except for electives. A visiting lecturer in the psychology department of a prestigious university was invited to speak on mind-body interaction and, thinking about her question of why men thought that female bodies having real minds were so difficult for so many males, she went.

The lecturer, Professor Ray Hayes, started by talking about

Descartes' form of the mind-body problem and about how it is that the mind can influence anything so alien as the body. Claudia surprised herself by saying out loud, "I'll say!" and the lecturer heard her. He looked up at her with a smile. The lecture was followed by a question-and-answer period.

"Tell me, Professor," Claudia asked, "Women have different bodies from men. Do they have different minds?"

The largely female audience, most of who had at one time or another been treated like fools by men, howled their delight at this question.

"Well, Ms.?"

"Claudia Harris."

"Well, Ms. Harris, I really don't know what to say. What do you think?"

"Well, as they say, this is a man's world. And that means, I suppose, that women's minds are different from men's minds."

The women in the audience cheered Claudia on with whistles and whoops. Professor Hayes looked at them with a blank stare of incomprehension, which soon reduced them to silence.

"As I said," Professor Hayes continued, "I don't think I know the answer to your very good question, Ms. Harris. But, if I may be permitted to hazard a guess, I would only do so with a conditional. And, that is as follows: If – and this is a big if – if sexual dimorphism is any indication and, further, if all that females think about is their bodies, then it would seem to follow, at least to me, that there might just possibly be a sort of mental dimorphism. I have not found this to be the case at all in the course of discharging my teaching duties."

The audience went wild over this answer. Finally! Here was a man who just did not care about the reproductive functions of rational, intelligent, educated men and women. Here was a man who both listened and talked.

The reception in the foyer, after the question period, lasted until security had to insist on dislodging the hotly debating students. Claudia never left Professor Hayes' side, and he seemed to like that arrangement. With a skill that hid itself, Ray Hayes fielded all questions back to the questioner and, when a conclusion was absolutely demanded, he helped Claudia give it. She realized this and enjoyed the charade immensely.

Claudia and Ray Hayes became lovers the next morning. They had gone to a diner after the question period was over. There, they talked and they looked at one another's faces, they got their second wind and they drank wine in his motel room, their very intelligent talk became spirited and, then, they grew tired again and they looked at their watches and saw it was three o'clock in the morning, and they lay down and they slept in one another's arms. And, nothing more. Not that night.

When Claudia awoke, she was untouched, but not unmoved.

"I find, Ray Hayes, that my woman's mind can think of nothing but your man's body. Does that make me a man in a woman's body?"

Ray laughed a quiet, deep, and rumbling laugh, which struck Claudia as belonging to a much bigger man, even to a fat man.

"Will you stand up and model yourself for me, Ray?" Claudia asked. "My mind is full of thoughts of your body."

Ray laughed again and stepped out from under the sheets.

He was magnificent.

At the Metropolitan Museum, Claudia had seen a replica of Zeus throwing a thunderbolt and its proportions had struck her as darkly elegant. When she had first seen that statue, she had thought of those myths where mortal women were sexually possessed by a god. And, here was such a god, Ray Hayes.

"*Mais, vous êtes magnifique!*" Claudia breathed.

Ray answered with an elegant shrug of his ivory shoulders and a very slightly raised eyebrow.

"Come back and take me, Ray Hayes," Claudia said, not quite meaning what she had said. Ray, however, took her at her word.

Professor Hayes was endlessly skillful and practiced in his taking, but that taking could not, by the furthest stretch of the imagination, be termed "love making." There was simply nothing of love in it. Even Claudia's abrupt falls from the heights of pleasure were performed in a sort of slow motion power-dive, with no turning to Ray for comfort. In the following weeks, Claudia became obsessed by his body, when they were together and, during the nights away from him, she found herself more and more preoccupied with her own body's openness to his touches and explorations.

Claudia told him this. It was their fourth meeting and she had just walked into his hotel room, taken off her coat and sat down. As he took off his tie and began to unbutton his shirt, he answered, "Well, since your mind is equally obsessed with your very female body and with my male body, it would seem, I think, that the mind is neither male nor female. Q.E.D." He paused, as he looked down to unhook his complicated belt-buckle and, once he had managed to open it, he asked her, with the slightest of raised eyebrows, "That is what you wanted, isn't it?"

"But, this means that my body, which is female, has no soul of its own!"

"Who needs a soul, Claudia? A mind will do just fine," Ray answered, as he carefully smoothed out the creases in his trouser-legs, before he hung them up in the closet.

"Oh, no, Ray, I don't like this at all. I miss a kind of shyness other men feel around me. They may be strutting roosters and you are elegant and beautiful, but I am a woman to them and they strut for me. Your pleasure is unisex. You aren't a lover...only a neurologist of pleasure. I want my body back, Ray. I miss it."

They were both quiet for a long time and, then, Claudia resumed. "No body, no soul. That's the way it is. And, you took my body. I know," she said hurriedly, as she saw Ray's ironic eyebrow shoot up, "I told you I wanted you to "take me," but I don't like it...the way you take my body. You leave me nothing to give. It's no longer mine to give and... love is a giving that takes."

"Well, as I said, Claudia, you don't need a soul. Only that wonderful body of yours and a mind to tell you what you can do with it, without overloading it." As Ray said this, he took off his undershirt.

"So...your mind only tells you how to budget your sensory input? Why am I an economist?"

"You want a job...honor...security...that sort of thing."

Claudia got up out of the chair, just as Ray stepped out of his under shorts and, slowly putting on her coat, said, with a slight raising of her left eyebrow, "I'll call you if I need to be jump-started, Ray. If my body is not stoked up enough with hormones, I'll give you a call. You are pretty useful that way, you know?"

"Thank you, Ms. Harris. I'll be sitting by my phone...fully dressed."

Claudia went home and entered into a lonely and joyless life, with neither lover nor pleasure. But, her body was hers.

\* \* \*

Marian Caton, Claudia's thesis advisor, was the only member of the economics department whose writing was as good as Claudia's. She had majored in classics as an undergraduate and had kept up her Greek and Latin, to the point where she could still sometimes team-teach with friends in classics for a change from her economics teaching routine. After a month of Claudia's unaccountably dull and uninspired papers, Marian called her into her office and suggested that they meet at her home for drinks. "You've never met my husband, and I think you'd be cheered up from whatever it is which is bothering you. If you could tell me what it is, I might be able to help...Ah, you're not pregnant, or anything like that, are you, Claudia?"

"No, nothing like that. But, it is pretty personal. But...well...I would like to have a drink with you...perhaps in a bar?"

"Of course. Can you meet me here tomorrow at, say, four, for happy hour?"

Claudia smiled a crooked smile and nodded, "Yes."

The next day, Marian drove them out to a small bar-and-grill in New Jersey and, after ordering beers and munchies, she said, "Claudia, I don't really like to meddle in my grad students' lives, but, I shall. You're about twenty-six?"

"Yes. Just."

"And, you don't need a mother any more. But, maybe an older sister or a friend?"

Claudia looked up at her advisor, frowned at the idea of telling her what the trouble was, and decided against speaking.

Seeing the doggedly silent look on Claudia's face, Marian said, "Claudia, you are the best student I've ever had, and I've invested in your future very heavily. Please, Claudia, try. Let me do whatever I can to get you back on track. There's not much time left before you'll be job-hunting, and I want to be able to guarantee prospective employers that you are going to finish your dissertation on schedule. Please try, Claudia."

*Naturally Bad Manners*

Just then, a man walked up to the bar that looked very much like Ray. Claudia saw him and, turning back to Marian, she told the whole story, leaving out only the more graphic details.

But they were not necessary.

"You know, Claudia, the Ray Hayes' of this world are the bane of the academic female's life. I've known one or two of them in my time, and I just happen to know who Professor Ray Hayes is. By the way, did he ever tell you much about himself?"

"Not really. I got the impression that personal history would offend this man. He seemed almost ashamed of having a life outside of his oh-so-personal life. Do you know what I mean by that?"

"Oh, yes, my dear, I know. Your...our, Ray Hayes is a psychologist, alright, but an experimental psychologist, and what he doesn't know about the central nervous system of higher mammals is not worth knowing. Were you aware of that?"

"I knew he was famous, but not for what...at least, not exactly. I knew he did experimental psychology and that he doesn't like theory. I mean, he really doesn't like theory...only practice," she finished and then, blushed crimson.

Marian looked at her steadily and continued, "Bad luck, Claudia. To the Ray Hayes' of this world, a woman, or a handsome young man, for that matter, is a certain composition of nerves leading to a brain, which is tickled into consciousness by whatever it is that those nerves send it. Not a very tender lover."

"No, no lover at all. I felt I was on an operating table. But, God! Does he know nerves," Claudia said with a broad smile, ending with another blush.

They were both silent for a long time and then Claudia resumed, "Now what? My mind is unisex, but my body has become a male neurologist's banjo. Do I have to marry a Williams boy and settle down with babies to be a woman again?" She paused and continued, frowning, "You know? That damned man really does have a soul or mind...or whatever...which is neither male nor female. But, I hated it. But, dammit, I still hate the idea of thinking like a woman. The idea of thinking like a woman repels me."

"Good. Stay repulsed, Claudia," Marian said and then ordered them each another bottle of beer. After they had each poured full glasses and taken a long drink, she continued, in a leisurely tone of voice, "Claudia, you are a good thinker. Remember what you are doing for your dissertation. You are the first person in this department ever to propose, let alone be permitted to write, a dissertation on the psychology of money. There have been some more or less interesting papers written on the socio-economic parameters of why people spend or save, but you are trying to think through the question of what money really is to people who have it or want it."

"Yeah. There's something so public and moral about money. And, yet, it's not just conventional. Or, if it is just conventional, then convention is more real than the people who make it up. That's what really gets to me."

"And, to me, Claudia. But, tell me, isn't your real interest centered on the relation between theory and practice, or, to be more precise, between what people do and what they think that makes them do it?"

"What?" Claudia asked, with a puzzled frown on her face.

"Well, perhaps I didn't say that too clearly. When you say money is conventional, but somehow more real than the people who created it intended it to be..."

Claudia sat up and interrupted with, "Ah! That's it! Money takes on a life of its own!"

"Well, I don't know. But, it becomes an odd combination of what one thinks it is and what it really is. What it really is has something to do with what one thinks it is."

Claudia was quiet for a long time and then she asked slowly and with many pauses, "And, how about my nerves?"

"Ah, yes...Your nerves. Look, Claudia, I am married to a very handsome man of forty-eight. I am only forty-five, but he is a much better looking forty-eight than I am a forty-five. As I'm sure you know, he's a theater producer in New York and away a lot of the time. For all I know, he may have affairs with those lovely young things he works with. I can't say I'd be amazed. But, this I do know, Claudia Harris. He has never, ever, given anything to any one of them that was, by right, only mine. Do you understand?"

"I think so."

"Well, let me assure you that, even at my aged forty-five, my husband's embraces are by no means unwelcome to me. I love the man dearly, and I wait for him to come home, where we can be husband and wife together. Now, Claudia, just let's suppose that I found out tomorrow that my husband and my closest female friend have been lovers for years, and that everyone knew except me, and that this made me a laughing-stock. What do you think I'd feel about his embraces, then?"

"I see. The same nerves would be excited, and the same brain-centers would be tickled...But, it would not be good at all...Not even pleasant, I suppose."

"Yes, not even pleasant. So, it seems that the impulses that my brain receives from my nerves are impulses that are not altogether just facts. I would find those ticklings into consciousness absolutely repellent...and certainly not pleasant."

"But, then, this means that pleasure is like money? What I mean is, pleasure is an odd combination of nerve impulses and what people think about them...Just like money! I'll be damned. Good Lord!" Claudia ended, with a look of wide-eyed amazement, which soon faded into a grin.

"Intelligence is a lovely, lively thing, but I don't really think it's either male or female."

"But, it certainly isn't unisexual, let alone bisexual," Claudia answered heatedly.

"True. My sense is that, when the person whose intelligence, or mind, or whatever, is thinking about things that concern him or her as a male or female, then the mind is more or less sexual. You say that this happened to you with Ray. Well, what about questions we face as rational, non-reproducing, non-love-making animals? And, economists, as such, don't reproduce the way men and women do."

"No," Claudia laughed, "They reproduce by writing articles and dissertations."

"But, if they are not dumb, some of the issues of economists' brains last much longer than their authors or even their authors' children."

"So, Ray didn't know about this other sort of reproduction? Odd..." Claudia mused.

"Oh, he knows. He is very widely published and very jealous of his stuff. Anyone who dares to cite him had better do so just right, or else the proud papa goes berserk. No, his problem is that he doesn't see where the body belongs."

"Where does it belong?" Claudia asked with a puzzled frown.

"In the same world as sexually dimorphous thinking. He's very intelligent, but he's a little crude...even sentimental. He is afraid to have us in two worlds at once. But, I, Marian Caton, the economist, wrangling with her younger sister economist, Claudia Harris, is a different Marian Caton than the one who wrangles with her auto-insurance salesman, when he tries to treat her like a dumb broad."

"Ah, so that's why Ray is so hot on the fact that even doing economics is sort of survival-exercise. He told me that it's only to make me rich and famous that I do this stuff. He says that being rich makes me feel secure and safe."

"Those tough guys tire me," Marian said, with a weary grin.

"If only he weren't so doctrinaire," Claudia said slowly and then snapped out of it. "Thank you, older sister. I hope to be smart enough someday to do this for some younger sister myself."

They settled down and talked more about Claudia's immediate strategies with her dissertation and so passed a very profitable hour. They split the bill and Marian drove Claudia home.

A short time before they arrived, Claudia turned to Marian and asked, "Do you really think that pleasure is so, well, theoretical? The very difficulty of making money puts a kind of check on our desires – no pun intended. Is there anything like that in nerves and pleasures?"

Marian pulled up to the curb in front of Claudia's house and turned off the ignition. She frowned in her effort to be precise in her answer to Claudia's question. "I think so. The nerves give us all sorts of messages and, depending on who and what we are...you know, the Ming dynasty Chinese males thought that the horribly deformed feet of their women were extremely erotic! Well, the world we live in somehow tunes our nerves so that we hear their messages in one way or another. Money is a sort of tuning device in the same way, I think. But, that's your baby, Claudia. Think about it and let me know what you come up with. I'm interested. Go to work now. Stop fretting and get on with it...okay? And, call on me any time, Claudia, day or night."

"Day or night?" Claudia asked, puzzled.

"Yes. You might begin to lose your nerve about your nerves. Call on me if that begins to happen, please."

*Naturally Bad Manners*

"Thank you, Marian. I will."

They shook hands gravely and Claudia went into her house, and into the most productive and least happy, period of her life. She was, she realized, suffering from something like withdrawal symptoms from Ray's minute attentions. "My God," she thought to herself, "that man is addictive. But, it sure isn't love."

The dissertation was finally completed and won honors. Then her sister, Megan, got married and Claudia was maid-of-honor. She was flirted with by men ten years her junior and by men old enough to be her father. She found that she liked the formalities of courtship, and that flirting was an art to be practiced. She practiced it and immediately became good at it. She was a natural.

During that last year of graduate school, Claudia was offered a one-year appointment at a small, up-state, college, Chaldes. She took it, was liked by the faculty and students and liked them. She became particularly attached to Michelle Winan, a biology teacher and self-proclaimed "lover of beautiful young women, not simply a lesbian, thank you!" and to Avram Bonapoggio, the Professor of Ancient Near East Studies. They both valued her friendship very strongly, and so, she was only mildly surprised when, shortly after her dissertation and its defense received honors, she was offered a tenure-track position at Chaldes. During the course of the little dinner party Michelle threw to celebrate the event, Bonapoggio mentioned casually to Claudia that an old student of his, named Stafford Wyatt, was going to spend part of the spring term as guest writer-in-residence and that Claudia might just like his company.

\* \* \*

Rabbi Avram Bonapoggio had been the perfect pilot to start Stafford on a road that would lead him to a medicinal poetry and a graceful therapeutics. His own family's safari, which had finally led him to settle, at least temporarily, at Williams College as a professor of Hebrew, began around 1460 with the slaughter, dispossession and dispersion of his ancestors by King Ferdinand and Queen Isabella of Spain. These entrepreneurs of rapine and pillage first despoiled and then scattered the oldest peoples of the Old World, and, when they had finished doing this, they used the money they had realized through their murderous enterprise to capitalize their rape and slaughter of the New World. Those of Bonapoggio's ancestors who survived the flight from the Iberian Peninsula settled in Italy – whence he came by his name – and, after a long and honorable sojourn there, other entrepreneurs of pillage scattered them yet again and this time they went back to the Middle East, but now to Turkey. "Nationalism" then drove them away, yet again, in 1920, and so the Bonapoggio family ended up in the New World. This New World to which the Bonapoggios had fled to escape the rebuilding of Turkey after the Ottoman Empire had crumbled with the end of WWI, was thus a country whose discovery had been partially financed by the dispossession of his ancestry some four hundred years earlier. "What a proof of the existence of God," Bonapoggio sometimes thought to himself, and then always added, "and of what a God!"

Professor Bonapoggio was the perfect complement to Stafford Wyatt. Although they had arrived at their conclusions in very different ways, each had a hunch that it was good for a human being to have a body and that the human spirit, no matter how exalted, needed flesh, no less than flesh needed spirit. Both sensed that the flesh's stupid, dogged and ponderous folly required the spirit's naughty immoderation; without it, flesh, they both saw, becomes merely bored humanity trying to regain its dimly remembered vitality by watching horror films, pornographic tapes, or by drinking too much vodka. On the other hand, without the terrible limitations imposed on it by that dull and limited flesh, the spirit is freed to become what can cheerfully murder twenty or more million humans, in order to redress old economic inequities, and to ensure a more equitable means of distribution of goods and services to the survivors. They both also understood that only powerful and wise charms could ever induce that uncongenial genie that is the human spirit to inhabit gracefully such a vessel as the grotesque human body could provide for it. Stafford had become a writer and craftsman of books full of discrete images and illusions of reality, and Avram Bonapoggio had become a scholar of Hebrew and its commentators. But, what made them most congenial, perhaps, was that both had spent a great deal of time considering the idea that to be a true human is to choose this or that good book as our mentor and that, if we fail so to choose, we are likely to become some sort of Calaban-like child of nature.

\* \* \*

Claudia and Stafford were unmarried, good-looking, and they both hated both lies and liars. Also, both of them sincerely loved Avram Bonapoggio, who sincerely loved both of them. Claudia had as much money as she had time to spend, and Stafford, although not rich, had much more than he had time to spend. The possession of like temperaments, sufficient money for shared needs, and mutual friends are as close to an erotically manifest destiny as most men and women will ever experience, or need to.

Claudia met Stafford at Bonapoggio's house for dinner before his lecture. She was seated just opposite him. As the host had foreseen, Claudia could look at Stafford, but, because the general conversation distracted her, she missed much of what he said to the other guests. Consequently, she was very interested in him before the lecture, an analysis of a poem by the sixteenth-century poet and Stafford's namesake, Thomas Wyatt.

Dinner was at last over and the guests trooped over to the lecture hall. After an introduction, which was full of praise to an extent that surprised all his colleagues, who had spent a good deal of time trying to earn even faint approval from the distinguished Professor Avram Bonapoggio, Stafford began his lecture by reading a poem of Thomas Wyatt's, copies of which he had passed out to the audience. That particular poem made Claudia extremely uncomfortable. It was one of Thomas Wyatt's translations from Petrarch, and it went:

> *The long love, that in my thought doeth harbour*
> *And in mine heart doeth keep his residence,*
> *Into my face presseth with bold pretence,*
> *And therein campeth, spreading his banner.*
> *She that me learneth to love and suffer,*
> *And wills that my trust and lust's negligence*
> *Be reigned by reason, shame and reverence,*
> *With his hardiness taketh displeasure.*
> *Wherewithal, unto the heart's forest he flieth,*

*Leaving his enterprise with pain and cry;*
*And there him hideth, and not appeareth.*
*What may I do when my master feareth*
*But, in the field with him to live and die?*
*For good is the life ending faithfully.*

When he had finished the reading, Stafford carefully showed his audience how Wyatt had made meter and emotion complement one another. But, Claudia heard none of this. She sat reading and re-reading the sentence:

*She that me learneth to love and suffer*
*And wills that my trust and lust's negligence*
*Be reigned by reason, shame and reverence,*
*With his hardiness taketh displeasure.*

"I'll say," Claudia murmured to herself under her breath. She then looked up sharply at Stafford as he pointed out, "Wyatt's use of sounds plays on our ears, like a guitarist's fingers on his strings."

"Oh God! Another Ray Hayes," she thought angrily to herself while Stafford continued, "Look at that first line: 'The long love, that in my thought doeth harbour.' Only the 't' and 'd' of the 'that,' and the 'thought doeth,' is jagged. All the other sounds flow from word to word. Even the 'g' and 'l' in 'long love' are swallowed, semi-silent, sounds, a sort of so-called 'glottal-stop.' But, look at line three: 'Into my face presseth with bold pretence.' Where are all the liquid 'l's?' The flow from word to word? That line three has nothing much other than sounds which fairly explode as they leave the mouth: 't,' 'f,' 'p,' 'b,' 'd,' and even, 'pre.'"

"Hmm," Claudia mused. "Ray only knew the t's and f's."

The lecture concluded with a challenge to the audience "to distinguish between the various parts of the mouth used to make certain sounds slip and slide softly and others 'bang,' 'knock,' and 'clash'."

As the question period opened, Claudia asked the first question.

"Mister Wyatt, is Thomas Wyatt saying that love, true love, is unreasonable, shameless, and irreverent?"

"Look at the last line," Stafford answered. "'For good is the life ending faithfully.' That sounds reasonable, moderate, and reverent, to me."

"But, that clashes with...oh...I see. That last stanza is the...well, the liquid to the first stanza's d's, p's, and t's?"

"I think so," Stafford answered, looking at Claudia very intently.

"So, this poem is about a clash between two sides of love? The one is blustering macho, and the other a...well..." Here, Claudia was at a loss for the right word.

"Perhaps the other is a courteous love?"

"Exactly. Yes...I like that. Yes," Claudia said in a rush, with an intensity that both interested and puzzled Stafford.

"I might even suggest," Stafford said after a moment, "that this sonnet of Petrarch's is about a horse and his rider."

Other questions were asked and the question period came to an end. Claudia had an early class the next day, and a few last-minute preparations to attend to, and so she said a hurried, somewhat flustered good-bye to Stafford.

"Thank you," she said, shaking his hand firmly and vigorously. "Your talk was very interesting to me and it helped me see something very personal and very important. I am grateful to you."

"Thank you for telling me," Stafford replied, a slight flush coloring his face.

"Good, he blushed. He's no expert on women's nerve endings," Claudia thought to herself as she walked the short distance between the college and the little house she rented.

Claudia woke the next morning feeling like her old, pre-Ray Hayes self. Her classes went well, and she was in a very good humor. After cleaning up odds and ends, she went home to prepare for Bonapoggio's dinner and the Dean's reception for Stafford that evening. His lecture had been a big hit and, with Bonapoggio's very strong backing, it seemed quite likely to everyone that Stafford would be offered the fall semester position as writer-in-residence and a permanent position after that. The faculty and student body were enthusiastic, and a rich friend of Bonapoggio's, so the rumor went, would help endow the position. So, Claudia's evening was set up. First, dinner at Bonapoggio's and then the Dean's reception for Stafford.

# CHAPTER 6

## Nurturing Nature's Manners

As Bonapoggio led Stafford gently by the elbow into his large living room for drinks prior to dinner, he told him that his guests were discussing the nature of Nature because of a recent article about gay rights that had polarized the faculty. Some said that homosexuality was a sickness; others said it was a choice; still others said it was a birthright. "Some men and women were simply born that way." This led, predictably enough, to the nature-versus-nurture controversy and, from there, to the nature of each. They were still hot on the trail of the nature of nature and so had not yet begun to argue over the nature of nurture, when Bonapoggio entered the room with Stafford. The first thing that struck Stafford's attention was the tableau of a little, twisted man who was loudly talking to a tall, beautiful woman and a very languid, willowy man.

"*Merde! Merde*! I say! Nothing but *mere*!" the little man shouted, waving his arms.

"You have that right," the languid man answered.

Bonapoggio interrupted by announcing to the group, "If I might, ladies and gentlemen, let me introduce the true cause célébre of this august gathering of wit, Mister Stafford Wyatt. Stafford, you remember Jim Dixon. A detective captain, he is of the Law, if not of the Prophets."

Jim shook Stafford's hand and said, "Stafford! I liked your lecture and I agree with you. Wyatt, the Elder, your namesake, is far greater a poet than old Howard, The Earl of Surrey. And, Petrarch! I love that man. Did you know that he carried a copy of St. Augustine's 'Confessions' with him, wherever he went?"

"No, I didn't. Perhaps we could get together and you might tell me something more about this?"

"I look forward to it."

The slender, willowy, man was introduced as "Patrick Ryan, a chemist," and then Bonapoggio introduced Stafford to the woman next to him. As Stafford shook her hand she said, "I am Michelle Winan. I teach biology." Stafford smiled and shook her hand. The group seemed very much at ease and, seeing that Stafford was at his ease, they continued their conversation while Bonapoggio retreated into the kitchen to oversee the last-minute preparations for dinner.

"Don't give me your damned chemicals again, Pat!" Rick said, picking up on the conversation just where Stafford's appearance had interrupted it. "Of course, they are useful on food can labels and headache remedies, but, otherwise, they are your stupid artifacts, of no earthly use to anyone." He then bolted a large cracker piled high with Bonapoggio's Caspian Beluga black caviar and then washed that down with a huge gulp of Piper-Hiedsieck champagne. He licked his fingers like a cat, belched like a bull and peered up at Pat, to see what he could say in return.

"You little toad!" was Pat's immediate response. "Looking at what you do in your chosen profession – ruining perfectly good canvases with bilious greens and tony oranges – you need those labels on food cans. Christ! Without labels on cans, you couldn't tell caviar from roach paste. And, look, my ignorant canvas-dauber, chemicals are not something I made up. Deity made them at the beginning of it all!" Here, Pat waved his hand in a grand circle and nearly emptied the contents of his champagne-flute on the assembly. "Give me," he continued, "this caviar, or that pâté and I'll give you back a few piles of pure chemical elements!"

"God in heaven! Give us a break!" shouted Rick gleefully. "So, Avram wasted all his time and money on you. Set you down in front of a display-case of sulfur, salt and whatever and you'll have your little feast. Ah, Petronius would love dining out with you! Soufflé of oxygen, followed by Crème de Tartaré then, roast of antimony, finished off with tastefully subtle, but filling, compote of hydrogen sulfide. Such a swank repast, my dear!" And, then he added, looking despondent, "And, they call us Germans Huns!" He ran over to the sideboard and threw his short arms around a beautifully worked silver tray laden with caviar. "Leave these! Oh, spare these!"

"Oh, you know what I mean," said Pat a little impatiently.

"Damned right I do!" Rick shot back. "Your damned elements have turned painting into the technique of smearing primary – that means elementary to you chemists – colors over everything. The damned hideous plastic chairs in your classrooms are even primary colors. The whole world looks like a goddamned day-care center!" Rick was beginning to become seriously excited.

Just then, Bonapoggio returned and, pointing out that the only primary colors in his house were to be found on the noses of his sloshed guests, announced dinner.

As the group began to file into the dining room, two people stood up whom Stafford had not seen before. They had been sitting in a matched pair of heavy leather armchairs; deep in conversation and Bonapoggio had taken it for granted that they would introduce themselves. They had, in fact, not heard Stafford come in. One was a very athletic-looking man in his middle thirties. His hair was graying at the temples and he was deeply tanned, which set off well a pair of very clear, steel-gray eyes. He sported a carefully styled mustache, which framed a sensuous pair of full, red lips. His partner was a tall woman with blazing green eyes, bronze-red hair and skin the color of café au lait. Stafford noticed that she walked on the balls of her feet. She was about thirty-five, or perhaps a bit younger. Bonapoggio introduced them as "Ted Simms, Political Science and his friend Laura Miller," and then led the way into the dining room. As he followed them in, he heard Laura say to Bonapoggio, "Mamman sends her regrets. She is still under the weather a bit." Her voice had that lovely lilt that identified its speaker as coming from somewhere in the Caribbean.

The host had planned to have Stafford sit with Claudia, Jim, Ted and Laura and for Mamman to sit with Rick, Pat and Michelle. But, Mamman's absence disarranged this plan. So, fearing for his china and crystal if he left the terrible gang of three alone without any moderating influence and remembering that Claudia would be at the Dean's reception later, Bonapoggio sat Stafford with the three. Claudia talked to Ted, Laura, and Jim, only once in a while getting caught as she looked appraisingly at Stafford.

Dinner was very good indeed, but uneventful. At one point, Rick asked Pat how he liked his potassium cyanide done, well or medium, but Pat was not interested in carrying on the conversation then. So, they spent the time making Stafford feel very welcome and comfortable. All had made it a point to read some of his work and all of them, whatever their individual tastes in poetry and drama, felt that this Stafford Wyatt could write. So, he felt genuinely welcome.

Bonapoggio's dinners were banquets. Guests always left later than they had planned and so it was that the group broke up to go to the Dean's house for the official reception a good deal later than anyone, except for their host, had intended. Since Laura had left a little early to look in on Mamman, Stafford, Claudia, Ted, Jim Dixon and Bonapoggio were the last to leave. Claudia was just saying to Stafford that she would see him at the reception, when the phone rang. Claudia paused for a moment and he came hurrying out with a grave face. "You know young Hurlock, the rugby player?"

"Oh sure," said Claudia, "Is he hurt?"

"I can't figure out what is going on. His roommate just called and said he had a stroke or something."

"A stroke? Hurlock? A rhinoceros couldn't give him a stroke!" Claudia answered, with a laugh.

"Well, I don't know what it is, but they have asked me to come over and see what is going on. He takes 'Ancient Near-East' with me and, although God knows he is no scholar, we get along. He wants to see me, for some odd reason. Ah...Claudia? Would you be so kind...?"

Claudia expressed a heartfelt delight in the prospect of chauffeuring the honored guest to the reception and, with Bonapoggio between them, they walked to her car.

"I presume you leave me with your full powers of attorney?" Claudia asked.

Bonapoggio kissed her on both cheeks and left, leaving Claudia and Stafford anything but bereft for his leaving – love him as they both did.

The five-minute ride to the Dean's house, where the formal college reception was being held, was both uneventful and informative to them. Claudia asked Stafford polite, interested questions about the odyssey that led had him to Chaldes College. His answers were at one and the same time exactly polite. She liked the thoughtfulness and precision in his responses to her background-seeking questions. But, they, all-too-soon for either of their tastes, arrived at the Dean's house and its reception line.

The silence that fell as they pulled up to the curb outside the Dean's house was acutely embarrassing for both of them. They had genuinely taken to one another and had not realized the extent of it until that moment. They mumbled, "Thank you very much for the ride," and "Oh, it's nothing," and both of them got out of the car a little disoriented.

The date of the reception being early April, the newly refreshed faculty had just come back from Spring Break and so it was not yet jaded by its labors – which one wicked wit once characterized as "the casting of false pearls before real swine." Being only recently returned, the faculty had not yet been able to recall accurately old grievances or to remember who was a particularly laughable horse's ass about this or that pet hobbyhorse of a theory. Consequently, this ceremony, which opened the academic spring season at Chaldes College with the celebration of Stafford Wyatt's appointment, began less guardedly and thus ended more acrimoniously, than the parties later in the term.

Avram Bonapoggio's dinners began after a time that suited the peculiar temper of American academics at play and therefore, they ended sufficiently late to satisfy his own European sense of what constituted an event. Thus, colleagues already in a more or less advanced state of inebriation greeted all the guests from his party. They pretty well ignored the guest of honor. This suited him completely, since it gave him freedom to roam about at his leisure and to snoop into the affairs of the faculty with whom he was to spend at least some part of his professional life. After meeting the Dean and his lady, the bursar and her husband – why, Stafford wondered, were men married to ladies, and women to husbands – Claudia introduced him around and they wandered into the large living room, where the main body of the faculty was assembled.

The essentially liberal or conservative nature of a regime is, perhaps, nowhere better revealed than in its posture toward ceremony. Thus, Easter in The Vatican City is a pandemonium, consisting of a vast surging, weeping and shouting crowd greeting a solitary figure on a balcony far above them. On its part, communist Moscow had celebrated its May Day with an orderly, goose-stepping, ceremonial, passion which Rome – Christian Rome, that is – never conceived of. And, even a fleeting glance at post-Mao Beijing, at six o'clock on any morning, rain or shine, will reveal several million rapt Chinese, dancing the slow, ceremonious paces of the Tai Chi war dance, in order to start the day with a polite invitation to the cosmos to guide them and help them to compose their bodies for the day's work, which happens to be required of them by their present historical regime – namely, The People's Democratic Republic of China. Whereas, allowing a few hours for the sun to make the trip westward, if at that same season and time of day we glance at Manhattan, we will see several hundred thousand semi-naked men and women, huffing and puffing, with starting eyes and curt "Coming through!"

But, in American academia, Beijing and Moscow are peaceably enough greeted by Manhattan, at least with respect to ceremony. At these occasions, all differences of rank, gender, political persuasion and, what makes Academe truly wonderful, all points of view, are gently nudged aside for an hour or so and the Marxist sits next to, even if he cannot, or will not, lie down with, the scholar of Saint Thomas Aquinas. Swords, if there were any to be had, could easily have been beaten into plowshares. But, this universal tolerance at Chaldes lacked the swords that could be found even in a mediocre service academy, just as it lacked those farmers who knew how to till, using the plowshares that academia's universal tolerance is so good at forging. So, since Chaldes College was neither West Point nor Texas Agricultural & Mechanical College, its faculty had to rest satisfied with, first, putting aside the barbs they charitably extracted from their witticisms and then, with flattening them into those vast stainless-steel trays that they loaded with – of all things – indigestible deviled ham sandwiches, as a sign of peace between them.

As Stafford and Claudia entered the room, the knot of faculty closest to them was in the midst of a heated debate, still about nature-versus-nurture.

"And, what, may we ask, does the newest luminary in our academic heaven think about this matter of nature and nurture?" asked a mischievous looking Claudia.

"Me?" Stafford answered, looking as if the question had never occurred to him before. "I'm a writer. I couldn't care less about other people's glands. I make my own literary bed and then my characters join me in it – glands and all."

"Do you entertain them there?" Michelle asked.

"Of course!" Stafford answered, "The bed my characters live in is the one I make for them. I am, as an author, only interested in what I, or someone else, create. But, really, running the risk of being just a bit of a bore, creating – God, how I hate that word, but English has no word for something like making-as-an-artifact...Where was I? Oh yes, creating is not quite a natural birth, is it?"

Claudia spoke up in the middle of the immense silence this sober remark caused within the din of drunken battle. "Sir! You are claiming for yourself the prerogative of my kind! You are claiming to take something out of yourself and to be able to form it into another separate, living being. This, sir, means war!"

"Well," Michelle broke in, "my science tells me that something called DNA controls the self-creation of the natural character from a fertilized egg. My science tells me – and, make no mistake about it!" she said rather truculently, "I love my science – that it's not a novelist who creates us living things, but a sort of molecule that can read another molecule. Yes! This molecule acts like the novelist and reader combined. One natural thing naturally writes and then it reads what it has naturally written. But, you know, I have problems, very personal problems with that."

Bonapoggio asked her, "Would you share those problems with us? I, for one, would be very interested, Michelle."

"Well, in a word, I have the appetite of a man, in the body of a woman," Michelle said, looking rather haughtily at the group.

Ted looked at her and whispered to Laura, who had returned, "What a mess! We find a place with all the comforts of home and we are mismatched! What an idea! Here is this beautiful woman, whose genes naturally misread her genetic code...and what a result! But, she says, all wrong. She has that beautiful female body and her father's soul! What a mess!"

Laura whispered back, "Ted, I would feel better at home with Mamman. I'll see you later. I love you." She went over to Bonapoggio, thanked him for a splendid evening of food and conversation, kissed him goodbye and left.

Turning back to Michelle, Bonapoggio said thoughtfully, "Although I am no scientist, I think I can claim to be a reader. The question of just what it is that reads the so-called message, that interests me. And, just what is that message? And, was it written before it had a reader? I wonder; can nature write a natural message that is a question? But, no reader, no question, I think."

"Ah!" said Stafford in a flash of insight, "a message is always a message to someone, from someone. But, then, what is DNA? The way you talk about reading the genetic code makes it seem to be some sort of natural stage direction. And, as if this weren't queer enough, we are told next that this text reads its own message, which it has sent to itself! It has a message in itself, to itself – as if that super-molecule is a sort of magazine article written by itself, for itself to read!"

"Alchemy! Oh rank, rank Alchemy! The dark arts are in ascendancy!" a very drunk Rick screeched, hands raised to heaven while he spoke.

"Oh, be quiet, thou indigestible tidbit in the guts of a termite!" shouted back Pat. And, then, to Stafford, "Please, continue. Nature's minimal jest must be expressed. Ha! I rhyme!"

"Nature's garbage can just fell down creation's stairs. We hear the clatter, but it doesn't matter. Fool!" Rick shot back.

"Well," continued Stafford, a little put off by this tomfoolery, "I am a writer and, whatever the DNA people wish to say about writing, it is something I know about. But, this talk of natural codes and natural messages and reading those natural messages, by God knows who or what; well, that strikes me as a very odd way of talking."

"Damned right," Rick said truculently and somewhat thickly. "Look at me, if you like. God's own ultimate particle, the original quark. Smaller than an electron. A dwarf. A midget's hangnail! That's my body! This snail's habitation is the message the reader got from the whatchamacallit – color-code? – laid down by the happy conjunction of my Mamma and Papa – two large and healthy humans, by the way! You guys tell me it's a chromosome – a color code. God! And, me a painter! As if I don't know more about color-codes than the biology boys, who couldn't paint the town red if they were drunk and disorderly! And, they're telling me that that little bedroom session between Mamma and Papa really cooked up the color-code and the blue-print, for this doll's house of a body I've got to live in? But, me? I mean me-me! That's no midget. But, that real me has come to be used to living in its ridiculous habitation."

Rick paused, looked around dramatically and continued, "Ladies and gentlemen of the jury. You don't know what you like, but you know art. I ask you, now that you are here, in Deity's gallery, viewing the results of his color-coding, what kind of palate did He see fit to prepare for our color-coded genes and what painter, pray tell, could have used that palate to paint us? Deity would have failed my Color 101 class!"

At this point, he belched loudly and began to hiccup violently. Pat, who took care of him at moments like this, sat down on his haunches and put an arm gently around Rick's narrow, hunched-up shoulders. Rick patted Pat's cheek and, laughing, when his hiccups subsided, sang to the tune of Pony Girl: "Molecule, molecule, Patrick Ryan, you're a fool."

Skipping out of Pat's roaring grasp, he hid behind a table that was surrounded by the husbands and ladies of several sub-deans and the bursar.

"Well," said Stafford, picking up the thread of his own thought, "the composition is, I suppose, the whole point of this sub-cellular hurly-burly. The final natural meaning of the message is the natural full-grown animal or plant."

"That's close enough," Michelle said. "And, then, what?"

"Well, it seems to me that there are natural misreadings."

"Mistranslations, you mean?" Michelle corrected.

"Good!" Stafford answered. "Mistranslations! Some of us are what happens when the DNA mistranslates itself...What an idea...a natural, living, mistranslation!"

"Exactly," breathed Bonapoggio, smiling beatifically. Michelle looked at Stafford with narrowed eyes and answered, "An interesting side light. How can there be mistranslations, viable mistranslations, which do very well? Rick says he's one and God knows he does okay."

"Well, speaking of the body constructed according to the DNA's instructions," Ted interjected, looking speculatively at Michelle's striking figure, "doesn't the message that was taken from the original instructions for constructing the body tell how to compose the real, living body, with all its tastes?"

"Go on," said both Pat and Michelle in unison.

"These living translations are very pleasant indeed," Stafford thought to himself, his eyes surveying the group and coming to rest on Claudia. "I think I shall enjoy reading my colleagues."

"Well," continued Ted, "it's our living, mature, bodies that are the final, edited translations performed by the genes on themselves. And, those grown, mature bodies...they really live and make real sense, in real human neighborhoods...you know, eco-systems, cities, families, clans, what have you. These are the neighborhoods of our adult human bodies."

"Exactly!" said Bonapoggio. "The living human being is a sort of DNA to his own life-space. Other humans living around him 'read him off,' if I may speak so, and the sum total of these readings is..."

"The body politic!" said Ted triumphantly.

"Lovely!" said Stafford, always on the lookout for a new metaphor.

"Then this means," Michelle said slowly, "that each of us can be a distinct message to the world around us, depending on the readers?"

"Ah," said Rick, "give me a ticket to Munchkin Land, where no one is taller than a bird-bath and I will be just one of the boys."

"Not quite," Bonapoggio answered seriously. "My dear Ulrich, you paint and you teach young men and women the tradition. You polish them until they shine. You weed them like a garden. My God! You are a magnificent chromosome!"

Everyone standing around clapped at this compliment. The group broke up to get more drinks.

They returned in a few minutes. Michelle resumed the discussion by saying to Rick, "I think that what Avram said a minute ago was very good. May I add to that?"

"Of course, Michelle," Rick answered.

"Well, you are a painter. Don't you, yourself, read the world off around you? You are more than a genetic message. You don't surround yourself with miniatures and images of yourself. You are always looking at beautiful things, not at yourself. You take them in their motion and, in painting them, you stop them for us, who missed them as they whizzed by. You read them. When you paint them on canvas, you take them out of their natural processes and you re-present them to us." She fell silent and the group waited for her to continue. After a long moment, she finished, "Because of what you and your kind do, Rick, I suppose that, as a biologist, I would say we have two quite distinct messages and two distinct readings. The first gives us the complex bodies of higher animals. But, you, Rick, your painter's reading of these bodies somehow completes that so-called natural reading. Only then and I really believe this Rick, only then is natural law completed."

"Ah, Michelle," Bonapoggio breathed softly.

"Exactly!" said a very excited Stafford. "But, exactly! When I write a dramatic incident, I take something that, at some level, really happens. I mean something that really happens all the time...day-to-day stuff. That so-called real world is just what really happens to happen. But, it doesn't satisfy. We don't buy it and we tinker with it, all the time. We take that world – and each generation does this anew, in different styles – we take that world into which we are born and we treat it as the DNA of literature. We re-read it off as we see it should be...you know?"

"Yes," said Bonapoggio. "I suppose that this is one reason why my own tradition insists that the same God who created the Heavens and the Earth and human beings, did not leave it at that. Much later, at Mount Sinai, He completed that primal creation for humans by giving them laws to live by in that same world He had created much earlier."

"Well," said a skeptical Ted, "the same story says that, when God threw Adam and Eve out of the garden into a relatively hostile world, that world was also God's creation...alongside Eden. I presume that the two sides of the one gate leading out of and back into Eden, were completed in the same act."

"Well, my Roman friend," said Bonapoggio, smiling and putting a friendly, relaxed arm around Ted's somewhat hunched-up shoulders, "original sin is a dark question for me. But, I think we can agree that the world outside of Eden was not the world God created for Adam and Eve, or for their children? Okay?"

"Okay...Yes, I guess we can have our separate pieces of unleavened cakes and still eat together," Ted said with mock gallantry, accompanied by a slight bow in Bonapoggio's direction. "But, Avram," he continued, "you certainly don't think the natural laws governing the universe and the moral laws governing human beings, are two totally distinct laws? You aren't saying that, are you?"

"You mean, because I said God created two distinct worlds? One in

Eden and the other outside it?"

"Yes," Ted answered.

"You bet!" Pat seconded. "The more modern, liberated, among us all agree that the laws of nature are the model for human law. We also agree that the famous Ten Commandments are pretty rational and sensible. But, you know this, Rabbi."

"And, " Claudia with a hint of irony in her voice, "surely, Rabbi Avram Bonapoggio believes that one and the same Deity gave us both nature and the moral law?"

"No question in my mind," Bonapoggio agreed jovially. "Here, Bertrand Russell lies down with the Pope and with the chief Rabbi!"

"What a mess," Pat said, crinkling his nose.

"Imagine the issue of that *ménage a trios*!" chimed in Rick. "We might call it Russell's Papal Bull!"

"Now that would be Russell's Paradox!" Michelle added.

"I think, gentlemen, that it would be more of a minotaur," Pat added; "the head of an ass, the Rabbinical feet of clay and the horns of a Papal dilemma."

"All very well, but look at my case, Avram," Ted insisted. "I was illegitimate in my natural birth. My natural conception was just like other men's conceptions and it was certainly natural. But, it was not legitimate! Not lawful! My so-called natural father and mother naturally gave me my genetic potential. But, they refused...un-naturally?...to recognize me as theirs–as if my conception didn't happen in natural time! They didn't expose me to the natural elements, as in the good old days. Instead, they gave me to an orphanage. There, another man obeyed what he saw as a super-natural injunction...With no natural ties to me, he adopted me...un-naturally, I guess. There's certainly no natural adoption. At any rate, he adopted me as his son in Christ and I took him as my father in Christ."

Ted paused for a moment and then continued. "And, this same Christ he worshipped was – in another persona – God, the Father, the Creator of the natural world. This celibate father of mine also believed that this Christ died to kill natural death. This was the Deity whose commands my adoptive father felt he was obeying when he took me as his son...me, who my natural parents got in the course of nature! My only father, I mean real father, was my father in the name of this most un-natural God, who became a man, chosen by himself to die, in order to kill death! I thank nature's God for His unnatural convention. It gave me a real, but celibate, father, when I had neither father nor mother."

"That true father adopted you," Claudia said quietly. "That means he opted to take you as his son. And, humans naturally have the power to opt for this or that, or even to reject, the options that nature presents in the form of unwanted children. Isn't that also nature at work in us?" she finished softly.

"Sure! But, how can we naturally opt to deny the issue of our natural desires? My natural parents did this to me. But, it was in the name of that prodigy of the other-than-natural, whom we call, 'The Christ,' that I found nature. When my natural mother and my natural father denied me, Mother Church bore me into legitimacy and when no one else would, Father Feeney molded me into my manhood," Ted finished breathlessly.

"And, Avram Bonapoggio became my teacher-father when I opted to turn my back on my parents' profession. I dis-opted them and adopted Avram as a sort of spiritual father," Stafford said to a beaming Bonapoggio.

During the lull this caused in the conversation, Pat asked Bonapoggio about Hurlock's illness.

"Oh, that idiot, Mustapha, whatever-his-name-is, fed Hurlock some brownies that were heavily laced with marijuana," Bonapoggio answered. After a moment's pause, he continued. "I don't like that Mustapha. I have heard very unpleasant stories about him. He goes into Manhattan, where he gets into all sorts of mischief that most of our students don't even know names for. He seems to have an unlimited amount of money and strange tastes on which to spend it. His last name is Kussi, or something like that. Is that Turkish?"

"I think I heard his father was Albanian and his passport is Turkish. Something exotic," Michelle answered and then continued with a smile, "He apparently wants to get into films and so, Stafford Wyatt, you are likely to become his teacher-father!"

"When do I meet this paragon of virtue and sanctified odor?" Stafford asked.

"In yet two days. Then shall ye see the minions of Creative Writing!" answered Rick.

"Well, I'll give him a bit of hell about this. That is not my idea of a joke. Can anybody prove it, by the way?" Stafford asked.

"No. He's been here a year and catastrophe follows him as boredom dogs the heels of edifying discourse," Rick answered. "But, no one's able to actually pin anything on him."

"Well, I'll do what I can to put the fear of God into him."

"Good luck!" Rick answered Stafford without conviction.

"Poor Hurlock!" continued Bonapoggio. "He is such an angel. He has probably never even smelled a drug. He does not even take sulfa drugs. He is healthy as a horse and twice as strong. He was really frightened by this stroke, as he called it. He said he lost his ability to shift his attention away from whatever caught it. He said he felt his limbs were made of iron."

Turning to Pat, Bonapoggio asked, "Is that what pot, as they call it, does to you?"

"I've never touched the stuff, but I have read up on it. I have a hunch that it affects your CNS – Central Nervous System, to you liberal artists – in such a way that your voluntary system is affected. As long as you don't want to do anything, it doesn't seem to have much affect. But, the moment the voluntary system tries to kick in, not much happens. My idea is that the dumber or more depressed someone is, the less the damned stuff does to him. Hurlock is smart and a gorgeous athlete. It would really affect him. Does that seem sensible to you, Michelle?"

"Absolutely. I think you are onto something about the depression and stupidity."

"Well," said Stafford, "I'll talk to Mr. Kussi soon. What is his first name?"

"Mustapha?" Bonapoggio asked.

"Yes, something like that," Rick answered.

"Well, I'll have a chat with Mustapha Kusi, or Kussi? or whatever, and I'll soon clear this up once and for all," Stafford answered.

He was wrong.

The Dean came in and hemmed and hawed until the faculty remembered that student advising began for some of them the next day and others had freshman orientation to attend to. Those of the faculty who had helped with summer pre-registration were free the next day.

The others had to be in their offices to counsel returning students majoring in their disciplines. Claudia and Bonapoggio had worked on freshman summer pre-registration and Stafford was too new to know anything to tell students. Thus, Bonapoggio invited Claudia and Stafford back to his house for a post-party omelet and "something light to drink," as he referred to his wonderful cordials and digestives. The lucky pair grinned at one another, pleased they were to be together a while longer. Then, turning to Ted Simms, who was slowly preparing to leave, Bonapoggio offered him a ride, but he said he wanted to walk.

"It's only a half-hour's walk. Thanks for a good evening and, Stafford, it was good to meet you. I liked your lecture."

Smiling a thin smile, he left.

* * *

Bonapoggio, Stafford and Claudia were making the short trip to Bonapoggio's, with Stafford riding in Claudia's car, following her host.

"Talk tonight was rather demanding," Claudia said to Stafford, as she drove.

"Yes. The molecule, color-code idea is somehow right. But, it's also somehow incomplete. There's more than that."

"It also seems as if there just ain't room in this here town for the both of them," Claudia observed tentatively.

"That's good. No one says that either gunslinger is not a good shot. They just can't be in the same town together. But, it might be deeper than that. By the way, did Avram by chance get around to telling you my mother was a biochemist and that for years, I thought of doing something in that general area?"

"No. He told me you once planned to go into medicine, but nothing about your family."

"Well, I was sent to schools where I learned a lot of good science, especially medical biology and chemistry. I had wonderful conversations about these things over the dinner table at home. All that came flooding back tonight and I feel a little disoriented...No," he continued, correcting himself after a moment's pause, "I guess I feel a little two-faced!"

"Two-faced?"

"Yes, just a little. Almost as if I converted to literature after being a worshipper of science for years," Stafford said, in a serious tone of voice, as they pulled up behind Bonapoggio's car. They went in together.

Bonapoggio's housekeeper, Mrs. Tintintolo, was a gray-haired, plump lady who looked like the dietician at a nursery school. She met them at the door and, being given her instructions, "To prepare something light; you know," went into the kitchen. They followed their host into his large, richly furnished library, whose Tiffany lamp cast a soft glow over the center of the room. Several sets of electrified brass sconces lighted the room's edges, so that even the titles of the books on the top shelves of the high, floor-to-ceiling bookcases were plainly visible to someone standing below.

"Champagne?" Bonapoggio asked.

"I would love some of your dark beer," Stafford answered. And, then, turning to Claudia, he said, "I became addicted to it when I studied with Avram at Williams. Do you know it?"

"Nonsense!" Bonapoggio interrupted. "This is one of the high moments of my life. You will have my best champagne!" As he popped the cork on his Piper-Hiedsieck, he put his arm around Stafford's shoulder and proposed a toast, "To your very good health, my dear friend." Then, after serving Claudia, he poured his own, clinked glasses with both of them, kissed Claudia's cheek to wish her special health and bade them to find a comfortable chair.

"In a second!" Claudia said, more than a little flushed. "I want to drink to the special health and welcome of Stafford Wyatt! Permit me, please...For your lecture, Stafford. It spoke to me." Raising her glass in a toast, she drank and then kissed his cheek.

"All this and champagne, Avram! You are too prodigal! My colleagues intoxicate me with their arguments. My fellow guest intoxicates me with a brush of her lips. And, now, champagne! Shall I ever be sober? Will the sun ever rise in a smooth arc from its Orient bed, if I am daily reeling with delight? How shall the day end, my friends, if its course is but a spiral from morning to night? How shall it find its Occident bed? Accidentally?"

"Incidentally, if at all," Claudia proposed.

Just then, Mrs. Tintintolo pushed in a butler's cart covered with platters of omelets, toast, coffee, pastry and bottles of liqueurs. After eating in comparative silence, as people do when the food is good and the hour late, they sat back in their deep leather chairs and looked at one another. Stafford finally had his dark beer, Claudia her Benedictine and Bonapoggio sipped a clear and fiery brandy he had shipped in from Arakova, not far from Delphi in Greece.

After a few minutes' of restoring quiet, Bonapoggio sighed deeply, turned to Stafford and asked him, "Do you think it is possible, Stafford, for a human being to consistently misread a text and come up with something that makes sense? Nature seems to."

"I don't know, Avram. I once knew a very good writer who committed suicide in something like that way...I mean, by doing something akin to intentionally mis-writing his own texts for others to, unknowingly, mis-read."

"Oh?" Claudia asked, "Real suicide or metaphorical suicide?"

"Well, you be the judge of that. I was reminded of this story earlier this evening. It's remarkable that you should bring it up in my mind again, Avram! What odd ideas...A naturally mis-translated text and a natural reader, who first mis-translates and, then, correctly reads, that mis-translation."

"Your story concerns a purposeful mis-translation?" Claudia asked, curled up in the comfortable depths of an immense leather armchair.

"Well, not quite. More an intended mis-writing to lead his readers into an intended mis-reading. The writer destroyed himself by his mis-writing. And, by God! I swear he was a writer!" Stafford was silent as he gathered his thoughts. Then, looking up, he began his story.

"When I was in Paris, a group of us met nearly every evening for a few hours. There were several painters, a composer, a few musicians and two writers, Jules Le Seur and I. He was a writer/philosopher, the only son of a very old, aristocratic family from the south of France and he had graduated with distinction in Philosophy from the Sorbonne. By the time he was twenty-two, my age at the time, he had gained a name for himself as an *explicateur* of texts, especially of so-called nihilistic writers."

"What a contradiction. A nihilist critic-artist, who creates artifacts," Bonapoggio drawled.

"Avram! Don't say anything more. You'll give away the

dénouement."

"Sorry. Continue, please."

"Well, Jules Le Seur was truly devastatingly handsome and..."

"...And that is why he was a nihilist?" Claudia broke in. "Terrific beauty can kill, I hear."

"You know, Claudia? That's not at all bad. I never thought about his remarkable beauty in that way. I knew it opened a number of possibilities that neither love nor money could have gotten him."

"Interesting. Do you think visible beauty is more powerful than love?" asked Claudia.

"I don't know...I may be special pleading as a writer, but, well...yes! I don't know...I think I think so. At any rate, Claudia, his good looks certainly slew a number of people around him. Or, to be more precise, those people seemed to lose their characteristic habits and defenses around him. He made them over and that is a sort of destruction, isn't it?"

"I suppose so. But, what do you think, Avram?" Claudia asked.

"I think the myth of Narcissus is, perhaps, the greatest of all the Greek myths. But, Stafford...continue."

"Well, he was very good looking and he had more lovers than I could count and very different from one another." Here, he stopped for a moment, and, then, shaking his head, continued. "He seemed to be totally indiscriminate in his tastes and conquests. As far as appetites and tastes were concerned, no one was beneath him as a partner. Gender, age, social condition, or looks were all one to him. No one seemed to displease him and I gather he didn't displease many of them!"

"What did this prodigy of non-discrimination write about?" asked Bonapoggio. "It is clear who his philosophy teachers were and what his philosophy was."

"What do you mean, Avram?" Claudia asked.

"Ah, my dear Claudia, have you not heard that only the power to annihilate entirely is true power? What is more, you have surely heard that Nature...slow, stupid and blind Nature...evolves all manner of questionable forms, but that only Homo can take pleasure in utterly annihilating the form and product of stupid, mindless and chance evolution?"

## Naturally Bad Manners

"He was sort of a psychological nihilist," Claudia said out loud, more to herself than to the others.

"Yes," Stafford said as he began again, "But he was really more. You know Stendhal's great remark, that the only way modern man can assert his existence is by committing suicide? Well, Jules Le Seur seemed to feel that whatever feelings he had that seemed natural or spontaneous were contemptible, and that he, Jules Le Seur, had to eliminate them completely in order to assert his control over his own nature. He thought that he could control his own nature if he could replace all his spontaneous affirmations and denials with his own creations–which were very often mere negations of that spontaneity. Nature, his nature, tells him this or that is lovely; he, the real Jules, says it is repellent. Whatever struck him as particularly loathsome and repellent drew him like a magnet. He embraced it, even when it gagged him to do so. This was Jules Le Seur. He was totally in charge!"

"But, why didn't he take the anarchist's route and become an assassin...you know, kill whoever attracted him?" Claudia asked.

"Because, my dear," Bonapoggio answered, "he was an aristocrat. But, please, on with your story. How did Jules overcome his own nature?"

"Well, this neglect of taste and discrimination didn't show itself in his writing. He was the envy of us all. His style was flawless, his diction perfect and his plots fascinating. He was genuinely learned and had a wonderful eye for detail. Like a wonderful spider, he could snare what looked like a gnat and use it to weave a wonderful web, in which he caught the attention of flighty listeners."

Stafford heard Claudia groan from her armchair and he bowed slightly in her direction by way of apology for his somewhat rococo simile.

"Didn't he use his writing to, well, redeem himself at all?" Claudia asked.

"No, he didn't. For a while, we hoped that he would come to see dramatic fiction as a form of rejecting the day-to-day, but a redeeming way of doing it, as you suggest, Claudia. When we told him this, he scoffed that this was only a child's way out of the dark. He claimed that artistic creations, especially fiction writing, only celebrate our fantasies. He said fiction was only a species of fairy-tale writing and, when we tried to remind him of the norms of common decency, he referred to them as 'nothing but the rotten fruit of folk mythology.'"

"So? What did he do?" Bonapoggio asked after a long moment's silence on Stafford's part.

"He created imperfection, in order to lead his readers to mis-read his stuff."

"He created imperfectly?" Claudia said by way of correction.

"No, Claudia, not at all. He saw that artistry was either sound or nothing. This man wasn't a soup-can or comic book painter. Those poseurs made their mark by what they didn't do and this flatters rich nouveaux *arrévistes* into feeling good about their own lack of talent. Le Seur did something…something terrible."

"Did he make something beautiful and then destroy it?" Bonapoggio asked.

"Not quite, Avram. He wrote fine, well-balanced stories, with superb character development, subtle plots and wonderful color. And, then, he surgically removed one whole character from the story, leaving an odd wound on the face of an otherwise exceptionally beautiful work."

Claudia and Bonapoggio grunted their surprise in unison, but said nothing.

Stafford continued, "Then, something very unexpected happened. He hadn't thought that more than a few people would read these stories and raise hell about them. But, this wasn't what happened at all. The *avant-garde* picked up on him, especially those weekend nihilists who are bank clerks from Monday to Friday. They ate his stuff up. He was delighted, of course, because they didn't even begin to see what he had done. They hailed him as 'Spontaneous! Of Unfettered Fantasy!' even as, 'Creativity Creating Itself!' They saw him as a radically absurd writer and this misunderstanding pleased him immensely. He gloated over it to us."

"A famous nihilist! What an idea," Claudia crowed.

"He became a literary celebrity and was lionized by all those readers who didn't have a clue as to what he was really doing. The stories almost made sense, but then didn't. After you read one, you found yourself worrying it like a dog chewing on a clean bone. You tried to adjust its parts in a way that would make it sit well with you. He claimed that his pleasure in receiving entirely negotiable royalty checks and getting rave reviews, which were all completely wrongheaded, was something like his pleasure in coupling with ancient, stinking prostitutes. He claimed, and we had to agree with him, that the degenerate old hags no more understood why he, the dashing, handsome, pomaded dandy would come to them for sex than the readers understood why he offered his damaged wares to them."

"He was fetid and they fêted him," punned a triumphant Claudia.

"Lovely!" Stafford and Bonapoggio said together.

"But, please, continue," Claudia asked.

"Well, he was wined and dined and beside himself with the wicked delight of his triumph. 'Just think!' he would brag to us, 'I can intentionally create an essentially incomplete artifact that is accepted with universal acclaim!'"

"Ah," Bonapoggio interrupted, "now I see why this evening's conversation reminded you of this story." He paused, sipped his brandy to help him compose his thoughts and continued, "Jules Le Seur's DNA! What an ungodly mess."

"Ungodly and unscientific," Claudia added with a whoop of delight. "Jules Le Seur, as the product produced by a natural biochemical reader, reading a color code that..." and here she lost the thread and looked beseechingly at Bonapoggio.

"...Which," Bonapoggio finished, "produces a product that miscodes the world around him because he rejects its, the world's, message."

"Not quite," Stafford interrupted. "It wasn't that he did not like the message. He denied it was a real message at all. The real message, he said, was an anti-message, a sort of intended random noise, whose only job was to jam up what seems to be real messages, but aren't."

"Ah, good. Now I see," Claudia said slowly. "Yes. He creates a message and then he de-constructs it perfectly to make it look like a perfect imitation of a real message."

"Or even a mockery of a real message?" Bonapoggio asked.

"Yes, good," said Claudia. "And, the oddest thing about this is that if you read the de-constructed message correctly, you get a false non-message!"

"Exactly!" Stafford said, jumping up from his chair and striding around the room. "Yes, exactly. That was the odd, low genius of the man. The better the reader, the worse the reading. You know? I imagine this was what Professor Vogel was talking about earlier this evening and why I remembered Jules, now."

"For the love of Heaven! Sit down and finish this story!" Bonapoggio ordered, gathering himself into a compact mass and retreating into the depths of his chair, his long legs curled beneath him.

Stafford sat down again and continued.

"Well, friends, Jules sold a series of these lobotomized stories. The character that he cut out after finishing the story, even after polishing it to a high luster...and please, be very clear about this point," he added with a serious expression on his face, "that character was not just lacking. He or she had been written into the story line with all the skill and verve that the very gifted and competent Jules could muster. And, he was a very good writer."

"And, so?" Bonapoggio asked by way of encouraging Stafford to continue, "After he had completed the story..."

"But, not just finished," Stafford insisted. "He really polished it to a high gloss."

"Then, Jules did away with his creation," Claudia said, at last fully grasping the situation. "The artist didn't want to be controlled, even by his own art. Good Lord! Even by his own art. He destroyed his own perfection in his artifact."

"Yes. He scarred it as soon as he had perfected it. He didn't destroy it. He scarred its loveliness," Stafford said in a low voice.

"What a truly terrible man," Bonapoggio said, gravely.

"Yes," Stafford agreed. "The man was a spiritual vandal alright. But, he didn't get away with it."

"Oh?" Bonapoggio and Claudia said in one breath.

"Well," Stafford continued, "Jules' terrible anti-artifacts faced his readers, from Paris to Aix, like a beautiful woman whose nose has been destroyed by leprosy. As I said, the radical intellectuals adored him and bought him out as fast as his new stuff appeared, okay?"

Stafford sat back in his chair and shut his eyes before continuing. Neither Claudia nor Bonapoggio disturbed his reverie.

"But, then," he continued after a few moments, "an article appeared in a small, but extremely influential right-wing Roman Catholic, review. In a very long, very closely argued article, the editor showed, even to me, who thought I knew better," Stafford said, waving his hand in front of his face in an odd dismissal gesture, as if he were shooing a mosquito away, "that Jules Le Seur was really writing about the impossibility of any life and hence of any literature about life, without the presence of The Holy Spirit!"

"Ah! Too wonderful!" Bonapoggio shouted, slapping his thigh and laughing in a deep, rich chuckle.

"But, true, Avram. This editor proved that the missing character revealed the presence of the invisible, immaterial Holy Spirit and that the odd, alarming craziness of the plot caused by the missing character represented human life's odd craziness...unless, that is, we recognize the invisible presence of the Holy Spirit. This reviewer argued, remarkably skillfully, that the missing character was there and that the plot only seemed so crazy because only the characters that were present were aware of it! Nice, eh?" Stafford finished up triumphantly.

"Wonderful!" Bonapoggio and Claudia agreed together.

"Go on, please!" Claudia begged.

"Well, Jules was beside himself with fury, but there was nothing he could do to counter the article. It was very skillfully argued, using all the techniques of literary analysis of which Jules was also a master. Indeed, the missing character in any given story did seem to move in and out of the remaining characters' lives. The plot was entirely senseless without the presupposition of the presence of that character. Can I have another drink, Avram? I'm dry. Claudia?"

They got new drinks and settled down while Stafford finished the story.

"Well, the particular story the reviewer had analyzed so persuasively was concerned with a Parisian degenerate who, as the French will do, decided to seek his salvation in self-degradation."

"You sound like an Englishman, Stafford," Bonapoggio chided him.

"Well, this story involves one well-to-do, pious church-going Auguste who has a crisis of faith when his sister, to whom he is very attached, dies of a particularly agonizing form of cancer. His priest and confessor can offer him no comfort in his distress, so he stops going to church and his club and begins to frequent low-class brothels. Among the clientele of one of the less savory of these, he stumbles upon a disaffected Roman Catholic, Paul, who persuades him that he is worshipping a false God, and that he should joyously pursue and embrace all those activities which his church found most sinful. August turns out to be a diligent student as Paul carefully guides him, step by step, away from his former oh-so bourgeois pleasures into the gross entertainment enjoyed by the true low-life of Paris. Paul finally introduces him to a disgusting burned out hag from the Algerian slums and, with Paul's constant coaching, he explored all manner of nastiness, some of it criminal, with her. The longer he did so, the more slack and degenerate his own manners became. The salons to which Auguste was invited were irritated by his behavior and the members of his club – to which he had belonged for years – began to consider expelling him. However, they bore up for a while under a steadily increasing torrent of filthy innuendoes and repulsive interpretations of the members' otherwise largely ignored peccadilloes. Then, Auguste began to tell them of his escapades with his hag. This was too much and all his friends finally abandoned him. He ended his miserable life by taking a strong poison mixed with a powerful emetic and he died a hideous and disgusting death at the communion rail of a large church packed for Easter Mass."

"What a dreadful story!" Claudia observed, drawing herself together in her deep armchair's depths for comfort.

"Well, after Jules had polished this tale to perfection, he surgically removed both Paul and the hag from it and August's descent into Hell seemed to be merely a matter of what happened to happen! No reason. No because. It just happened. Life's like that."

"And?" Bonapoggio prompted.

"Well, first, other Catholic conservative literary journals picked up on Jules' story about Auguste and other less conservative journals and reviews soon jumped aboard the bandwagon. In a few months, Jules was the darling of the Catholic Right and damned viciously by the intellectuals of the Left."

"The former allies, what did they do?" Claudia asked.

"Well," Stafford said, laughing softly, "they cursed Jules for a Jesuit!"

"And, the final issue of all this?" Bonapoggio asked, "What did a just, but witty Heaven visit on our entirely independent friend, pray tell?"

"No light recompense," Stafford answered quietly. "Jules was beside himself with rage. He snapped at everything and everyone. Soon, he began to accuse us of being part of a huge conspiracy against him."

"Ah," nodded Bonapoggio, "they all do. When Deity leaves His Heaven for the Earth, it is, according to the Jules Le Seurs of this world, only in order to form conspiracies, eh? But, what did happen?"

"Well, the original model for the story's prostitute was, as I think I've said, from the worst Algerian slum in Paris. Her real-life pimp was a greasy young man with no gift for charity or kindness...all business. Jules was also very tight with his money and so, when the hag was no longer useful as his literary model, he simply dumped her, without a word."

"Not exactly a trusting, solid relationship," Claudia observed from the depths of her chair.

"No, but the pimp was somewhat sentimental when it came to the whereabouts of his regular customers and he missed the income provided by Jules' visits. The pimp's hag had disappeared from the story Jules had originally written her into and then written her back out of. At the same time, Jules disappeared from the hag's life. But, whereas her disappearance from his story brought him universal acclaim from the Catholic Right, her pimp was not so pleased."

"The man was obviously not much into literature," Bonapoggio remarked.

"But, the story character...what was she like, Stafford?" Claudia asked.

"She was a disgusting, degenerate, hideous hag before Jules excised her from the action of the story. Then, by her absence in his story, she became an angel of God, in her very absence! Nice, eh?"

"Yes, very nice," Claudia echoed.

"Well, to make a long story not much longer," Stafford said, as he heard the grandfather's clock strike one, "the pimp missed Jules' trade, and sought him out and, finally, traced him to his house in a very nice quarter of Paris. The pimp rang the bell at Jules' front door and, quite by chance, Jules himself, rather than his butler, answered it. Since Jules was sure by then that everyone was conspiring against him, he saw the completely unexpected resurrection of the pimp as just another chapter in the universal plot to make him wretched. When he opened the front door and saw the pimp, he was beside himself with fury. He kicked the pimp down his front stairs. But, the pimp had brought the hag with him. When she saw her pimp lying groaning at the foot of the front steps, she pulled a knife and expertly cut Jules' throat, from ear to ear. He was dead before he hit the ground. The pimp and his hag disappeared from view and have never been heard of or seen again."

"But, Stafford...That's wonderful!" Claudia cried out getting to her feet in her excitement. "The missing character! The character Jules thought he had absolute artistic power over as her creator! She returned!"

"Twice! The nihilists saw the lack simply as a lack and they loved it! Real affirmation, they said. But, my dear, the Catholic Right saw that lack as a spiritual presence! That was the hag's first return from the nowhere to which her creator had banished her," Stafford gloated, rubbing his hands together in delight.

"Poor man. Heaven warned him and he ignored the warning," Bonapoggio said reflectively.

"Yes," Stafford said, getting up out of his chair and stretching. "Jules' fate made me think I saw that I was facing a sort of logic that, well..." He strode back and forth several times, his head bent and his hands in his pockets. "Well, I think Jules was destroyed by a sort of divine logic. I don't know how to say it differently."

Bonapoggio surprised both Stafford and Claudia by intoning, "Oh thou Tubalcain, be ye a great artificer and great Nimrod, be ye a mighty hunter before the face of the Lord."

"And, what was the hag's second resurrection?" Claudia asked, as they began to drift toward the front door.

"She came back and cut his throat."

"Ah, of course."

Bonapoggio announced at the door, "Since Stafford is staying here for the time being, perhaps you could let him see you home. He can follow you to your house and see you in. It's too late to go home alone."

"Good Lord! This town is as safe as can be," Claudia answered automatically.

*Naturally Bad Manners*

"I'd rather like it, if you wouldn't mind," Stafford answered plaintively.

"Of course. It would be my pleasure."

Bonapoggio gave Stafford a key to the front door and told him there was no hurry for him to return. Claudia kissed Bonapoggio on both cheeks, thanked him for a true feast of food and good conversation and ended with her thanks, "for a privileged introduction to Stafford Wyatt."

Bonapoggio smiled them out.

Once they were in her car, Claudia insisted that he take her car for a few days. "The college is only a few blocks and I'd enjoy the walk for a week or two, or until whenever you get your own car."

Stafford accepted at once and Claudia drove them to her house.

After they left the car and reached her front steps, Stafford, very awkwardly, as it seemed to him—although very charmingly, as it appeared to Claudia—asked, "Might I meet you for dinner this Thursday?"

"Yes. I'd like that."

Then, as he turned to go, Claudia asked him, "Might I kiss you 'thanks' for a fine evening. Now? I'd rather not wait until Thursday."

"Yes. I'd like that."

So, Claudia kissed him.

Her kiss was neither particularly urgent, nor afire with any burning desire. It was direct, simple and entirely compelling to Stafford. That was how she had intended it to be. As clear and abrupt as a telegram, it said to him: "I think I will come to love you, Stafford. 'Stop'."

Then they began to look at each other.

No treasure-hunter ever studied a faded, water-stained, map more closely than they examined one another's face. Looking closely at someone is not as carefree and effortless as kissing that same someone, because no one who is not an elephant or an anteater can simultaneously kiss and look. Kissing must have an end, but not looking. So, if a police cruiser had not pulled up to the curb to investigate the activity taking place on Dr. Harris' front steps, Dr. Harris and Mr. Wyatt might still be there, gazing at one another from sightless, because eyeless, sockets. But, the sharp CB-voice of the police radio dispatcher crackling out of the cruiser's window broke, if only for a time, the potentially lethal charm each treasure-hunter's face held for the other. Claudia called out, "All's well, officers. Thank you," and the cruiser moved on.

"You know, Stafford Wyatt," Claudia said, sitting down comfortably on the top step and motioning him to join her, "up to now, with one exception, the men I've known have treated me like a beautiful Circasian captive, or like a rock star, or..." She frowned and was silent.

"Oh?" Stafford responded, taking advantage of the nearby streetlight to trace the line of her lower jaw, from just below her delicate earlobe to her stubborn chin.

"Yes. The one sort expected me to swoon over the back of their Yamaha motorcycles. The other sort begged me, with the most amazingly silly smiles and head-bobbing, to have pity on their normal, healthy, male desires and, of course, their hopeless adoration for me. Another just toyed."

"Hmm?" Stafford responded, as he admired her fine broad brow, ending in the slight dip that began her wonderful straight nose.

Looking around suddenly, Claudia saw that he'd been painting her into his imagination, where she would remain for a more leisurely inspection when time and occasion permitted. Some men had undressed her with their eyes and one man had coolly looked at her with the eye of a surgeon. Some leered at her and others smiled lovesick grins. But, Stafford was the first man who had really studied her face. Rick Vogel had done a number of quick portrait-sketches of her, but he had "measured" her face; to Rick, her face was a face, but not her face, the face of Claudia Harris.

Claudia put out her hand and touched Stafford's cheek. He moved his head slightly in her direction and gently took her index finger between his teeth. Letting go in a moment, he then held her right hand in his and then kissed the tip of each finger, then each joint of each finger, then, her palm and her wrist.

He then held her hand and said, "I'm afraid I'm quite dizzy."

"I was telling you something important about me, Stafford. Or, at least, important to me. Okay?" she chided, gently taking her hand back, but stroking his cheek with it, in a gesture of reassurance.

"I'm sorry," Stafford answered, sounding genuinely contrite.

"Oh, I'm not. Never shall this hand know soap or water, or those usages, great or small, poetic or very much otherwise, which are customary for the right hand of a right-handed person. But, what I began to say was that I am very wary about love these days. No fault of yours, God knows!"

Stafford looked at her for a long moment and then said, "I'm sorry, Claudia."

"I was very dumb. There were candidates and I pretended they were real candidates who I really wanted in the race. It's that simple."

"Look at me, Claudia."

She did and saw that Stafford was looking at her with his head slightly cocked to one side.

"If I were to say that I am glad, I'd sound like a fool. So, I'll say nothing, except to thank you for telling me."

"Thank you, Stafford."

He answered, in a matter-of-fact tone of voice, "You're welcome. May I kiss you again?"

"No, Stafford. I'm deeply tired. I would fall into your arms and I don't want to do that. I want to return embrace for embrace, breath for breath. I know you understand," Claudia ended and Stafford thought that he had never been so elegantly complimented or slyly turned down.

Claudia stood up, opened her front door and they shook hands goodnight. Then, just before letting go of her hand, Stafford brought it up to his lips. She returned the gesture and they released hands.

As she entered her house, Claudia turned around and, over her shoulder, asked, "Until next Thursday night? Say, six? Here? I could give you a drink and then dinner."

"I'd like that very much. But, don't plan to cook, or do anything spectacularly domestic and feminine. I'd sit on my haunches like a dog and howl at the kitchen ceiling."

They touched hands again and, after Claudia disconnected her car keys from her key ring and gave them to Stafford, he left.

After she shut the door, Claudia prepared for bed in slow motion. She was relieved to note that her body was not tingling to be touched by Stafford and she thought that, perhaps, she loved him most of all for the way he rode his urgency. As she prepared to put on her nightgown, after she had taken off all her clothes, she first looked at herself in her full-length mirror. Then, looking herself straight in the eye, she said out loud to herself, "Never be simply naked to Stafford, Claudia. This is your body. Keep it and only share it, sometimes, in return for his loan of his body. That way, you'll never again be without a body. Or a soul!"

Sighing deeply, as she realized how very premature such thoughts were, she put on her gown, got into bed and fell asleep at once.

# CHAPTER 7

## Dreams

But, we are not to think that such a night, beginning in such an auspicious way for Stafford Wyatt and Claudia Harris, was to be altogether dreamless. Stafford, who seldom dreamed, woke up the morning after the late evening at Bonapoggio's with a sense that he had dreamed, but he could not remember of what. Claudia dreamed and remembered.

In her dream, Claudia found herself exulting in the nakedness with which her God had clothed her, each living curve and each luminous highlight of each curve reflecting the flesh and bones her God had sculpted out of Stafford's sleeping flesh. Numbers of the lower creatures came up to her and they watched, as she posed, proudly displaying herself as her God's youngest creation and all the living rest of that creation sang together in a chorus.

Not all. For, among her viewers was a Komodo-Dragon-like creature, a terrible lizard. When its long, constantly flicking tongue touched the thighs and hips of the newly created, newly dreamed Claudia, it made her wince and, what was even worse, the lizard's breath stank terribly. He spoke in a rattling whisper that made her think he did not want the other animals to hear what he was saying and he spoke, again and again, of the folly of her joyful exultation in the unclothed beauty with which she had been created by her God. Then the dragon's rattling whisper became Ray Hayes' voice and it spoke to her, saying, "Oh, foolish Claudia! Youngest artifact of the Maker! Why will you always flaunt your shameless nakedness?"

"What is it you say, Lizard? Has not our Lord God, the Father of us all, has He not told us to tend our gardens? Are we not to exult in its many beauties? And, am I, Claudia, not the youngest creation of our Lord's great bounty? Why should I not be joyful in my beauty? Did not our Lord God sculpt me, of all creation, out of living flesh? Am I not a very special beauty, this creation out of living flesh? And, shame? I do not know what that word means, Lizard."

Claudia laughed because she was happy and she spun on her left foot, with her right arm out in front of her, her left arm bent at the elbow, so that her hand was over her head and her wrist bent downward. The lizard's tail lashed back and forth, while her other spectators, from the smallest, songful cricket to the great honey-bears, who stood on their hind legs and roared their approval to high Heaven, made manifest their delight in her beauty.

"Oh, shameless Claudia, young and foolish as you are, why do you rejoice in what you have? Has not the Maker left you pale and hairless? Where are your shimmering feathers? Where are your gossamer wings? Where are your great, green scales, like mine? You are only half-complete, young and foolish Claudia."

"Not yet completed?" Claudia called back, stopping in mid-twirl. "There is yet more to come? Shall I be yet more beautiful and so yet more exalted in my beauty? How could that be, lizard?"

"Oh young, foolish and naked Claudia! You are naked as the newborn mouse! Shall you not be yet further completed by the Maker?"

"But, how shall this beauty of mine be further completed?" Claudia demanded. She executed a fine spin, with one arm over her head and the other on her hip, ending with a bow. The great tiger, watching this from nearby, lashed his tail in his delight and his eyes blazed to see her dance so.

"Ha, oh, mouse! Shall Stafford have his Claudia and Claudia have nothing?" the lizard hissed, moving closer, to keep what he was saying more confidential.

"Hmm," said Claudia, interested for the first time. "What could I have which would be, to me, what I am, to Stafford? Am I not a new shape of his flesh, sculpted out of his lovely side?"

"Ah, dear Claudia...not-quite-complete-Claudia...I am only the lizard. Oh, of course, I've been here longer even than Stafford. But, the Maker has insisted that your Stafford should rule over me and my kind. How is it to be me who is to tell you what you must know to be complete in your beauty?" And, the fetid breath of the whispering lizard drove Claudia back a few steps.

"What is this nakedness you talk of, Stinking-Breath? I know my

## Naturally Bad Manners

excellent beauty that my Lord and my God gave me when He sculpted me out of Stafford's side. I know Stafford's wonderful eyes and his delightful thighs. But, this nakedness of yours. What is it? What does it name? Are you naked, Lizard?"

The terrible beast hemmed and hawed and scratched his chin with his hind leg and his great claws slashed the air as he did so. "Well, you see, Claudia, youngest and most foolish child of creation, only you and your Stafford are naked! Of course, you should not be naked and my ancient wisdom tells me that you will not be naked forever, either of you. We dragons...er, lizards, we have our beautiful scales and the honey bear here has his long, soft hair, which you grasp when you ride on his back. Only you and Stafford and, of course, the newborn mouse are ever naked, Claudia, newest and least-perfected of the Maker's undertakings...Oh, yes, that mouse, you may have noticed," the beast continued reflectively, " gets covered with hair as soon as he can! How about you, young and beautiful – no! Almost beautiful, but still naked – Claudia?"

Claudia frowned. No, not Claudia, but the Claudia who, although known only to the real Claudia, was not the real Claudia. She, the dream-Claudia, frowned as she pictured thoughts the real Claudia had never before imagined. She thought to herself, "The lizard is most surely not at all beautiful. He cannot dance and his breath stinks. But, he does seem to know about this nakedness, whatever it is."

Turning to the dragon, Claudia smiled and thereby clothed her doubt in her very beautiful smile.

The lizard, now become a true dragon, knew this at once. Furiously flicking his great tail from side to side, uprooting a number of blossoming rose-bushes thereby and his great, golden, irises showing only the narrowest of slits, the terrible beast advanced toward Claudia and flicked her familiarly all over her body with his long, cold, forked tongue.

Claudia no longer gloried in her beauty. She covered her shapely breasts with her right hand and she covered her lower belly, where it met her thighs, with her left hand. Her lovely hands and arms now hid the beauty of her nakedness, as her beauty had hidden her doubt about her nakedness. As she stared at the terrible beast, she heard a swish, as when the hawk plummeted past her in his rapturous plunge with which he answered the glory of her beauty as she danced and a shadow descended over the fiercely triumphant head of the dragon. Stafford, blazing in the glory of his beauty, which Claudia now saw as his own beauty, rather than the beauty given to him by the Maker as He molded Stafford out of clay, hit the dragon where his head broadens out from his neck. The subtle beast fell, vomited blood for a while and then lay still.

"Why, dearest Claudia, are you standing in that awkward position? Where are your lovely and joyful dances? Why do you press your arms to your sides, rather than throwing them out in an ecstasy of joy and celebration of God the Father's gift of such great beauty?"

Once again, Claudia smiled to hide something, this time her fear and Stafford knew it at once. He wept and all of animate creation groaned. The alarm clock rang and one of the Claudias woke up, announcing out loud, "I will live with Stafford Wyatt, if he asks me to, but I'll be damned before I merely spend nights with him. Dammit! My body isn't going to be a party-favor for our Friday night meetings. He's got somehow to live with my nakedness and I've got to learn to live with his...Oh, damn you, Ray."

Claudia realized that if she saw Stafford that evening she would probably tell him her dream and that this was a very bad idea. So, after a leisurely breakfast and several hours of school-preparation, Claudia called her best friend, Laura Miller and asked her to come over to visit.

"I really do need your good sense, Laura. Can you come over this afternoon? Say, at two?"

Laura arrived a little after two. Coffee was poured and Claudia brought a light snack out from the refrigerator and they nibbled and drank coffee as Laura wandered around the kitchen. Claudia sat down.

"Man-problems, Claudia?"

"No. I've asked you to come to tell you that dreams come true, sometimes. Did you know that?"

"Shall the daughter of La Videnta not know that? Not for a moment did I think you had called me over to discuss stocks."

"As a matter of fact, you know you're much better at stocks than I am. But, no. I didn't call about stocks. I'm in a man-quandary. Or, I think that's what it is. But, Laura, I might say some things in passing that sound as if I'm prying into your life. I'm not. It just happens that

## Naturally Bad Manners

our cases might turn out to be somewhat parallel."

"Go on."

Then, seeing Claudia stammer and search for an opening, Laura bent over and, kissing her on the cheek, said, "Claudia, my dear. Be of good cheer. You are in love and your best friend, Laura, whose mother is the wise woman, La Videnta, will advise you as well as she can. Looking at your eyes, I will guess that you are in love. You know that I am in love with Ted and that your best friend, me, will not marry the man she loves. Is that part of your problem?"

"I suppose. But, I promise! I didn't call because of you and Ted. I would have called anyhow. I promise. You are so smart! How do you do it? And, don't tell me you're the daughter of a witch."

"Ah, but, Querida, I am the daughter of a witch," Laura said, her eyes twinkling with fun. "And, Beautiful Circasian Maiden, please remember that I am black and that Sheba was also black. She, alone, among all the daughters of men, was most famously fit to consort with the great, wise Solomon."

"You are mocha and you are beautiful."

"But, come now and tell the wise woman, Laura, all."

Claudia told Laura her dream, leaving out no detail or impression. She ended her recital with a description of her first waking thoughts.

"So, you see why I am a little shy about saying I would live with Stafford, but not be merely lovers?"

"I see. You have not been with a man since Ray Hayes? Some time now."

Reaching over the table, Laura took Claudia's chin in her hand. After studying her face from a number of angles, she let her go and said, patting her cheek gently, "Yours is a severe beauty. A real beauty, but very severe. Most men would not abide it peacefully. They must either conquer you or, what is yet more boring, worship you. How about this Stafford of yours?"

"He doesn't do either. And, he spends a great deal of time really studying my face. He seems to love it."

"Well, Claudia. Like Caesar's Gaul, which we both learned to hate in Parochial School, I am divided into three parts. I am of Africa, of Spain and of the Carib Indians who, perhaps you know, were cannibals."

Claudia looked interested, but said nothing.

"So, the Carib Indian in me is your dragon–Ray Hayes, perhaps? The African in me is you, before your dragon made you wise. The terrible Spanish in me makes the Carib cannibal and the African, for all its tumultuous mystery, look tame! The Spaniard has the avarice of the Carthaginian and the subtlety of the Berber, together with the savagery of the Celt. But, enough of this psycho-geography. Mamman says that since Lotario died before we had a son, I cannot remarry until she dies. So, until then, I only live with Ted."

"Oh, Laura, I'm sorry. I didn't mean to pry. Really."

"Do be quiet, Claudia. And, do not be sorry! Let me tell you a little about Ted and me. It might help for you to know."

Laura paused, took a long pull on her coffee cup, sat back in her chair and, looking directly at Claudia, began. "You see, Ted was an unwanted child and his father and mother, who were not married to one another, put him in an orphanage when he was just a baby. The lack of love for him during those first few years made him all too susceptible to it later. Like an albino, he blisters easily. So, he loves me with a sobbing intensity that frightens and, sometimes, even repels, me. But, then, he sometimes looks at me as if I were the veil hung between him and some very great and beautiful mystery. This ravaged me and I cared for his grief and fear as well as I could. He is becoming used to loving me now. And, only the world stands between us. Before, I stood as a door between Ted and his mysteries. I love him, Claudia. But, he is so dark. So sad sometimes. But, he is a good man, a deeply good man. When he can take me as his own, we will marry...somehow. But, first, he must sacrifice his fear and his grief. These two passions have no place in love, I think."

"Right you are. And, I am afraid. I know it sounds crazy, but the idea of being in front of a man without clothes frightens me, since Ray."

"Oh?" Laura said as she got up and poured them each more coffee. She sat down and continued after a long pause. "Let me tell you a little about me and my courtship. I was only 16 when my Lotario began to court me. I was a Spanish virgin and I remained a virgin until I married. And, Claudia! That was not the custom where I lived. A woman who was betrothed to a man–engaged, as you say here–was a lover with her intended. If he ran out, he was a dead man. Her relatives would not bear such shame. And, Claudia, you are a doctor of economics and a professor. I was the daughter of Mamman and the wonderfully handsome Lotario was quite a catch. There was no question, Claudia, that he would have married me, whether or not we became lovers. Everyone, including Lotario, was too afraid of Mamman, of La Videnta. And, Lotario was mad about me. No. I was very safe indeed."

"So, you stayed a virgin until you were married?" Claudia asked, very interested.

"Oh, yes. Lotario begged me, first on one knee and then on both knees. And, then, Claudia, once he prostrated himself before me. Before me! The daughter of a weed-woman...like a saint! When I still said, no, he stood up with his hands before him and growled like a bear. I still said no! And, then, he swore he was dying with desire for me."

"Why did you say no?" Claudia asked, a little upset and feeling a very unexpected sympathy for Lotario.

"I am no longer sixteen, but I am not so ugly?" Laura asked, with a blank expression on her face.

"No, you goose. You are not so ugly," Claudia said, as she got up and went around the table to where Laura sat. She hugged her tightly and kissed her cheeks.

"Ah, but Querida Mia! At sixteen, I was so beautiful!" Laura said and fell silent. Claudia studied her fine figure and strong face of twenty-eight and thought to herself that, indeed, Laura must have been very beautiful at sixteen. Laura aroused herself out of her reverie and, with a penetrating look at Claudia, seemed to make up her mind about something.

"Claudia. I am going to tell you something I have never told anyone. This is only ours. Yours and mine."

"Of course, Laura."

"Well, Mamman would bring home goats, pigeons, doves and the like, for her healing-sessions. Her patients would buy them from her and Mamman would sacrifice them to the spirit whose presence had made the patient sick. It was my job to care for these beasts until it was time for their sacrifice. I fed and comforted them with patting, scratching and little crooning noises. But, on the day they were to be killed, they became restless. I swear to you, Claudia. I am speaking the truth."

"I believe you, Laura. Why wouldn't I?" Claudia reassured her. "Go on. Please?"

"Well, the healing sacrifices always took place at seven o'clock in the evening. The sun sets about six, year-round, in the tropics and it is quite dark by a little after seven. And, by three in the afternoon of that day, my pets were panicked. Oh, Claudia, I loved them so! But, I loved Mamman and she trusted me and, Claudia, most of these patients of hers got well. I thought my heart would break."

"Oh, Laura," was all that Claudia could whisper.

"Well," Laura continued, patting Claudia's hand, "I took off my clothes and I danced for them."

"Oh, Laura!"

"Yes. And, Claudia, they were quieted."

"You had nothing else to give them."

"No, my dear Gringa! Not at all. I gave them the best thing I had! I gave them the sight of my dancing in celebration of my beauty."

Claudia looked stricken. "What an ass I am."

"My joy in those dances saved me from the distress I felt because I had kept those lovely animals for death. They may have sensed my joy or...or at least sensed that I was no longer distressed."

"And, your Lotario?"

"Ah! My Lotario. His illness was not fatal and we both knew it. He howled like a dog and crawled on his belly like a snake, but he would live and he would have me. We both knew it. He was very beautiful, Claudia. I would have danced for his beauty, but he was, as is the way with men, too stupid to know this. But, I pretended not to be moved by his howling or by his tears. Not even by some very nice presents that I accepted from him and then shut the door on him. He finally threatened to kill himself–I think that was the advice an uncle of his gave him. I told him that Mamman would oblige me by bringing him back to life, so that I could torment him further."

"And?"

"After several months of this, on a blazing Caribbean night, I heard a gentle knock on the door. Lotario always banged on it as if he would break it down. So, I opened it, thinking to find one of Mamman's

## Naturally Bad Manners

patients and there was Lotario, in a white linen suit. In one hand, he carried a small bunch of native flowers, which he must have picked himself. He had a Panama hat in the other hand. Oh, Claudia! He was so fine-looking that I nearly fainted. He said, in a voice that sounded like a morgue-attendant, 'It is I, Lotario Ursina, Angelina. I have come to ask for the honor of your hand in marriage. Father Gomez feels that this union is appropriate and will prove to be most fruitful. If you will have me, I will work hard to make you rich and happy. I know that you are Mamman's daughter and thus I will never raise my hand to you in anger, as is the custom with the other island men. I will try to give you all those things you need to make you envied by your near kinsmen and respected by your neighbors.'"

Laura stopped, poured them each a little fresh coffee and continued. "I asked him, 'Why is it that you do me such an honor?' but, I did not invite him into Mamman's hut. He answered, still standing in the doorway, 'Your beauty touches me to the heart and, I swear it on the body of my mother, Rachael Ursina, I cannot live much longer without the joy of your wifely embraces.'"

"What a proposal!" Claudia said, getting up and stretching. "What next?"

"I was very impressed, but not overwhelmed by his words. But, Claudia, he was so beautiful. That overwhelmed me, but he would not keep quiet long enough for me to succumb and I was the woman who had danced away the fears of beasts about to be killed. Dear Lotario was not much better. If only he had known how beautiful he was!"

Laura stopped, looked out the window at the distance and absent-mindedly sipped her coffee. She began to smile and resumed, "I asked him, 'Why do you tell me these things? Am I a nun that I should pray for your recovery from this terrible illness? Or, if you seek medicine, see Mamman, not me. Prayers from a nun and medicine from Mamman. I am neither a weed-woman nor a nun'."

"Laura! You were so cruel!" Claudia said in a distressed voice.

"Ah, Claudia. I told you. I was speaking as a Spaniard. He insisted and I chided him for his very unholy desire to couple with a nun. Worse! First to marry her in a Catholic Church and then couple with her. He replied, 'Angelina,' for that was the name he called me by, 'you are very beautiful and, as I have heard, you dance naked before La

Videnta's beasts to comfort them and make their last hours sweet.'

"'You have heard that?' I asked back sharply. 'But,' he continued, ignoring my stupid question, 'I wish to hold you in marriage and no goat or dove can offer you that!' I started to object, but Lotario motioned me quiet and continued, 'I do not wish to embrace your nakedness, Angelina, no matter how wonderful it may prove to be. There are splendid harlots too, you know? I want your nakedness clothed in God's Holy Catholic law. With that law around you like the Virgin Mother's mantle, I will have your beauty as no goat ever beheld it.'

"Well, I thought to myself, this man is indeed a Spaniard. I have met my match. So, dear Claudia, I married Lotario."

"And, did he find you beautiful in marriage?" Claudia asked with a smile.

"Oh, yes. He found me beautiful and I took great care to go to him clothed in that mantle. And, Claudia, never go to your Stafford Wyatt stripped of whatever mantle it is you have thrown around your shoulders for him."

"What would I look like if I were to appear to Stafford stripped and bare?" Claudia asked with a deep frown.

"Like a naked woman. Nothing else. Nothing special."

"And, so?" Claudia asked, very much interested in what Laura's answer might be.

"And, that would be the coupling of beasts, my dear Claudia. My Lotario was correct in that. My doves and my goats were somewhat quieted by my dancing, but I believe, truly, that it was my joy that quieted them and certainly not my nakedness. Lotario was too Spanish to know about these things, but even he saw that I must come to him clothed in something."

"Then why did he try to persuade you to be his lover before you were married?" Claudia asked softly.

"Pooh! That was the Spaniard again. I had to want him. But, he did not even begin to suspect that I did! Or that, if he had truly offered himself to me, I would have accepted and taken him for my own."

"And, why didn't you?" Claudia asked, puzzled.

"Oh, because Lotario was not his own to give. He and I went to Father Gomez, who, in his Catholic wisdom, knew how to give Lotario to me and me to Lotario, even if we did not possess ourselves. Do you understand what I am saying, Claudia?"

"I'm not really sure I do. Perhaps I'm too Spanish?" Claudia answered, with a rueful smile.

"You? God in Heaven. I don't think so. No, Claudia. Someday, and I think it might be soon, you'll be yours to give because you made yourself yours to give."

"And, you, Laura?"

"Ah! It is not so easy to be raised by an island weed-woman and also go to a good British Catholic Parochial girls' school. I suppose nature is a sort of God to me. But, then, Mamman's cures are very good, you know? I sometimes think that we humans, with our medicines and our religions, have woven a mantle to cast over nature's very shoulders, the way we girls used to weave and embroider beautiful mantles for the Blessed Virgin Mary's Feast of the Assumption. Remember? We took last year's mantle off the statue in the Mary-Chapel, put it away and then placed the new one on her."

"The way each generation expresses itself?"

"Ah. Good. I have never thought about it that way. Yes. Very much so, I think. But, you, Claudia, you have a real sense of mantle-styles. No. I am not making a joke at your expense," Laura said, very seriously and even a little sternly, as Claudia laughed merrily at the idea of shopping for a mantle.

"What I am trying to tell you, Claudia, is that you are not like Lotario. You can choose your mantle. He used the one he happened to have available. So it is with most of us."

Here Laura indicated that she was ready to go. She turned at the door and said, "Congratulations on your sense of style!" and left.

\* \* \*

Although he had enjoyed no such nocturnal adventures as had Claudia, Stafford was also somewhat overwrought that morning. He spent several hours that morning preparing himself to meet Claudia at six that evening. First, he asked himself what it might mean to meet Claudia Harris at six, that very evening. He concentrated on her and at once found himself jotting down the following thoughts:

About how lovely her jaw and hair were. About the way a runaway curl often escaped her mass of hair and how that curl had plastered itself in an inverted question mark above her wonderfully arched left eyebrow. That she used no perfume and only faintly smelled of violets – a good eau de cologne? That this was the way Doctor Claudia Harris, Ph.D., presented herself to non-economists – what did fellow economists think about this woman? That this was a particularly wonderful way to package an economist – he would never have thought of it, in a million years, for one of his own characters. That she was the first woman he had even met, after Doctor Lydia Wyatt, M.D., who had style, brains and smelled good. He never thought of Claudia undressed. When he experimentally tried to, he could not. He did not know why.

"Well," he thought, a little ashamed of himself, "it's a good thing she's not a character in a book of mine." He then blanked out with respect to his preparation, only noting a monarch butterfly sitting on the window ledge, the sounds of quarreling birds and the ticking of his watch.

Then it struck him. "I want to marry Claudia! Oh, my God! What if anything happened to her? So this is what those poems I've been translating for the last ten years are about!"

He felt like a fool and, after staring out the window blankly for a long time, he realized he was prepared for the evening.

Bonapoggio met Stafford in his study for a drink and a visit before his date with Claudia. The day was clear and bright. Bonapoggio had placed a large bouquet of gladioli in a cut-crystal vase in front of his study window. The predominant impression their mass gave the viewer was of a snowy white field for a deep, rich, red to splash on. The cut-crystal vase refracted blues, oranges and reds around the room. The afternoon sun raked the blossoms and then settled into a pool of light on the floor.

Such a journey the light from the sun takes to get to that crystal vase! And such a gentle ending to it. Beginning, so we are assured, in unimaginably ferocious atomic holocausts taking place on the surface of the sun, that light had sped from its terrible source and winged Earthward for nearly two minutes until, one hundred and ninety-three million miles later, it was captivated by Professor Bonapoggio's bouquet of red and white gladioli. It raked them farewell, sped on yet

## Naturally Bad Manners

a little and then reformed within the pool of rose, blue and ivory it located on Bonapoggio's fine old carpet and, leaving that pool as a dragonfly dips into the surface of a still pond, without seeming to disturb its glassy calm, it finally charmed the eye of a poet.

After they had each sipped their drinks for a few moments and Stafford had settled down, he surveyed the spectacle of light and color before him and he began to muse out loud. "Avram, I sometimes envy the painters. My writing can never capture this."

"And, just what is it, would you say, the painter can capture that you cannot?"

"Well, something of the given quality of what we see. In writing, we are always going through something. A painter gives it all at once," Stafford answered slowly, searching for words as he spoke.

"I am not so sure, Stafford. But, let us suppose what you say, that what you, in your writer's way and the painter, in his painter's way, are doing is presenting something of the petals to someone who is not here. What I mean is," he continued, as Stafford prepared to interrupt him, "the petals capture and then, transform, the sunlight. Isn't that what we see, or write about, or paint for others? About a given-off something? – The stress is on the given-off part."

"Ah, but according to what we learn in college optics, what we see is a leftover. The objects absorb what they can and what we see is the rest, what they don't absorb."

"The visible world then becomes a collection of crumbs," Bonapoggio remarked dryly.

Stafford had periodic qualms about leaving science and one struck him now.

"But, Avram! The petals absorb light. You know both the theory and the experimental confirmation as well as I do."

"But, Stafford, all you are saying can be re-said in what I feel is a saner way of describing what we actually see and, what we actually see is the result of what the petals do and do not do. You say, 'They hold something back and they do not hold back something else.' Well, instead, let us say they give something off and do not give something else off. What strikes us is the result of the petal's ah...discrimination." He finished with a slight shrug and, after a moment's pause, he continued. "And, look, my friend, you know the peacock's tail is what it is because the physical structure of its feathers refracts light – no less than this crystal bowl. What you see when you look at that proud marvel is an artifact of the peacock's feathers...not colored dust."

"So, you're saying that the petals really take some things and give off or, perhaps it's better to say, give back, some other thing?" Stafford asked, a little vexed he had not remembered the example of the peacock's tail himself.

"What I am trying to say is that the petals conceive the light in both senses of conceiving – to receive and then to give off."

"That is what conceive means, isn't it?" Stafford asked, slapping his forehead in mock amazement. "So," he continued, "the very activity of truly viewing something..."

"...Is an act of conceiving a conception?" Bonapoggio finished, with a mischievous grin.

"And, then, a poet, writer, or painter, goes one step further than when you merely gaze at the flowers," Stafford said slowly.

"He takes the conception and he re-conceives it. Re-conception is a poem, eh?" Bonapoggio said, with an elegant wave of his hand.

As Stafford was about to answer, Bonapoggio began again, saying excitedly, "Yes! To be more precise, when you write about what you see, or what you have thought through, you do exactly, in your human way, what a gladiolus does in its, ah, flowery, way. You are a human. It is a gladiolus. To write, even to speak, is to take something from the world around you, make it yours and, only then, give it back to the world – in a more perfect form? Yes...I think so. But, it has then come from you, the poet. You have caught it and held it. It no longer belongs to the temporal order of God's primal creation in six days...But, what am I, Rabbi Avram Bonapoggio, saying?" he finished, slapping his forehead.

Stafford thought for a long time, while they both sat stock-still. He then looked up and said, "You seem to be saying that human speech is fundamentally a kind of light. Our way of showing to others whatever it is in us that catches things going by. Is this it? Is that what you mean?"

Bonapoggio smiled and continued, "To return to Orthodoxy, the first recorded words of Deity were, "Let there be light." Now, surely, we agree that this book, Genesis, is not particularly interesting as a physics textbook, Stafford."

"What do you mean?" Stafford asked, with a puzzled frown.

"Are we not safe in assuming it was written for the edification and instruction of human beings, as human beings, concerning their relations with one another and with their Creator? I mean, their relations with one another, as distinct from their relations with the rest of Creation. Why else would a book separate the categories of creation so carefully? And, why else would it begin with light? And, with a light that was created within a great darkness, Stafford? And," he continued, "is not the essence of darkness..."

"...The absence of light?" Stafford asked tentatively.

"Well, perhaps I was thinking about the quintessence of darkness. Is not the quintessence of darkness the entirely unmarked and unremarked passage of events, of genesis and dying, without leaving any trace?"

"Ah, not even a perception!" Stafford answered, now very excited. "And, " he continued, getting up and walking around the room waving his hands, "that would mean that to truly perceive something is to speak somehow?"

"Remember, though. We can always remain silent concerning what we perceive. But, my hunch," Bonapoggio said shrugging modestly, "is that this book, Genesis – written for non-physicists – means to make us question, because of its very oddness, what light is to us humans, as humans."

"Good. Why else put it first?"

"Exactly. It seems to me that the flower, when it emblazons the light, colors it and gives it to us as its color. The color belongs to the flower, not to the light. That is an imprecise way of speaking, Newton or no. It is a colored flower and we see it because of what the flower's blossom has done to light. And, likewise, our speech is the way we give off what has come to us from elsewhere."

"So," Stafford continued the thought slowly, "when the Genesis story tells us that God gave Adam the task of naming the animals in the garden, he was ah..."

Here Stafford hesitated and then said, very slowly, "...God was presented as placing Adam between...is that the right preposition, 'between?'...Creation and its Creator?"

Bonapoggio's smile was a delight to behold, but Stafford was too preoccupied with his own thoughts to notice it. He continued, "But that would mean, Avram, that mere speech, let alone true writing and dramatic poetry, is a very high form of creation?"

"Of mediation," Bonapoggio corrected, looking out of his study window.

"So, modern art and poetry are dark? No, I have it...not dark so much, as pre-creative!" continued Stafford. "Being so immediate, they can't mediate. They deny the fact of humans!"

"Perhaps they think they are pre-human?" Bonapoggio answered.

"How could anyone be pre-human?"

"As the story goes, we sometimes seem to get our days mixed up. Perhaps that is why the storyteller gives us that strange picture of a naked Eve talking to a serpent. In the order of creation, the serpent is pre-human. It seems that the price we must pay for being in a created world with other creatures, is that we tend to edge onto their temporality – if I may be permitted to speak so."

"Yes," Stafford answered slowly. "I remember reading Jane Goodall, the chimp lady, ponder whether our human incest-prohibition was not being foreshadowed when the chimp, Flo, comes into heat and receives all the males in the troop, one by one, except for her offspring."

"So, totally empty space is black because there is nothing in it. It is not a medium. Ha!" Bonapoggio went on triumphantly, in answer to some question Stafford had not heard asked.

"And, isn't a certain kind of modern art non-mediating and, therefore, dark?" Stafford continued the thought Bonapoggio had introduced.

"I think so, "Bonapoggio replied. "The darkness it proclaims is, in the end, a terrible contempt for the world facing us. It rejects all, even possible, worlds when it rejects the luminosity of existences. There is nothing there to catch the light. How odd," he continued slowly, "that things catch light. As if light were some homeless bird. Hmm."

"So, Jules Le Seur was not alone in his outer space?" Stafford asked himself quietly.

The two friends were lost in thought until the grandfather clock in the entrance-hall struck five. Stafford had to finish his preparations for

*Naturally Bad Manners*

the evening with Claudia.

* * *

Stafford had Bonapoggio's car for the event. At six o'clock sharp, he pulled up in front of Claudia's house, and, as he rang the bell, he reflected that the birth pangs of a serious – perhaps, for him, *the* serious? – love was barely short of excruciating. He smiled to himself as he knocked on the door, realizing that, if he did not begin to breathe regularly, he would turn blue as a newborn baby and Claudia would find him balled up in the fetal position on her top step. He breathed deeply several times, smoothed his perfectly groomed hair and began to knock again, when he heard Claudia opening the door.

Claudia opened the door and looked at Stafford with alarm.

"Are you alright, Stafford?"

Stafford laughed his relief at seeing her there in front of him, entered and, as they walked into the garden terrace, he confessed his last thoughts. Claudia's delighted laughter broke the ice and, after a few sips of whiskey, Stafford looked at her with his writer's eye.

Her color scheme was perfect. She wore a lemon-yellow dress of very heavy cotton and reminded him of a great butterfly.

"How appropriate," he thought to himself. "When I look at her, I get butterflies." However, what he said out loud was, "*Mais, ma chére. Vous êtes très bien jolie*! So lovely!"

Claudia had been looking at him while he had been looking at her. He was elegantly dressed in a light blue, raw silk suit that made his blue eyes seem gray. His soft yellow ascot picked out the highlights in his blonde hair.

"I wish it were Easter," Claudia said in a low, breathy, voice that nearly made Stafford's knees buckle. "I would love everyone to see us arm in arm." Then the question struck her as to why lovers ever got undressed if they looked like Stafford Wyatt and her. But, she said nothing.

Looking intently into her eyes, Stafford said, "Avram and I have been talking about painting, writing and speech, as ways of taking the natural world and making it ours. Clothes are a very powerful way of doing that. In the wrong state of undress, we lose our world, I think.

But, you, Claudia! Not only does your clothing make your natural body yours, but it makes me quite pregnant with the sight of you, all clothed as you are."

He delivered this in a voice that, to Claudia, seemed more appropriate to a funeral parlor than a bedroom.

"I am deeply complimented, Mister Wyatt. But, although I am deeply honored, I don't think I shall presently return the compliment, at least not exactly."

They both laughed. Stafford then cocked his head and, looking appreciatively at Claudia, asked, "How can I be pregnant with your presence? Are you a fact that I, Stafford Wyatt, can conceive of?"

"What else is a lover, Stafford Wyatt?"

"So...I am not mad about you and I am not aflame with desire for you, eh? I am simply pregnant with you? I am full of you? Ah, Claudia, I think I am going into labor."

"Dear Stafford," Claudia said, as she went to him and laid her hand gently on his shoulder, "you need obstetrical care. Let's see. O.B.G.Y. That's Obstetrics-Gynecology. What's the opposite of Gynecology?"

"Anthropology? No. Ah...Andrecology. That's it! So, now we need a department of medicine, called O-B-A-N, for pregnant males."

"Good. I'll be your OBAN physician. Perhaps when the time comes, I can be your midwife, too..."

Hearing what she had just said, Claudia blurted out, with her hand to her mouth, "Stafford! Have I just proposed to you?"

"Yes! And, I accept, Claudia Harris."

"Now, just what is it I've proposed?"

"You have proposed and I accept, that you become my personal, very private, OBAN physician and my beginning-mid-and-end wife. That is what you proposed and that is what I accept."

They properly celebrated the event with toasts, embraces, popping of corks and this and that, bubbling over and the like. And, although it was a most fruitful night for them both, Stafford left as pregnant as he had come. At any rate, they did not parade their clothes that night. Nor did Stafford sleep over. Love had banished sleep.

They played during the next two days before Stafford had to return to New York. The first afternoon was perfect weather, so they had a picnic and then an old movie at a theater whose offerings were particularly aimed at Chaldes students and teachers. Sunday, they took a long drive in Claudia's car and told one another all those things that only new lovers tell each other – odd things, like stories about a dog one of them particularly loved and had been run over by a milk truck and not thought of again until the moment of the sad story's recounting.

It had been a perfect weekend with Stafford. He was everything Claudia had always missed in her lovers and he was both witty and ironic.

As they said goodbye at the train station Sunday night, Claudia thought she had finally met a male whose own work and profession fulfilled him, so that he would not have to claw at her professional life. As they kissed their final goodbye before the train pulled out, Claudia whispered into his ear, "Thank you, Stafford. You have helped me re-assemble the bits and pieces another man unglued. I was the shadow of a promise and now I've got shape and form. Thank you, my love."

She was surprised by his response. He looked at her as if she had pulled a rabbit out of a hat. His eyes glazed over and, abstracted, he gently squeezed her hand and formally thanked her. She waved a tentative goodbye as he disappeared into the train and wondered if he was always this way when saying goodbye.

When he had found an empty seat and gotten settled in it, he took a large pad of unlined paper from his briefcase.

"The shadow of a promise; now, I've got shape and form," he intoned to himself, quoting Claudia. "Nice."

He scribbled furiously and was totally unaware of the fact when the train pulled into the station, three hours later. He had a rough draft of a poem and, by five o'clock the next morning, a semi-polished draft. He slept until noon, ate a light brunch and then immediately got back to work on it. Consulting his Sappho, he corrected his meters, stresses, consonants and assonances. By Tuesday noon he had the poem he wanted; it wasn't Sappho, but it was a Sapphic. He typed it and mailed it to Claudia. It read:

> *PYGMALIAN: A SAPPHIC*
> *Here you stand, a promise and shadow,*
> *Consecrated formerly, born once,*
> *Just begun in the heat of conception,*

*Now consummated.*
*Limbs entwined began, in a moment,*
*Place and Time. The chisel and mallet,*
*Laid aside, the ivory, still breathless,*
*Lacked gracious movement.*
*Place and Time: How dark, lacking motion,*
*Lacking breath; an echo entwined in*
*Mists, until the light of desire,*
*Chaos-informing,*
*Shapes anew the forms of the artists –*
*Loving father, most gracious mother.*
*Join your love and be consummated,*
*Daughter and sister.*

Claudia received this on Thursday and, reading it rapidly for sense, stepped backwards feeling for a chair. She was white with fury.

"That bastard and his 'chisel.' Ray was open and straight about what he wanted. This one's trying to whistle me out of a tree into his net, like a bird."

She continued walking backwards, feeling for a chair with her hand until she came to one and sat down. Re-reading the poem, she began to cry. She soon got up, went into the bathroom, tore the poem into shreds and flushed it down the toilet. Then she walked back into her living room and called Ray.

"Hi, it's Claudia. Busy tomorrow?"

"No," Ray's voice on the phone answered. "I've been expecting your call. You held out longer than I thought."

Claudia was furious, but not as angry as she had been at Stafford. Where Ray had played with her, Stafford had made a fool of her.

"Come on over. Say at seven tomorrow and an evening in?"

"Seven it is."

She hung up and walked over to a mirror and looked at herself.

"Do you know what you're doing? Christ! Don't! Don't!"

But, then she remembered the line, "Here you stand, a promise and shadow," completely forgetting she had given it to Stafford as she kissed him goodbye.

"A 'promise,' huh? A 'shadow,' huh? A 'promise!' A promissory note Mr. Wyatt is going to pay off for me. I'm a bad debt! His bad debt! I'll be damned if I am!"

She then called up a senior student of hers and told him that she would not be able to make the economic club's weekly meeting the next evening.

In New York, Stafford was beside himself with anticipation. "That's a good poem," he said out loud to himself. "I hope she'll be pleased...Of course she will...she gave me the tag-line!"

Then a little cloud of doubt passed over the sunshine of his optimism.

"Hmm. That promise and shadow. I wonder...No, she gave me the line herself."

Walking over to his desk, he picked up the phone to call Claudia to make sure. He wanted to go up a week early, so he could visit with her for a day or two before his last lecture.

As he began to dial her number, he saw his key ring on the phone table. He still had her front-door key, which he had used to bring groceries in before she got home. He had forgotten to give this spare key back to her. A bright idea then struck him.

"I'll go up with a bunch of flowers and surprise her."

Then, remembering that she usually stayed at the college late on Friday nights because of the economics club meetings, he made up his mind.

"I'll go up a little early and get there at around eight, put flowers in a conspicuous place and surprise her."

Since the train arrived in Chaldes at seven thirty every night, he saw he could make it.

"Perfect!"

At seven thirty-three, Stafford entered Chaldes' Train-Station Mall. He headed for the little flower shop named, Advance Warning. He entered, nodded to the fifty-year-old bleached blonde behind the counter looking at the screen of a miniature TV set and walked over to the display cases, where a bouquet on the bottom shelf caught his eye. It was a large bunch of blood-red roses, mixed with a spray of pale blue forget-me-nots. He was delighted by the mixture of passionate red of the roses and the plaintive blue of the forget-me-nots. He put down his suitcase and knelt, to get a better look. The bleached blonde, however, saw a young male who seemed to be saying his prayers in front of her display case – right in the middle of a very important development in the prime-time soap she was watching. Just then, Stafford made up his mind and avoided a confrontation with security by asking her for the bouquet.

A few minutes in a taxi and the very self-satisfied Stafford paid his fare and got out in front of Claudia's house. He reached her front door with a suitcase in one hand and the vase of flowers in the other. For a moment, he wondered why the living room lights were on, but he shrugged and put the key in the lock just as a fire engine raced by with its sirens wailing and its horns blaring.

As he opened the door, Stafford saw Claudia sitting on the couch with a man kneeling at her knees. They were fully dressed. Claudia was sobbing and her right hand was over her face, with her left arm tightly pressed against her side. As it dawned on Ray that her sobbing groans were not out of anticipation, he looked up and asked, "Claudia?"

The next instant, Stafford's own, "Claudia!" rang out.

Claudia opened her eyes. She saw Stafford standing in the open doorway, a vase with roses and forget-me-nots in one hand and her key in his other hand. His suitcase was behind him on the top step. Pushing Ray away, Claudia ran upstairs to her bedroom, without a word. Ray stood up and, for the first time in his life, actually felt like a fool. He left the house without closing the front door. Stafford's foot shot out behind him and slammed it shut. He then softly walked up the stairs and sat down on the top step outside Claudia's shut bedroom door, still clutching the vase of roses and forget-me-nots. Neither of them spoke for a long moment.

"Stafford, Dammit! Why did you write that stupid poem? Promise and shadow! Me! Claudia R. Harris, Ph.D., with highest honors! Teacher-of-the-year, my first year of full-time teaching. Me! A Promise and a shadow. Me!" Claudia shrieked her rage and despair through the door. "And, you, of all people."

"Claudia, you know I didn't mean that. How could I? Please, Claudia, I was asking you to leave your mother and father and consummate yourself with me as your new family."

His plea met with complete silence. After a long pause he heard Claudia say quietly, "Go on. I'm listening."

"What more can I say? I want you to be with me and me to be with you. Apart from you, Claudia, I'm only a promise and shadow of the me I become when I'm with you. Oh, God, Claudia. I don't want to make you into anything. I want to be something different with you. I want to be what I am when I'm with you. I swear to you, that's all the poem was about. Please, Claudia, believe me."

Truly cruel men and women delight in rage. It, above all other passions, perhaps, feeds on itself. Men and women who are not cruel are incapable of taking any pleasure in it. In their case, it blows over like a July wind full of leaves, branches and dust, heralding the end of a long, dry, hot spell. The sun is blotted out; the trees show the silver underside of their leaves; the birds hide and are altogether quiet and, miles away, one can see the misty squall-line and its streamers of rain embroidered on the storm-curtain the distance has pulled over itself as it enjoys its hurried shower before entertaining the sun again. And, so, Claudia's rage began to spend itself as Stafford sat silent and downcast on the top step outside her bedroom door.

Claudia opened the door and came out. Looking up into her face, Stafford reached up and handed her the vase of flowers. She took them. Giving him a hand, she helped him to stand.

"I love and admire you, Claudia. And, I really do see why you are so angry with me. I think I would be, too, if you did to me what I have done to you. But, it was a misdirection, not an insult."

Claudia nodded a very small assent.

"Look," he continued, "you love your work and your profession and I love mine. We love and there is a tension, even contradiction, between those two loves."

"I know, Stafford," Claudia said, more gently than she felt. "And," she continued quietly, after a long pause, "not even marriage resolves that contradiction."

"I know. You have children, become angry with your husband because you have stretch-marks and he doesn't and because you are too tired to welcome him home at five-thirty."

They stood next to each other without speaking. Then, Stafford said, "I'll go to Avram's house now, Claudia. Can I use your phone?"

Claudia nodded her assent and Stafford continued, "I meant it when I asked you to marry me. But, we need some time to sort some things out, okay?"

"Yes. I still want to marry you, too, Stafford, but I'm a fool about some things that are my business. I've still got to work at them. I'm sorry. Don't mistrust me. Please, Stafford, I think I'm beginning to be cured."

She began to cry silently. Stafford gave her his shoulder to lean on and, after a few minutes, they gently kissed and Claudia returned to her room while Stafford rang Bonapoggio and asked if he could spend the night with him. It was fine with him and, leaving the flowers, Stafford left with a, "Goodbye for now. I love you," called up the stairs.

\* \* \*

Stafford returned to New York City and Claudia heard nothing from him for several days. But, two days later, she received a letter from Ray that was surprising only because he had the nerve to send it. In it, he pointed out it was Claudia who initiated their affair in the very beginning; that, when she broke it off without explanation, he didn't remind her of the fact that she had started the whole thing; that, when she called him breathlessly to come over for dinner and the evening, he had not crowed or reminded her of any of this; that she seemed more like a twit of a shop girl than a Ph.D. economist; that she talked about her soul – whatever the hell that is – at the drop of a garter-belt...And, on and on it went. Precisely because it was so just and accurate an account of what both of them already knew to be true, it was merely bitchy to send it at all. Claudia felt better after reading it. She now missed Stafford without any reservation.

After he had written this silly letter, Ray Hayes had deliberated for several hours about sending it. Shaking with an anger born of indecision, Ray finally walked out of his office and, taking the stairs two at a time from the third floor, strode across campus, over to the multi-purpose center, where the post office was located. Rather than give it to the mailman behind the counter—he could give it back if he changed his mind—Ray dropped it into the slot, turned on his heel and walked back to his car. He was halfway home when it hit him: He was deeply in love with Claudia and he had treated her like a laboratory rat. Now he had insulted her. He had never said, "I love you" to her.

Ray Hayes was not practiced in sorrow or regret. He raged against Claudia; he raged against modern women; he raged against his own parents; then, when he was finished with his raging, he looked at himself.

"Ah, our neurology. One little problem. That Goddamned vagus nerve; it begins in the brain stem, just below the brain, but then it wanders all over the place. Yes, Ray Hayes, you ass! It wanders. One branch wanders down to the heart, Ray Hayes. But you never wandered. Never, Ray Hayes, not even once! Oh, Christ! Why didn't you wander...just once...down to the heart?"

Then, Ray Hayes cried for the first time since he was twelve years old. When he had cried himself out, he drove back to his lab, looked at his pharmacopoeia and picked out a number of ways to kill himself. But, he was in no mood to be clinical and clean.

"You're already too clinical and sterile, Ray, my boy. For Christ's sake, don't die like one of Professor Hayes' rats! Die like a messy human bastard...just what you are."

He drove back home, took a gun, stuck it into his mouth and blew the back of his head off.

\* \* \*

Stafford and Claudia missed each other, but each was too shaken to be sure as to just how to start mending fences. The last of Stafford's master classes was in a week and he had to come to Chaldes for them. Claudia knew this and both looked forward to the event and dreaded it. What was the right course to take between a posturing gesture of haughtiness and inappropriate signals indicating unintended surrender? Then she remembered Marian Caton's offers of friendship. She called and told her the whole story. Marian's answer was short and to the point. "Get a mutual friend to invite you both over for dinner, you goose."

"Marian! You are a genius," Claudia answered. After repeated thanks, she hung up and called Bonapoggio.

"But, I would love to, my dear Claudia. Why did you not call earlier? Uncle Pandarus will fix you both," was his immediate answer.

Stafford received an invitation to a pre-lecture dinner-party at

Bonapoggio's house, to take place the next evening. There was no question of his not accepting it.

The day for the reconciliation arrived, along with Stafford Wyatt. He taught his master class and carefully avoided Claudia's part of campus. Since she did not teach on Fridays, a fact Stafford had forgotten, he wasted a great deal of time making large detours around the Henry Mulligan Social Science Resources Center, which, on that particular Friday, seemed to him to have acquired the power to lie squarely between wherever he was and wherever he needed to be. On her part, Claudia was in Lake Placid, shopping with Laura and throwing away money with both hands. They shopped themselves out and were then manicured and coiffured in the best boutique in town. They drank lunch at the best restaurant in town and flirted outrageously with its incredibly handsome *maitre d'* and arrived back in Chaldes barely an hour before Bonapoggio's dinner party was to begin. Laura and Ted had other plans for the evening so, with promises that all would be related over lunch the next day – "No," Laura interrupted herself, "Who knows? You may be déshabile at the time, ma chére! Well, whenever..." They kissed goodbye and parted. Claudia began to rush, but then remembered that Bonapoggio's six o'clock sharp meant "Sometime between seven-thirty and eight." So, with an hour to spare, she took a nap and had an outrageous dream in which a naked George Strauss and she played hide and seek with Stafford and Ray, both of whom were dressed as bishops, with crooked staffs of office and swinging incense-braziers, whose smoke smelled like the perfume she was wearing.

Claudia arrived at Bonapoggio's door just as Stafford pulled up in his rented car. She waved and he beckoned her to come over to his car and get in. She did so and, when she had shut her door, he took her shoulders and gravely kissed her full on the mouth.

"A kiss of peace, Claudia? I have to go to Paris for a summer workshop I've been asked to teach. When I return…"

Claudia stroked his cheek in response.

They entered together and saw at once that Bonapoggio had outdone himself for the occasion. It turned out that he had even gone so far as to spend that morning at the market and had designed the meal around the freshest produce and the most well aged beef he could find. Since it was late spring, new peas were in. The wine was fine old Bordeaux and dessert was a very light French-Algerian pastry, smothered in heavy cream and topped off with fresh strawberries.

Bonapoggio had invited Rick and Michelle as accents for Stafford and Claudia. It worked perfectly. The conversation centered on the role of art in hiding nature behind a veil of illusion so that humans can live their human lives. Michelle was tempted to argue against this point, but looking at the evil glint in Rick's eye, daring her to defend the natural and spontaneous, she thought better of it. Rather, she pressed the battle into Rick's camp by casually asking him which was the true him in which he lived so artfully. Rick grinned and pointed out that by his sublime disregard for his twisted dwarf's body, he rendered that body inoperative to make him particularly unhappy and that he, "just like you, my lovely young lover of lovely young women, with your lovely person, which so many men would love to love, render inoperative your peculiarly feminine loveliness."

"Your point," Michelle admitted, as she grinned at Rick's boldness.

"Well," Bonapoggio observed, "each of us is something of an artist. As President Lincoln once pointed out, a man over forty is responsible for his own face. If I understand President Lincoln's *mot*, a man's character etches itself on his face. He is responsible for what he faces so intently that it can etch his face. Yes, that is it! When we face this or that in the course of our lives, this gives us our characters and also permits what we have faced to etch those characters onto our characters. Yes, I like that. What each of us faces etches our face in return."

"Well, I'm not a bad portrait painter," Rick answered, "and I carefully paint those things in my subjects' faces that are etched there, as you say, Avram, by his or her characteristic activities. I never paint someone I know nothing about."

"How about young faces, Rick. They're beautiful, aren't they?" Michelle asked, with a slight edge in her voice.

"*Touché*! Yes, young people are beautiful. What I try to do with them can only be done after I have had them sit with me and chat. They drink some soda and then eat something. By doing this, I get something of an idea as to what they might be willing to face, in their future. But, you're right. It's tricky. Sometimes I get a young subject whose future is written all over his or her face. As the Greek said, 'Character is destiny.' And, some people are born with faces full of it. But, not too many!"

"You know?" Claudia broke in slowly, "Really beautiful people tend to have trouble here. They already have such form and shape in their faces, that they tend to face down the world, rather than face it to be etched by it."

"You are so right!" Rick almost shouted. "Also, the very ugly. It's very hard to find a man or woman who was strikingly beautiful at twenty who still has a fine face at, say, forty-five. Usually, their faces are that of a ravaged beauty. They are only aged beauties. The world didn't etch their faces...only aged them. Same thing with the uglies. Me? If I live long enough...Who knows? If the beauties get ugly, perhaps, just perhaps..."

"Stop it, Dammit, Rick!" Michelle blurted out angrily. "That's not true. Your face is fine. It shows what you love and faced because you loved it. No, Dammit! Your face is fine!"

The whole table sat stunned. Michelle never complimented anyone, except her prey and certainly not a man, certainly not the Rick Vogels of this world. Even Bonapoggio was caught off guard. Mrs. Tintintolo saved the day by announcing that coffee was ready in the living room. Since they only had forty-five minutes to drink it and then get to the hall for Stafford's lecture, the rest of the conversation was school gossip, except for Bonapoggio's *entre nous* announcement that he had a pretty good idea Stafford was going to be offered the chair for the coming fall. Claudia could not suppress a crooked grin.

"Where will you live, Stafford?" Rick asked.

"Oh, that depends..." Stafford answered nonchalantly, not looking at Claudia by looking over her head. Claudia took this, rightly, as a re-opening of marital negotiations.

The lecture was at nine o'clock. Everyone complained at the lateness of the hour, but the buzzed grievances floated on the air of the lecture-hall foyer like a swarm of gnats floating on whatever it is that keeps them sufficiently together to have people call them a swarm. Stafford's lecture had the provocative title, "Dionysus: The Therapeutic Mask," and so, although no one had the slightest idea what it was to be about, the hall was filled. The lecture turned out to be a big success

## Naturally Bad Manners

with the audience and Bonapoggio thought to himself, "Good. The Dean will surely offer Stafford the Chair."

The lecture knocked Claudia for a loop. She knew Bonapoggio would never tell Stafford the details of her affair with Ray and she knew she had never brought it up with Stafford. He had seen Ray kneeling at her feet, but had never seemed to make much of it. But, Stafford's closing remarks were, she felt, (but knew better), written to her as Ray's toy. Stafford's talk was so careful, so civil, and so thoughtful, that she felt healed by listening to it. He finished the lecture by saying: "The precondition for any and all leisure is trust. The highest fruit of human leisure, the finest use of it is, I think, to transform that trust into knowledge. The opposite of leisure is not work. Indeed, leisure, especially, has difficult work at its very center – something akin to what we call the arts, both liberal and fine.

"As I have tried to argue, a very great use of leisure is theater. Theater is to be looked at. It is intended to be seen. As theater, it addresses itself primarily to our visual consciousness and it perfects that very consciousness by making it public. In so doing, it fulfills to perfection its polar opposite and very first intimation, the dreams a sleeper dreams in a solitary realm, where only the phantoms of his life that he shares with others in the light of day can penetrate. Good theater borrows those casual intruders into our nocturnal solitude and introduces them for approval or disapproval to the waking spectators, who are also the sharers of our waking sunlight. Theater, as it were, 'civilizes' our dreams by teaching us to distinguish between those dreams that belong only to our solitude and those dreams that also belong to our world of shared sunlight. To the extent that theater does this to the phantoms of our solitary dreams, it transforms that solitary consciousness we experience in dreaming into a shared, civil consciousness. That shared, civil consciousness is conscience."

Here, Claudia drew back into herself and thought, "Oh God! Exactly! Ray had no conscience. He was all consciousness. God bless you, Stafford Wyatt!"

Stafford continued in his slow, easy rhythm, "Conscienceless theater is anti-theater."

Here, Claudia thought to herself, "Yes and conscienceless love-making is anti-love!"

"That anti-theater dissolves off, that is to say, unmasks, the civil dress of our politely transformed dreams and carelessly presents our sleeping consciousness to the prying, careless, eyes of strangers. Thus, conscienceless, unmasking theater is merely pornographic theater."

"Oh, Stafford! For the love of God! Stop it!" Claudia heard herself say out loud, but in a whisper that no one seemed to hear.

"Such theater demands of its spectators that they publicly unmask and thereby share all their dreams – the more private, the better. Beyond this terrible anti-Dionysian demand lies the most monstrously extreme of tyrannies, in which our waking life becomes a nightmare. The violence associated with Dionysus, the deity of theater, reminds us that conscience is the guardian of consciousness and thus its mask.

"If this be the case, then Dionysus, the deity of theater, is also the deity of civilized consciousness – a fact not lost on Euripides. Dionysus' dual realm is the underworld of solitary and often outrageous dreams, together with that small portion of the dream-realm that is properly permitted to see the shared light of day. It is only as masked that we humans see the true light of day. Unmasked, we live in a world of nightmare horrors; unmasked, we are no more real than the insubstantial phantoms of dreams, than those phantoms whose very insubstantiality is proven by the fact that they cannot withstand the light of day. Thus, it appears that the mask of Dionysus is precisely that in our dream-phantoms that permits some of them to be perceived in the light of day. Dionysus, the God of theater, is the deity of the properly visible – of the properly shared. Of the civil. Thank you."

During the applause that followed, Bonapoggio looked at the Dean, who nodded his assent to Stafford. Bonapoggio's former student was going to be offered the newly endowed Chair.

After the question period, there was a little reception for the speaker in the foyer. The Dean pulled Stafford aside and asked if he would be interested in holding the newly endowed Chair of Creative Writing, and Stafford, carefully coached by Bonapoggio, looked astonished and accepted the offer as if it were the last thing in the world he expected. The Dean liked him. He called for silence and announced the appointment for the following fall. Everyone clapped their approval and Claudia, realizing she was beyond civil behavior, shook Stafford's hand solemnly and left.

# CHAPTER 8

## Illusions and Realities

J.J. Rufus had made his huge fortune because he instinctively understood impulse buying. At age thirty-one, his daughter, Claudia Rufus Harris, a Ph.D. economist, had just begun to ask herself about this uneconomic activity of impulsively spending money.

Throughout the rest of an unusually hot June, Claudia gnawed at the task of understanding impulse buying as a dog gnaws a bone. She went to the library and looked up books under the headings of "Impulse Buying," "Impulse Shopping," and even, "The Psychology of Excess Spending." She took them out and she read them. They were interesting, but not very helpful. This occupied June and the first part of July.

On a sweltering day in mid-July, Claudia wandered around in the air-conditioned, dehumidified, psychology stacks. Idly looking at the backs of books in one particularly cool bay, she was struck by the title of one of them: "Too Much and Too Little." She took it down and looked at the long *précis* on the back cover: "This book examines in detail why the rich and the poor both spend a disproportionately large share of their income on non-necessities..." Claudia looked up with an absent-minded grin and, exactly at eye-level on the shelf in front of her, she saw: "Neurological Foundations of Sex-Therapy." Its author was Ray Hayes. Claudia carefully replaced "Too Much and Too Little" and left the library. Halfway home, she was caught in the most violent thunderstorm she had ever experienced. The sky was inky black and its forks of lightning looked like the veins of an immense, black, nature god, coursing living light through the veins and arteries of its great, potent body, which arced over the Earth. She heard herself howl with joy in response to the Earth-shaking thunderclaps and she arrived home soaking wet and largely cleansed of her ignorance.

After a warm shower and a cup of coffee, she wrote to Marian Caton.

"Dear Marian:

I missed something else in the dissertation you didn't point out! I only talked about spending money. What a fool I am. Earning money, really working for it, puts a form on our desires, a set of boundaries. (Does loving a particular man give form to general sexual desires? I think so.) The thing that made me open to Ray Hayes and to missing the rich and the poor, is that I believe – or used to believe–that individuals can control their appetites and their desires all by themselves! God! What a fool I am. One night with Ray and I knew that only organic considerations put limits to the amount of pleasure one can experience with a man. I hated it, but it seemed so 'natural!'

"And, those middle-class slobs who spend their lives working to keep ends together and the kids in braces and shoes! I took them as examples of real people. They were naturally prudent and moderate. Everyone else was a sociopath. (Am I a crypto-Marxist?) Well, I am a fool. Those middle-class slobs are hard working because they are willing to make a list of priorities and then to live by them and work for them. THE BUDGET! God love them. THE BUDGET! I didn't have to budget sex and it never occurred to me that we all have to budget money–except for the very rich and the very poor.

Thank you, Marian. I owe you a lot. Please, call on me if ever I can repay you. Thanks.

Love, Claudia"

The rest of that summer was taken up with daily fourteen-hour stints at her desk, rewriting her dissertation. Most of the rewrite was done in light of what she and Marian had discussed and what she had seen in the library. In this revised form of her dissertation, the very rich and the very poor figured prominently. Claudia took a wicked delight in pointing out how similar the effects of poverty and great riches were on the soul of the American consumer. Then, one day, in late August, Claudia found herself obsessed with a sentence she had written: "Too much and too little affect a human in the same way." She crossed it out and then wrote it down again, four times. She was just about to cross it out again, when the telephone rang. It was Stafford. He was at Kennedy Airport, just in from Paris.

"Hello, Claudia? This is Stafford."

"Oh, God, am I ever glad to hear from you! I won't cross it out!"

"Cross what out?"

"I'll tell you all about it when you get here. Come up now, tonight. You can rent a car and be here before midnight. Please?"

"I can accept no 'pleases' from the woman I love, Claudia. Never. No! Ask me impolitely. Order me to come to you and I'll ride my red cow, as she jumps over your blue moon."

"Professor Wyatt, circumstances and road conditions permitting, might it not be a not-bad idea for you to fly to your lover's arms with all haste, both due and undue? Said lover has chased the rats from her cellar and she has chased all suitors...that is, all but you, Stafford...from in front of her sofa. Okay?"

"Okay. See you by midnight, the Gods permitting, concurring, agreeing, not-forfending, bestowing their blessings..."

"Oh, be quiet and be swift."

He was both and, around eleven-fifteen, Claudia heard the doorbell. She opened the door and Stafford was there.

"Let me say, dear man, before kissing stops all speech, that I've learned something this summer. There is not one, and I mean not one, impulse in the human soul, no matter how natural, that doesn't need to be thoroughly domesticated."

"You talk like a poet, Claudia."

Walking up to him, she placed her hands on either side of his head and, quietly looking into his eyes, said, "Stafford, I've worked and I've claimed myself and I am now mine to give. I give myself to you. And, " she added with a frown, "don't think I'm asking you to take me. I'm not. I'm asking you to receive me."

"We'll exchange gifts."

Stafford moved in with Bonapoggio the next morning. After several trips to his old Manhattan apartment to collect his things, he was comfortably settled in his friend's house. Then, several days into the new fall term, Ted and Laura threw a dinner party for Stafford. After it was over, he walked Claudia home and again asked her to marry him.

"I think I'd like that, Stafford Wyatt. Let's sleep on it." Waking the next morning, Claudia said, without opening her eyes, "Yes, I think it's a good idea, Stafford Wyatt."

He kissed her and got up to make coffee. He had a number of appointments that afternoon, so he had to change clothes. After coffee and toast, they said goodbye and Stafford went home and spent the morning arranging his schedule.

Laura was the first of Claudia's close friends to hear the news and Bonapoggio was the first of Stafford's close friends to hear it. Laura raced over to Claudia's and the two kissed, hugged, and blubbered – something that involves a mixture of laughing and crying that few males, who tend to whimper at such times, ever master. When they had finished, they began the cycle all over again. Then, Laura, when her composure allowed, called a seamstress friend in Manhattan, a fellow islander and asked her to come up and stay in Chaldes a few days to make Claudia's wedding dress. The first and most important thing out of the way, she turned back to Claudia. Until that very moment, it had not occurred to Claudia that marriage to Stafford presupposed actually marrying him, a process whereby one ceases to be unmarried through the process of marrying. She panicked and froze. Laura sat her down and poured them both nine-thirty in the morning brandies. While Claudia dumbly sipped hers, Laura made a number of phone calls and furiously scribbled notes, dates and lists on the back of envelopes. Claudia vaguely heard the names, Avram, Ted, Father Ryan, Pat, and Michelle.

After thirty minutes of this, Laura made strong coffee and they settled down around the kitchen table.

"Good news, child. You are going to be married to one Stafford Wyatt on Friday, October fifth, at three o'clock in the afternoon."

Claudia's smile of thanks would have been more appropriate if Laura had told her that she had found a good dentist to do her root canals.

"Teresa, my seamstress friend, will be here on Monday to begin fitting your gown. We'll go up to Lake Placid this weekend to get material."

A considerably more animated smile met this news.

"Oh, and Father Ryan at Immaculate Conception will do the honors."

For the first time, Claudia began to giggle and then the two of them shrieked with laughter.

"My God! Immaculate Conception! What a place to be married in!"

This began another cycle of hugs, kisses and blubbering.

"I'm matron of honor, okay?"

This, too, was greeted by kisses and thanks.

"Avram...Oh God! He's...Can he...will he do it, at Immaculate Conception? It would break Stafford's heart if..."

They looked bug-eyed at each other and, then, Laura called him. He told her, in no uncertain terms, that, as a New York State inspected and licensed rabbi, he would be welcome because of the recent flurry of ecumenical papers presently coming from Rome.

"But," he concluded, somewhat hyperbolically, "I would have converted–if just for the day–to be at the marriage ceremony uniting two such beloved friends. I'll be there, if it requires a Papal dispensation–co-signed, of course, by the Grand Rabbi of Jerusalem, that excellent and ancient Jebusite city, which was very ancient when Rome's founder, Aeneas, was still but a gleam in his great-great-great-grandfather's eye."

"He'll be there," Laura said, as she put back the receiver.

"Good," Claudia said, getting into the spirit of the thing.

"Hmm," Laura said, "I wonder...Shall he be best man? Well, Stafford can decide. I suppose your father will give you away? You'll have to call them and, as I remember, you have brothers and sisters..."

The phone bill for that day would have made a significant dent in the national debt. Bonapoggio set about locating suitable formal clothing for the male side of Stafford's party–meaning white ties and tails. An appointment was made to satisfy the sovereign state of New York that neither Professor Stafford Wyatt, a published, chaired writer, nor Professor Claudia R. Harris, a Ph.D. economist, so in love with one another, so elegant, so solicitous in all things, had any venereal diseases. Their blood tests were set for ten o'clock Tuesday morning. Then, Stafford called his mother's only surviving sister, Aunt Adele and invited her to represent his family at the wedding. She accepted and was told she could stay with his best man, Professor Avram Bonapoggio. Before Stafford hung up, Aunt Adele got his address and his phone number at Bonapoggio's and a promise not to buy Claudia an engagement ring. A day later, Stafford received a registered package in the morning mail. He opened it and found an antique, square-cut, emerald ring for Claudia. The enclosed card read: "To Claudia Harris, from Stafford's mother's family. Good Luck! See you at the wedding.

Adele Smythe."

Stafford went to the phone and called Claudia to ask her for dinner so that he could give her an engagement ring. He was told she had to prepare an exam for her nine o'clock Intro class the next morning. "I'd love to see it, Stafford. But, I can't until tomorrow night. It'll keep, won't it? I hear tell that genuine jewels last forever."

"Avram!" Stafford shouted when he hung up. "What a woman! I call her for dinner so I can give her jewels and she has to give a test!"

"You are a very lucky man, Stafford Wyatt."

Stafford had his own work to do for his new classes and so he returned to his room. After several hours, Mrs. Tintintolo tapped on his door and told him lunch was ready. He went downstairs and found a smug-looking Bonapoggio. He was standing in front of the sideboard, which was covered with lunch foods. Both men preferred small breakfasts and large lunches.

They loaded up their plates, sat down and began to eat and talk.

"Bless you, Stafford. She is a fine woman and I am happy for the both of you. Be a good friend and she will be a good wife."

"Thank you, Avram. I'll try," Stafford answered gravely. Then, more brightly, he asked, "You've known me for at least eleven years. What do you think about this marriage? I hate to put you in my father's place." Apologizing more than he intended to, he continued, "But my father didn't know me much as a college student and writer. He died before he and Claudia could have met."

"But, Stafford! I am delighted and complimented to be your surrogate father–your uncle, as it were. I opt to be your father and that makes me your ad-opted father."

He was silent a long moment. Then, looking up at Stafford, he said, "I think you and Claudia are very good for one another. How long is it you have known each other?"

"Somewhat over a year."

"Oh. It seems longer. Well, in that time you have both blossomed. As the saying goes, 'You two are made for one another,' eh?"

He stopped short and, grunting, cocked his head and repeated himself: "You two are made for each other. Hmm," he continued, "a rather pious sentiment, don't you think?"

Stafford responded by grinning like a schoolboy and asking, "If two people are really made for each other, why do they have to marry? If the Creator made Darby for Joan and Stafford for Claudia, didn't He, at the same moment, ah...'super-naturally' marry us to one another before we were even born?"

"You never know," Bonapoggio answered, his head cocked to one side, studying Stafford's face. "I am a scholar-rabbi who has elected seldom to perform the marriage-rite of my creed. But, I will hazard a guess...but only as a scholar. Do you understand?"

"Go on, please," Stafford said, as Bonapoggio seemed to lose himself in a deep study.

Bonapoggio was silent for a long time. Then, looking appraisingly at Stafford, he seemed to make his mind up about something.

"Stafford, are you aware of how few religions have not required some form of human sacrifice?"

Stafford thought for a long moment and finally answered, "I'm afraid my own has a rather dismal record. The so-called 'acts-of-faith'..."

"Yes, the 'autos de fe...Terrible."

"Very terrible. They required us to burn men and women alive."

Sucking on his upper lip, Stafford looked at his hands and was silent. Then, he continued, "But what has this to do with marriage ceremonies? I know our St. Paul said, it's better to marry than to burn, but..." Here, he shrugged at his lack of comprehension and Bonapoggio picked up the thread of conversation.

"Suppose our human institutions are our way of thanking Heaven for birth, marriage, and so on...and even for death. Could it be, Stafford, that even burial rites are the way we give and I mean actively give, our dead humans back to Heaven, rather than, say, ripping their still beating hearts out of their chests...the Aztecs' way of giving humans to Heaven?"

"So you think the two rituals of burial and marriage are not altogether different?"

"Not altogether."

"Well, the upshot of this happy talk seems to be that I did well in asking Claudia to marry and stay with me, until death does us part!"

Stafford sat bolt upright as he heard the grandfather's clock chime two o'clock.

"Avram! I don't have time to get married in the next month! I can't marry in front of my master-classes. Not even in front of some student reading John Donne! And, where would we live? How can we have any time together?"

"Tut, tut. Now, Stafford. Your Uncle Pandarus is a man of many sides and some of these are of this world. I happen to own a nice investment property in the country, on Lauder Road. It is too big for me, so I have been looking for a couple to rent it to. So, now that you will be a you-plural, perhaps you two could fill it up for the next score or so of years? It would be a fine place for parties, and, Stafford, it has a duck pond and a swimming pool. Not an Olympic one, but then I am not into things Olympian, am I? At any rate, the rent is cheap, because I got it at an auction during a snowstorm last winter. It was a forced liquidation of an estate and the sale date was a legal deadline. I can let you have it for three hundred and fifty dollars a month."

Stafford looked at Bonapoggio with wide-eyed amazement.

"Avram! What a treat! But, only three fifty? Are you sure?"

"Yes, I am sure. It truly cost me next to nothing. I was the only person bidding."

"What sort of Earth-magic did you come up with to bring down that storm?"

"Goetry, 'earth-magic,' as you mere mortals term it, is not exactly my style. As I recall, the first king of Israel got lost in it. No, the snow was so deep that day that I could not drive to the auction that night from college. I had decided to spend the night in a dormitory room. Then, I heard the town's salt trucks and realized they went near to where the auction was being held at City Hall. It was a tax-auction. I demanded and got a ride on one and arrived in plenty of time. The sheriff was not too pleased, but he could do nothing. So, shall we shake on it? A large house, a duck pond, a swimming pool, all on about twenty partially-wooded acres?"

"I'd marry Lucretia Borgia, if that place came as part of the package."

"Say one word further and I will have to charge more to keep you from some terrible folly."

"Could I start living there at once and get it a little ready for Claudia?"

"Instanter," Bonapoggio exclaimed. "When I bought it, there was a great deal of furniture with it and I have added some more. It is not completely furnished, but it is not bad as a start. So, as soon as it is convenient, write me a check and I will get a lease written to protect you."

"To protect me?" Stafford asked, with a look of bewilderment on his face.

"Well, Stafford, I might someday take it into my head to run off to Morocco with the Dean's...ah...lady. The bank holding the mortgage would have to honor your lease."

"Between friends, Avram, we don't need a lease, do we?"

"Stafford, if you, that house and Claudia, were all made for each other, would you need a lease?"

"Only with the original maker of me, the house and Claudia."

"*Bon!* But, Stafford, the matter of the lease...I first really noticed you when I saw what fine work you did on your translations. Translations, Stafford. Did you not take someone else's writing, in someone else's language and put it into your words, into your language? Is that not what you gave me in return for my encouragement and help with a word or phrase? I think so."

"Ah, in these terms, a lease would be the reverse process. We'll do two things, okay? You take your intent for me to live in your house and I'll take my intent to live there and pay you my money for it. Together, we agree on a common language to express that intent. The language is not of our own choosing. It's the language of the law. That's interesting," Stafford ended. He then looked at his watch, a habit he had begun to cultivate since becoming employed. Jumping up, he said, "It's time. Out of the garden, into the bread-by-the-sweat-of-my-brow world of gainful occupation. I've got to go. My student...ah, that...ah...Mister Kussi is it? He's coming to see me this afternoon. My office is a mess. I've still got to empty my crates of books. We could perhaps have a drink before I meet with Claudia tonight?"

"I would like that very much. *Arrivederci.*"

"Adios, Rabbi," Stafford said with a grin and sped out the door.

The drive to the college reminded Stafford of his first introduction to Chaldes.

"I think I'm going to make friends here," he said out loud to himself.

He was in a very good mood. Craning his neck to see the neo-Mesopotamian and Classical-Revival mansions through the early fall foliage, he found himself uncomfortably awed by his sudden sense of the incredible persistence of ancient human conventions–even these grotesque, self-conscious, misconstructions had been committed in very ancient architectural styles. Being a thinker who enjoys thinking and who, consequently, talks to himself, Stafford began by chattering to himself and then, as he got into the swing of it, he began arguing with himself. "What's so comical about these houses? Don't you resurrect classical meters and themes for your stuff? Why can't they?"

"Yeah!" he assured himself, "but that's to keep me in shape."

"Nah! You like the stuff."

"Well, okay...But, still..."

"No stills about it. You like those meters and themes. Why shouldn't they like those styles?"

Stafford became conscious that he was not arguing against himself, but against a spectral critic of his writing. He smiled and started over again.

"No, I write because I love the English language as it is, today."

"So, why read and copy poets who died years ago?"

"They give me a language. Their language. I use it to write my language. It's as Avram said. What a sly fox. I wonder why he never married. Perhaps he did. Hmm."

Stafford was enjoying this dialogue and he was speeding. Before long, he was in front of the college. He pulled into the parking lot of the administration building, Tome Hall, and was prepared, by his reflections concerning Mansion Row, which he had just been driving past to be charitable about the monstrosity now facing him.

But, he was still repelled by it. Tome Hall was a warning against embarking onto the seas of higher education, rather than an invitation to sail on it. Stafford thought to himself that it should have a huge wrought-iron archway over the entrance path with the admonition, "Lose Grace, as well as Hope, All Ye Who Dare Think of Entering Here!"

As he rounded Tome Hall–The Crows' Roost, as everyone except the president referred it to–Stafford smiled at the autumn scene before

*Naturally Bad Manners*

him. The quad was full of students in various stages of ascent – from the designer-jeans, worn, like leper's-bells, by freshmen, announcing thereby their ignorance of style, to the haute monde costumes of the upper-classes. An occasional sartorial insurgent sported a meticulously styled head of hair and pre-owned clothing bought in a New York City shop that catered exclusively to the tastefully discriminating rebel. The old elms and maples were beginning to lose their summery brightness and the gay colors and sounds of students lounging under them were sweetly muted by this autumnal melancholy. Since this was Stafford's first time on campus without a guide, he felt free and very employed. An occasional female noticed him, checking whatever it is that a twenty-year-old checks when she sees a handsome male at least ten years older than she. Then she either smiled a "Good morning sir," or a "Well, well! What do we have here?" depending on her deeply unexamined taste, forgotten experience, or unnoticed mood of the moment. Enough of them flashed a brilliantly surprised smile to put Stafford into a very good mood for his first counseling session with Mr. Kussi of Hurlock-and-marijuana fame.

Stafford's office was located off of a large reception room presided over by a secretary-typist, Vikki LaRosa. She was a dream. She loved to work, never experienced a grouch in her life, never had a bad day and was a very good typist. Her hair was a glorious gold, dramatically set off by her ebony black roots, which matched her eyebrows. She had been introduced to Stafford several days earlier and was now fully prepared to meet him. She was dressed to show off her full figure and doused in the very best "parfum" sold by the Rite-Price Drug chain. Its scent hit him as he opened the hall door and entered the reception room on his way to his office. He saw, smelled, coolly nodded hello and made for his office, with its stale, but parfum-free, air. Once in it, he shut the door and ruefully reflected that there was no way into his office other than through the sweet chemical fog outside his door. He hoped Vikki would soon tire of the chase. If not, Claudia would have to come up and vamp him in front of her.

Collecting himself and surveying the piles of boxes on the floor, he returned to the door and said to Vikki, "I have an appointment with a Mr. Kussi in the next half hour. Please let me know when he comes in."

Vikki replied, "His name is Sussi– with an S." She had heard many unpleasant things about Mr. Sussi and made a face of displeasure at his name.

Stafford went back into his office, opened a window and took a deep breath of air. Then, he sat down at his desk and slowly surveyed his office. It was large and high ceilinged. One of its two corner windows faced the quad and the other, the library. The bookshelves were empty and his cartons of books had not been touched since they were deposited on the floor by the college help. He was itching to unpack them, but he first needed to open a bank account and buy a car.

"I can't go on mooching forever," he said to himself as he called a short-term car rental agency. This would permit him to take his time in looking for a good used car. He found nothing and decided to call the bursar and ask for help. She knew. In a matter of minutes, Stafford was talking to the highly recommended Jim Stiles at the Route 32 Foreign Car Sales Center. He was told that there was a real beauty of a used Jaguar convertible just waiting for the right owner. The price was well within Stafford's range, the warranty sound and Jim Stiles' reputation good. He said he thought he would come out and look at it. Would Mr. Stiles hold onto it? He would and Stafford hung up and shouted, "Great!" as he turned his full attention to the stack of boxes.

Just as he was picking up the first stack of books from one of the cartons, Vikki opened his door a crack to tell him Mister Sussi had arrived. Stafford told her to keep Mister Sussi waiting for a minute, but Sussi barged past her, darted over to Stafford, and rattled out, "Ah, permit me, Mister Wyatt, permit me, please!" and grabbed the books from Stafford's hands. In the course of pulling them away from the astonished Stafford, he collapsed the stack and the books in it went flying around the office.

"Be careful!" roared Stafford to the small, pasty-faced, round-shouldered catastrophe. But, before he could retrieve the scattered books, Sussi was running about the room. He stepped on the spines of those books that had landed face down and, to judge from the sound, broke them.

"My God! Stop it!" Stafford shouted, horrified to see this whirlwind of destruction doing its best to demolish every book on the floor, "Stop, dammit it to hell, STOP!"

## Naturally Bad Manners

Sussi responded by reaching down to grab a book lying open on its spine with its leaves up and ripped several of its pages out. Stafford could see that this particular book was his rare edition of Thomas Wyatt's poems. His parents had given it to him as a gesture of encouragement, after he told them he was going to be a writer, rather than practice medicine. It was a prized possession. Seeing Sussi rip out its pages, he grabbed him by the collar and sharply yanked him back. The book killer hung limp and then, wriggling free, turned around with a broad smile and, extending his hand to Stafford said, "Permit me, Mister Wyatt, I am Mustapha Sussi and I have come to chat a bit with you, about our writing, you know?"

Stafford was lightheaded with fury. However, he indicated a chair in a distant corner and sat behind his desk, only permitting himself to growl out, "Do not touch those books again. Do you understand? They are mine."

Sussi looked around at the books as if he had just noticed them. Turning to Stafford, he said, "Ah, a literary man or, shall say," he corrected himself with the fingers of his left hand on his breast and his right hand pointing to Stafford with palm up, "a man of letters? Such a man needs many friends, eh, Mister Wyatt? Why, my own uncle, Ibrahim Sussi–do you know his work, by the way? No? Pity. Indeed, a great pity, for both of you, of course. Ah, well, at any rate, Uncle Ibrahim is a very famous man of letters and he has a library many times this size. Yes," Sussi added slowly, running his eyes over the stack of cartons piled on Stafford's floor, "a man of letters needs a very large library. But, of course! What a fool I am!" he said, slapping his forehead, "this is merely a few of your less choice volumes. Who would dare entrust real books to the vermin who work for the college?"

Stafford answered slowly, "I believe we are here to discuss your course of writing studies with me, Mister Sussi."

"That's Mus-ta-pha, if you please. I presume I can call you Staff. Stafford has a repellently formal ring to it, don't you think, Staff?"

"Mister Sussi, Mister Wyatt is my full name, Mister being, for our purposes, my first name. A staff is a stick. Thank you."

"Ah, *tres charmant! Vous êtes tres...*

"I am here to teach you to write English, Mister Sussi and that will be the language of instruction. Thank you."

*"Aber, Ihrer Schweitzerische Bleibung..."*

"Mister Sussi, I speak fluent German and French, but only when I am in Germany, Switzerland, Austria, or France. Only sentimental fools, or scoundrels and, perhaps, aged expatiates, reminisce in the various tongues they happen to know. I lived in Switzerland, because my parents wished me to; in France, because I wished to; and now I am here in Chaldes, New York, because I was offered a position as writer-in-residence in the English language. I chose to come here and, if you would be so kind as to stop wasting my time, I will find out whether I am any good at my new job."

Sussi began to interrupt with protestations of love for America and its quaint, New-World ways, but Stafford held up a hand and continued as if he had not heard, "Therefore, Mister Sussi, if you wish to work with me, see to it that we meet at precisely scheduled times, for periods of precisely determined length and, be clear about this, Mister Sussi, if you are incomplete in even one assignment, I shall no longer be able to work with you. You will then have to seek elsewhere for a tutor."

"Look here, Mister Wyatt, I pay your pittance of a salary and..."

"Oh, be quiet. You don't pay one red cent of my salary. I am the holder of an endowed chair. And, one more peep out of you, and we will have to call it quits, Mister Sussi."

Sussi sullenly got up to leave, but then Stafford stood up and addressed him coldly.

"And, one more thing, Mister Sussi. It would be very unwise for you to lace anyone else's food with marijuana. Mister Hurlock..."

Sussi growled out a particularly unpolished curse and spat on the floor in front of Stafford, who automatically responded by taking a step toward Sussi. Then, to his amazement, Stafford saw Sussi go into a Karate-stance and begin to advance menacingly. Stafford laughed and said, "Get out of here, Sussi...Out!"

Sussi remembered who and where, he was and straightened up from his crouch. He stalked out the door and slammed it hard behind him. A moment later, a very disturbed Vikki rushed in and, seeing Stafford unharmed, giggled out, "The things that guy said about you!"

"Miss LaRosa, none of this happened, do you understand?"

"Yes, Mister Wyatt."

"Then, you understand I shall be very angry if any gossip about this gets around?"

"Yes, Mister Wyatt."

"Good. Now, please, get me Professor Bonapoggio on the phone. I'll take it in here."

Shaking his head, Stafford went back into his office and began to clean up the mess. An inspiration hit him after two or three minutes spent at his dismal task. He poked his head out the door and asked Vikki where the liquor was kept. She pointed to a steel locker in the corner and Stafford soon had a stiff, although iceless, whiskey and soda as he began to tell Bonapoggio what had happened. Stafford felt that perhaps he had done something to contribute to the mess with Sussi. This was, after all, his first teaching position. Bonapoggio impatiently cut him short and, with a choice oath, guaranteed Stafford that this Mustapha "Kussi" – or whatever he was called – would not be on campus long. Stafford had done nothing wrong. When Stafford remarked that the name was spelt with an S, Bonapoggio thought he was referring to the two S's in Kussi.

After a moment's talk about the bank and Jim Stiles' generally good reputation, Stafford hung up and drove Bonapoggio's car to Route 33 Motors. The Jaguar was a thing of dark-blue beauty, and Stafford drove it back to campus, while a student, one he had commandeered to go with him, drove Bonapoggio's car back to the Tome Hall faculty-and-staff-only parking lot.

\* \* \*

Stafford and Claudia met the next evening and went to dinner at a famous local Alsatian restaurant of Bonapoggio's choosing, Le Lapin. It was the first time Claudia had seen his new pre-owned Jaguar. The soft fall evening permitted them to drive with the top down. Stafford wore a light blue wool blazer with a russet ascot and Claudia, a blazing red dress, with a deep blue raw silk evening jacket. In her ears, she wore a pair of diamond pendants that Laura had loaned her for the occasion.

Bonapoggio's choice of restaurants had been somewhat mischievous. Here, couples that were not married to one another met to arrange trysts. But, Le Lapin had style and it boasted of a cuisine that did a great deal to help its dinner guests overcome most of their stray scruples. Erotic conspiracy perfumed the air of Le Lapin and the wines from its cellars were as fragrant and subtle as whispered endearments and no less pungent than their replies.

After exchanging unintentionally pleading glances across their small table, glances that made the other clients close enough to observe them in the cool dimness of the room, the least bit impatient with their own naughty counterfeit loves, Stafford took out an envelope, along with a small, expertly wrapped jewelry-box. Holding the box just out of Claudia's eager reach, Stafford took her outstretched hand and gravely asked if she would still marry him. She threw back her head and laughingly informed him that it was women's folly to betroth themselves to any man; for, all men, without exception, were idiots. She proceeded to support this assertion by referring to the preparations of the last few days; to the probable size of her phone bill, which, to pay, would require her to marry in order to save on taxes; to her fancy for him, no matter how misguided; and, finally, saying that, "Stafford, if, because of some peculiarly masculine indisposition, you were to grow long hair all over your face and long claws on your fingers, I would still marry you."

"Then, it's still on?"

Claudia nodded and Stafford gave her the box, which she unwrapped. But, just as she was about to open the box itself, he asked, "Let me have it before you see it. Please?"

Claudia pouted and said she wanted to open it. But, Stafford insisted. He took the box back and, before she could see the ring, slipped it onto her left hand ring finger.

Claudia was speechless. She shook her head and waved her hand slowly back and forth to see it better and to let its facets catch the dim light. Then, she looked over at him and said, "It's beautiful, Stafford. A fine complement to our love's elegance. I'll wear it proudly as a reminder."

She got up and, going around the table, lightly kissed him on the mouth, something one did not do in Le Lapin! Then, she sat back down and reached across the table for the envelope.

"And, this?" she asked, sitting back. "Am I being told that I don't add up until you do the sum?"

"No, it's my footnote to the other one."

"Okay, but I'm going to read it out loud, just in case. Let's see. Move the candle closer, will you? Hmm ... the title is promising! She then read out loud in a low voice:

> *"Love's Domestic Economies: A Second Thought*
> *Having loved you, I have borrowed all the finery of*
> *my soul,*
> *And, though, in the folly of the Stock Exchange, I am*
> *titled in the Banker's role,*
> *All my real estate is truly swallowed up in my*
> *default of sense.*
> *But, if we merge and liquidate our debt,*
> *I can save my failing, ailing fortunes yet."*

Claudia's eyes misted and she said, "Oh, Stafford! I accept your offer to merge and I totally forgive your debt."

"I hereby assert, represent, promise and swear never to go into such debt again. Thank you, Claudia."

"Speaking of debt, when are we going to honeymoon?" Claudia asked, changing the subject from Stafford's debts to his credits.

"Well, my private students are okay. As writer-in-residence, I'm not expected to meet with them on any prearranged schedules, other than the ones I make up with them. I hadn't planned to see anyone for a couple of weeks. As for you, fellow professor, I have a hunch about how you might economize on your teaching so you can go away for a few days' honeymoon right after we're married. The Dean told Avram that old Professor Wilson would be delighted to substitute for you. Is that okay? I don't want to interfere. I'm just bringing an offer from Avram and the Dean."

"Is that okay? I would let a pro-football ticket scalper teach those classes for me during that time! But, Wilson is very good. His age forced him to retire and he hates it. He's a good economist and a wonderful teacher."

"Good!"

"Better than good. I can do what I am always telling my students can't be done. I'll eat my cake and have it, too."

Claudia moved her hand and the candle's light was caught in her ring.

"Oh, Stafford, it is so beautiful."

"Tell me, Claudia. How do you love me?" Stafford asked with a flourish.

"How do I love you? Why...naturally. And, Mister Wyatt, speaking of nature, the call thereof beckons me away from the table and my natural love for you. Nature does get around, don't she?"

So it was that nature's call intervened by mocking nature's true calling. They both left to obey a natural imperative of a different order. And, each of them walked through a set of doors where ordinary, cheating men and women became Gentlemen and Ladies, just because they were answering THE call of Nature.

When they returned, they were somewhat deflated by what they had seen in the course of their trips. The paths taken by nature's prompting threaded through a maze of dimly candle-lit tables, occupied by couples whose attachments to one another had very little to do with nature. Many of these tables entertained couples animated by the willful, unnatural and unspontaneous promptings of that self-image-making that primarily nourishes itself from the potency of the drama of sexual infidelity, hardly the natural culmination of natural desire. This dreary scene struck them as the scenes of the first circle of Hell must have struck Dante. They looked glumly at one another. Claudia frowned and asked Stafford, "Why the hell does anyone get married? Will we, you, I grow cold and bored?"

She continued, after a brief pause, "There was a lot written during the sixties and seventies about sexual fidelity and jealousy. I wonder...?"

She trailed off and looked at Stafford, who asked, "What do you wonder?"

"I wonder if marriage only gives a partner in it the right to complain if the other one cheats. Is that what it's all about?"

Looking at the other tables around them, they grunted in unison. The flickering candlelight and the very low, diffuse side lighting made it difficult to recognize anyone from more than a few feet away. It was only their trips to the Gentlemen's and Ladies' rooms that made it possible for them to see their fellow guests at all clearly.

*Naturally Bad Manners*

Stafford was more than a little depressed. The exhilaration of giving Claudia her engagement ring was wearing off and he was somewhat hung-over emotionally. The present conversation was not helping. To top it all off, his knowledge of that radical liberation-literature of the past decades was minimal and he suspected, correctly, that Claudia's question was colored by her knowledge of it. He was largely ignorant of it because, during most of those years, he was either a pre-med student who was also reading Catullus, or even naughtier Provençal poets (whose concept of liberation was not that of the main lights of the sixties and seventies), or he was in the Williams College biology labs, doing comparative anatomy and demonstrating affinities between widely different species, using a kind of demonstration that effectively kept him off the streets. And, even as a child, he had traveled with his father to uncivil places and unenlightened localities where questions of cosmic justice and injustice were replaced by humbler worries: were their passports in order? Would the customs officials require larger bribes this year? Would the local strongman protect them if someone accused Doctor Wyatt of witchcraft? He knew, vaguely, what Claudia was asking, but he was unprepared to answer her.

For her part, Claudia had spent her college years reading numbers of the new, groundbreaking, highly controversial paperbacks then being published and hotly discussed on college campuses. These, of course, included the feminist and radical literature of the period. The burning issues she discussed with her friends at college included, among others, sexism, the neurophysiology of the female and how this set them off apart from males, the parallels between male exploitation of women and the capitalists' exploitation of the workers.

But, the list of topics she had discussed also included very personal discussions of sexual mores and tastes and whether morality and tastes were not merely "culturally induced," an expression that set Claudia's teeth on edge. Since the Harris household was fond of long, heated, after-dinner debates, this sort of heady discussion was bread-and-butter to Claudia long before she got to college. But, she soon found out that the initially general, initially theoretical challenges animating these sexual dialectics always led to principles concerning admissible sexual behavior. From there, in small, easy steps that could be followed even by those of her friends who were much less astute than she, Claudia found that what had been proposed initially as general principles of sexual behavior had become quasi-logical mandates to engage in certain kinds of sexual behavior.

And, so, nineteen-year-old Claudia Harris had come to grips with the mind-body problem. All those sexual principles, rooted in abstruse theories concerning the randomness of the evolution of sexual dimorphism; of the higher mammals; even of society itself! All those theories based on those general principles had turned out to contain a moral imperative to have, and to positively enjoy having, sexual relations with members of the same sex.

Claudia had been amazed. A naturally skilled dialectician, with years of practice gained from her family's after-dinner conversations, she had long since come to consider hypothetical cases brought up for discussion as indispensable ways to illuminate otherwise obscure points at issue. The usual number of school-girl crushes on older girls at her Parochial School, together with a wide range of poetry reading, had given her a clear sense concerning the trustworthiness of her disinclination in that direction. Female sexuality was, for Claudia Harris, a matter involving males.

Not that Claudia had ever been offended by the propositions of her fellow students; it was the pretentiousness of the pedigrees of those propositions that put her off. She would say, "For God's sake! Ask me outright and I'll answer you outright. But, don't try to seduce me with schoolroom sophistries. Theories of evolution tell others and me a lot about why some animals are born mobile and open-eyed blind and helpless. They don't tell me why I should go to bed with you."

This stance puzzled her friends. They saw that Claudia accepted their tastes at their evaluation, but acted on their proposals at her evaluation. Claudia had insisted that she was no less entitled to her tastes than they were to theirs. After a large number of complex responses to her simple, but altogether firm, refusals, Claudia had begun to grow weary of the tyranny of this new intellectual sexual order.

Late one night, after her drinking/debating friends had been particularly articulate in the defense of their "life-style," she realized that she had begun to feel lonely around these people. But, at the same time, she realized both that they were the most interesting group on campus and that the males at nearby colleges were crude and stupid when it came to being friends with women. When everyone but a particularly close friend, Jane Childress, had left for the night, Claudia settled back in her college-issue chair, took a slug of wine and frowned. Jane did the same and, putting down her glass, said to Claudia, "You know, Claudia? You're too up tight. You bring too much of your Catholic schooling to college with you."

Claudia had had enough. Slapping the table with the flat of her hand, she answered, "Why in the name of God need my imperatives be the same as your principles? You people are damned tyrants!"

"Well, what the hell do you base your actions and choices on?" Jane shot back.

"On what I happen to believe," Claudia answered, without seeing what she was opening herself up for.

"And, why do you believe one thing rather than another?"

"No reason. I just do," Claudia responded airily.

Jane was furious. "No reason?" she shouted, slamming her palm down on the tabletop. "Did the nuns tell you what to believe, Claudia?" she taunted. And, then, by way of a final dismissal, "You sound like some twit in a medieval nunnery."

"That's garbage-talk, Jane. You have no right to talk to me that way. I don't talk to you that way, okay?"

The moment she heard what she had said through Claudia's ears, Jane was ashamed of herself.

"I'm sorry Claudia. It's just that I really care for you and I know you understand the way I feel for you. You know it isn't sick or anything. But, you are so cool! How can you understand and still not agree? With most people, either they're into it, or they hate it. But, you don't do either."

Claudia looked at Jane quietly. She was silent for a long time, obviously reflecting on how to respond to her friend's difficult question. After a while, she answered, slowly and deliberately, "You know, Jane? I don't understand either the way you are, or the way I am. To me, understanding doesn't seem to be the problem. I don't really understand me either. But, I think I see something in myself. And, I think I catch a glimpse of who and what you are...even a clear glimpse, sometimes. And, Jane," she continued quickly, laying a sympathetic hand on her arm, "I didn't think any of this out. I sort of figured it out...you know, the way you figure out who someone you meet for the first time looks like? You don't think that out. You figure it out, you know?"

"I think so," Jane said, slowly and barely audibly.

"As I see it," Claudia continued, "you don't love me as you do because of anything you think or have thought. Do you?"

"No, I guess not," Jane answered slowly. Then, after a long pause, she looked up at Claudia sharply and asked, with a note of desperation in her voice, "Do you believe that you and I could ever be lovers, Claudia?"

Claudia sat up very straight in her chair and put her arms around her own body, each hand under the opposite arm. She slowly took in the scene of disarray on the table in front of her, its spilled ashtrays, old Chianti bottles sprouting colorful candles, books and several newly emptied wine-bottles from which, its drinkers of earlier that evening had imagined, could be imbibed new and hitherto unsuspected, truths. Sensing her own inability to answer both appropriately and precisely, Claudia took another pull on her glass and settled back into her chair.

"Jane, I suppose I believe that God, or something, cares for us humans and I believe that, I think, because the same people who told me that, also told me a lot of other things that have turned out to be true. I don't believe anything the Nazis said about the Jews and I don't believe anything the Klan says about blacks. I do believe that, well, for instance, that I have a father and a mother and that my reasons for believing it are good reasons. But, I don't see anything in myself that would make me believe that you and I could ever become lovers."

"Do you believe your father is really your father?" Jane asked, with a sophomoric grin on her face.

"Do you believe you really asked that?" Claudia answered, with a crooked grin.

"Okay, point well-taken. But, suppose, just suppose, you don't want to be lovers with me, now, only because you were taught to believe it's wrong," Jane answered, sitting up and looking triumphant.

"But, Jane, even if that's why...and I really don't think so...you know? But, even if that's why, so what? What else do I have? Do you have? Does anyone have? Darwin's theories? What the hell does a one-celled protozoan have to do with you, sitting opposite me, here and now? What imperative can I find in theories of chance, got that? Chance! Selection? So what if sexual dimorphism is only the way CHANCE hit on the way nature selected for maximum survival of our remote ancestors? So...? What the hell does that have to do with you and me...here...now? I like that stuff and I get straight A's in it. You know that. But, it doesn't tell me a damned thing about murder, rape, incest, or my sexual tastes. Should it?"

"Damned! Damned! Damned!" Jane sobbed, biting her hand. "My damned analyst tells me it doesn't matter and that I should read De Beauvoir on the second sex. My psychology teachers and my sociology teachers tell me sexual preference is a cultural phenomenon. My priest tells me I am a sinner and my parents pretend I'll grow out of this phase, as they call it. My brother knows better and calls me a creep and Claudia, I am in love with you! Head-over-heels in love with you. It really matters to me. It ain't a phase. I ain't a creep and..." Jane couldn't remember the rest of the list.

"...And, it's beside the point what the others say," Claudia finished for her.

"You're damned right! Those bastards! They all talk as if I'm suffering from a problem...which will go away like a virus or, if not, I'll learn to adjust to it, as if I had just gotten a wooden leg. They aren't in love with you...or with anyone!"

Her tears flowed in earnest. They slowly trickled over her high cheekbones, down to her chin and, sparkling for a moment in the candlelight, fell onto her blouse. Her total and open despair touched Claudia deeply and she took Jane into her arms as she had held her little sisters when a puppy had died, or a favorite doll had been broken.

This act of friendship broke down Jane's last defenses against her admission to herself of how unhappy and alone she really was. She cried uncontrollably, burying her face in Claudia's bosom like a tired child. Claudia led her to the bed and made her lie down. Again acting like a loving big sister, Claudia comforted her unhappy friend and they fell asleep in one another's arms.

Thus, when Stafford and Claudia questioned each other concerning the need for marriage in general that night, at Le Lapin, they had very different answers.

Each of them begged the other to begin.

Finally, Stafford grinned and said, "Alright, then, let me make a fool of myself and get it over with. The sooner in this, ah, relationship you see my folly, the better. So, in twenty-five words or less I, Stafford Wyatt, drunk as I am with a love, whose ardor is only somewhat dampened with spirituous liquors, will say, without equivocation, or hope of correction..."

"God, how you do go on."

"...Why two adults who want each other are willing to act like a sponge to sop up each other's soul. And, this, my love, they attempt to pull off through the use of an odd institution, whose principle goal seems to me now, at this very drunken, love-crazed second," and here Stafford wagged his finger in Claudia's face and she bit it, "ouch! To keep the pair of ever-loving fools in that extreme physical nearness...I forget what I was going to say," he finished with a silly grin.

"Get on with it!" Claudia demanded, looking very fierce.

"Well, I guess they want to be near each other's bodies. But, why get married for that?"

"Well asked, Professor Wyatt, well asked."

Just as Stafford opened his mouth to continue, the main course arrived. They had each ordered Lobster Rockefeller and it was served by an ancient waiter, who announced, in a high-pitched falsetto, "I 'em culled 'On-ree."

Henri's enormous skull was as absent of hair as an egg. His ears were sharply pointed and he had enormous wattles under his chin. Once he was safely out of earshot, Claudia gravely announced that she just happened to know that Henri was only thirty-six years old, but that bachelorhood and its attendant tastes for solitary pleasures, had rendered the man old before his time. "And, so, Stafford Wyatt, marry me and avoid Henri's fate."

With a semi-filled mouth and an expression of amazed delight, Stafford answered, "M'darlin', if Henri will serve this dish every night, I'll insist that you bring him home with you as your little brother. Marital fidelity be blowed, I always say. It's culinary fidelity that counts!" Stafford said, in a voice loud enough to amaze and somewhat alarm, the discreetly buzzing couples seated at tables on either side of theirs.

*Naturally Bad Manners*

While Stafford was carrying on, Claudia leisurely picked out choice bits of lobster, and first popped one into her mouth and then one into his. With a beatific smile on her face, she asked, "Why don't we have a Lobster Rockefeller cult-marriage on the order of the bald-headed guys at the airports...what are they called? Never mind. Since to rule is to serve, our faithful servant can be The Excellent, Wise and Most Subtile Guru Henri and we can all live and eat communally!"

And, so they carried on, each new course provoking yet more imaginative answers to their question, why marry? –Which soon became, Why marriage?, and finally ended up, WHY! By the end of the meal, they had agreed to found a Culinary Ashram, whose thousands of devotees included Henri as Guru and they themselves as his ministers of Love, Education and Haute Cuisine. They decided that this Ashram should include the cattlemen who supplied their beef; the watermen who supplied their lobsters; the butchers who prepared it for the cooks; then, the farmers and grocers who provided the artichokes, mushrooms, and brussel sprouts; and so on, down to the masters of the truffle-pigs who snuffled out that fungoid wonder. Champagne with desert made them raucous and only their response to Nature's bidding saved them from the terrible glance of Henri's displeasure.

Something about the ambiance of those rooms restored the giddy pair to this planet, where they could enjoy their coffees and brandies. Their reaction to these goodies proved Rick Vogel's contention that physical chemistry is a fraud. For, although coffee and brandy are liquids and dampen linen tablecloths when spilled onto them, when poured into Stafford and Claudia, they did nothing to dampen their spirits.

Then all of a sudden, they realized that they had to be alone with each other. Stafford signaled Henri for the check, but the Madame of Le Lapin appeared and explained that there was none. Bonapoggio had given them this evening. The whooping pair left a sizable tip and went out into the midnight air of an upper New York State September night.

The stars were dazzling, and the air had that pungent scent of drying leaves that, after the rains of October, would become sweetly heavy. It had become too cool to leave the car top open, so they closed it, got in and were immediately locked in the most intimate embrace a five-speed, stick-shift, English sports-car permits to a pair of vertebrates who do not happen to be snakes. After a few anything-but-breathless moments, the lower edge of the steering wheel digging into Stafford's left kidney conspired with an extremely threatening gear-shift to break them apart amid peals of laughter.

"Truly," Claudia sing-singed, "a triumph in a Jaguar is a triumph!"

Since neither of them had classes the next day, they agreed to try an all-night road house that several of the faculty had told Claudia about. Stafford asked her if she would like to drive his new, pre-owned Jaguar. Claudia answered, "Yes, indeed!" and, changing places via the doors, she slid into the driver's seat and drove them off.

After a few miles of silence, during which Claudia got the feel of the car, she said, "Stafford, I'd like to ask you a question. It's a little strange, but it's been on my mind. Do you mind?"

"Of course not. What is it?"

"Well, I've been held and kissed before...both. But, you hold differently. Others tended to make me feel they were holding on because maybe I'd get away if they didn't. Not you. It's really different with you. I never feel encircled. Do you know what I'm saying?"

"Is anything wrong with it?"

"God, no! It was the straw that broke the back of any camelard resistance I might have had to the idea of marrying you. But, it is strange ...well, different. No, Stafford, I like it very much. I guess we women tend to be either somewhat passive, or inviting and men respond by being insistent, or something like that. You don't. I noticed that right away and I've never felt passive or inviting when I'm around you."

Stafford did not answer right away. He made a quiet, humming noise and, after a few moments answered.

"You know? I think coming from a family of doctors has really made a difference."

"Oh? How?"

"Well, long before I ever thought about holding a woman in my arms, I'd seen lockjaw patients bent backwards, shrieking to be put out of their agonies. I've seen dying men and women twitching their way to death and others, gaping wide-eyed at its approach. I've seen some," and here, Stafford paused and took a deep breath that had something of a sigh in it, "even screaming that death had no place here among the living. Furious with their sense of the injustice of the very existence of death, here in the world into we are born so alive!"

Stafford finished in a low, thoughtful tone of voice. "So, my love, I don't like my body to be picked up and shaken, like a cat shakes a mouse. To me love...damn! This sounds just the opposite of what I really mean, is ...well, to me, the essence of love is that the body is in command."

"You mean just the opposite, don't you? Those other...those other men grab to control bodies. You don't. Doesn't that mean that the body isn't in control with you?"

"I know. That's why I said it sounds the opposite."

"Please, go on. I have a hunch that I have a hunch."

"Well, you know the talk about letting go and being spontaneous?"

"Everyone knows that talk."

"Well, maybe I'm too clinical, but, 'Letting go and being spontaneous,' sounds to me like diarrhea."

"You are a doctor's brat."

Stafford was quiet for a few moments and then said, with a start, "I think I know what marriage means to me."

"Oh?"

"Yes. Marriage is...well, like the soul of my body when I'm in love...Or is that the body of my soul?"

"I don't follow you."

"What I think I mean is, when I used to make love with someone who just happened to feel the same and nothing else was between us, desire was..." Here Stafford faltered.

"Yes? Go on."

"It sounds backwards, but when all you have is naked bodies ready to make love, desire is too...well...spiritual. Do I make any sense at all?"

"Do you mean it's all up to you two?" Claudia asked, beginning to follow Stafford's odd train of thought.

"Yes! That's it! Good. When two people are together and all they have for one another, since that's all they brought with them, is their bare bodies, they're too alone. People have desires. Bodies don't...I mean not by themselves. Bodies by themselves are what I saw when I saw lockjaw victims."

"Now I think I see. In other words," Claudia picked up the thread, "they leave their jobs, their families, their church and all that behind?"

"Yes. Good!"

"Ah," Claudia said, with a slight swerve of the wheel, "that's how principles become moral imperatives and why people go to bed, of all things, to help out the war-effort."

"I don't think I follow."

Claudia told him about her experiences in college, ending with the beginning of her friendship with Jane Childress.

"So," she continued, "what those metaphysical seducers are really doing is trying to make a bond between themselves and the prospective lover, but using more than their naked bodies."

"You know, I think that's it. Good."

"So...that means that the institution of marriage is a body that is animated by two souls," Claudia finished, not entirely sure of her conclusion, or how she got to it.

Both of them were silent for a few minutes. Then, she continued, "You really do mean self-control in a sort of medical way when you talk about love and self-control. Hmm ... without something like marriage, the body, sooner or later, tends to be just a body that is totally predisposed, as a body, toward the more-or-less-total answering predisposition of the other lover's body."

"You said it better than I could have," Stafford said, as the all-night roadhouse came into view.

The rest of the night was spent drinking to dampen the intolerably giddy hilarity of love, dancing close; nibbling earlobes, and that general dizziness that lovers feel when they hold each other close in public.

When they arrived back at Claudia's, they were on the verge of collapse from exhaustion and excitement. They parted after promising those things that such people in such a state promise because they really mean them and fail to deliver, because no mere human being could. Claudia made her way to bed, strewing her clothes about her as she went. She did not remember her head hitting her pillow. And, on his part, Stafford did not remember very much about the drive home. He did, however, remember to drink two large glasses of water, with four aspirins, a falsely hope-inspiring bit of drunk's magic taught to him in Paris by a drinking friend and he remembered to leave a note forbidding anyone, on any pretext, to wake him before noon.

# CHAPTER 9

## Natural Bodies

By eight o'clock that morning, Stafford was having dreams that would have warmed Freud's heart. By nine o'clock, he was having dreams that Freud never dreamed of, but that would have delighted the heart of a fifteenth-century Dominican Inquisitor. By ten o'clock, his dreams were all Jung and Hesiod, involving waterspouts of colors and day-glow orange eagles plummeting down out of electric blue skies onto violet lakes to capture enormously chesty mermaids. By eleven o'clock, Stafford Wyatt's sleep had become a mere mockery of sleep. Outside his window, the piercing song of a white-crowned sparrow jostled him into a semi-wakeful state that was further shoved, so he dreamed, into a fully sensate condition by the raucous shriek of a blue-jay swearing at a nearby, marauding cat.

Stafford was in a rage. He sat bolt upright, and there was Bonapoggio, silhouetted against the light filtering down through the trees that arched overhead to form a high-roofed glade. His teacher and friend had thick, cherry-red lips and a thin line of spittle trickled down from the corners of his mouth and met at the tip of his goateed chin. Except for an odd pair of chaps, which appeared to be covered by a silky down, Bonapoggio was naked. His feet, however, had pointed slippers on them. No! Sharp little hooves!

"Good God!" thought Stafford out loud, and Bonapoggio sprouted a long, gray beard and a halo that sat on top of a cunning pair of baby-goat's horns, which barely broke through his gleaming, silver locks.

"What the hell?" Stafford shouted next, and Bonapoggio's long gray beard receded into a short, glossy, blue-black goatee. His baby-goat's horns became long and curved sideways over his suddenly long, floppy ears. His loins became enveloped in a long, winding, scaly, tail that left a forked penis fully in evidence.

"Avram!" he cried out and Bonapoggio, looking much more like himself, beckoned Stafford to follow him. Upon getting up, Stafford discovered that he no longer walked on the soles of his feet. Rather, he followed his teacher on horny toes, his knees bending backwards, rather than forwards. He had the legs of a goat.

"Crap! I'm digitigrade!" he said, and at once found himself up to his hocks in cow manure. Bonapoggio stalked on ahead, his now-massive shoulders covered by a thick leather mantel, which was decorated with a myriad of small, iron disks. A conical helmet covered his head and his beard, reaching halfway to his navel, was a mass of tight, Assyrian curls. "Nimrod!" Stafford thought, but he said nothing.

He and Bonapoggio each carried a huge spear, its great, flat, man-killing head supporting a butterfly-net. Nimrod turned around and, in a terrible voice, shrieked, "Shh! Quiet! They're coming!"

"What?" shouted Stafford, at the top of his voice. Nimrod, looking more and more like Bonapoggio, looked sadly at him, and Stafford saw himself as a six-foot long phallus, with a butterfly-net hanging limply from its leather head. Bonapoggio, now looking very much like the chaplain at The American School in Switzerland, hissed for silence and pointed over Stafford's head. Stafford whirled around and saw a dancing swarm of letters that, as they came closer, spelled out, "How do I love you? Let me count the ways." With a single sweep of his net, Stafford scooped up the whole swarm. The letters buzzed and squawked in their captivity. Then, Bonapoggio laid down a white bed sheet and Stafford shook the letters out onto it. They fell haphazardly and made up the line, "Don't do that!" Stafford then realized that he was naked, except for his academic mortarboard and that he was seeing the sheet through its tassel. Bonapoggio, in a flowing gown and holding stone tablets in the crook of one arm, used his free hand to rip off Stafford's mortarboard. He hissed him into silence, at the same time pointing over his head. An enormous monarch butterfly danced into view on a stairway-to-heaven of sunlight. Stafford offered his left hand, with palm up and fingers naturally curved. The beauty fluttered its lovely wings and settled on the extreme tips of his index, middle, and ring fingers. Slowly fanning the air, like a conductor drawing elegance out of competence, the butterfly grew huge, but not heavy. Its broad-veined, fanning wings came closer to Stafford's cheek, and there was Claudia, her exquisite body perched weightlessly on his left hand, her wings progressively blotting out more and more of anything except their nasturtium-orange pools of color, each of which was outlined by its net work of soot-black veins.

What amazing and lovely sounds that network of veins seined up from the clear air! Vaguely aware that Chaucer and the Latin poets were among their authors and that he, Stafford, was their editor, the first song, "In all my youth, in all my chance, Claudia takes me in her governance," was swept out of the thin, clear air by those slowly fanning wings.

Claudia's face became huge. Her enormous orange wings were now barely visible out of the corners of his eyes. She gazed into his eyes with a dreadful intensity and the veins on her gently fanning wings netted,

"Made of desire's blood, and love's kisses, of jewels, of flames, and of flashes of the sun,

Tomorrow, the bride will unfold, unashamed, from the wet cluster, from the crimson bud."

Claudia's eyes now sparkled so brightly that their glare blinded him for a moment, but he could still feel the slight breeze of her fanning wings. Then he heard yet other lines from the Pervigilium Veneris:

> *He has been bidden go forth unarmed,*
> *Has been bidden go forth naked.*
> *But take heed, nymphs, because Cupid is fair;*
> *Love naked is complete; Love unarmed is the same.*

Stafford, floating lightly on the billows of his exhausted sleep, heard himself give a strangled sob. Up from what depths of what soul had Claudia's wings seined that verse?

Claudia receded from the center of his perspective. Now, she frantically fluttered up under the great down-curved petals of a Turk's-Cap lily. Sunlight came streaking down to meet the backward-bent petals of the blossom. Claudia's wings took her up under it and she grasped its long, curved stamens and rested there. Her wings very slowly closed above her lovely back, until they were finally only a little open and blazing bubbles of sunlight filled up the inner space between her wings with a glowing fluid. As she slowly opened her wings, that sparkling liquid congealed into a shower of articulate speech. And, when that articulate brightness found eloquent tongue as it slid down the great curved pistils into Claudia's open mouth, Stafford heard an infinite chorus of voices chanting, ordering, begging, shouting, whispering, sobbing, and laughing, in what he knew was every tongue mankind had ever spoken, or would ever speak.

Then, Bonapoggio came forward through the garden, mincing on his sharp, dainty doe's feet. He caught Claudia's waist and her articulate wings dissolved into arms, legs, and thighs. In her tousled hair, she wore a Turk's-Cap lily, its red-orange upturned petals framing her still, white face, with its sapphire blue eyes. She wore nothing else. Hand in hand, Stafford, Bonapoggio and Claudia danced through the green glade formed by the great trees, whose uppermost branches met high above them.

And, what a dance! Its beat was the throb of the cicada's chorus on a hot July night. But, sweet! Oh, God, how sweet the melody they danced to. Its flavor was the liquid love-song of the spring blue jay, and its elaboration was the sigh of a May breeze in an apple orchard. Everything Stafford had ever loved was there before him. The gracious, mighty trees, dancing in place to celebrate August's quiet, and the coming fall's blazing funeral, dappled the strong light. And, the dancers' nakedness was simplified by its obscurity in that light. They danced together and the cicada, crickets, and jays fiddled and sang, and the trees waved their late summer's sigh of culmination. As Bonapoggio spun around, revealing an enormous erection, Stafford woke up.

\* \* \*

Time. Clocks are said to keep it–as if a clock's possessor who happens to be running late and is in need of more time, could negotiate with his clock for a temporary loan. The Swiss sell it, the French waste it, Americans say it is money and Stafford and Claudia almost entirely forgot its existence. While their colleagues and students were obediently circling left and circling right and keeping time with all their might to the tick-tock of the Tome Hall clock, now coming together as teacher and students, now dividing right and left at the end of an hour's instruction and then reassembling around dining-room tables to eat,

Claudia and Stafford drifted down slow stretches of those shallow waters that marked their hours apart. While they were together, they shot through deep rapids, being spun dizzily by dark eddies of apprehension and then hurled against barely submerged shoals of near-misunderstandings. And so Newton was proven wrong: there is no "true, absolute and mathematical time," flowing equitably, somewhere up there. For the ill tempered and peevish, time is a series of discreet and totally unconnected insults and offenses floating down a universal drainage-ditch, which runs just under their crinkled-up noses. For the man of business, time is a choppy bay, where the winds change from moment to moment, and only occasionally permit him to enjoy a calm and quiet interlude. To the serene and wise, time is just the opposite–the hawk's slow, effortless, circling glide, which is broken only by an occasional break-neck dive, down to the surface of busy Earth for the capture of a delectable tidbit to meditate on later. And, then, one time it was the nighttime before the time they were to be married and the next day was time for their wedding, and Stafford Wyatt was joined in holy matrimony to Claudia R. Harris.

After Father Ryan had performed the ceremony, Bonapoggio, at Father Ryan's suggestion, gave a short benediction from the chancel steps. (As Father Ryan had pointed out to a slightly scandalized Rabbi Avram Bonapoggio in the rectory before the service, "You know, Rabbi, Holy Water is thicker than blood.")

Bonapoggio's benediction was short and somber. It began with a selection from "The Book of Judges," concerning Samson as a teller of riddles: "And, out of the eater came forth meat; and out of the strong came forth sweetness"–a dead lion's carcass inhabited by a swarm of honeybees.

Looking up, Bonapoggio addressed the newlyweds standing before him.

"My beloved friends, the mighty Samson had a lamentable taste for Philistine women and, at the same time, a clear sense that a Philistine is someone who can neither abide, nor solve, riddles. The intimacy of the marriage state tempts all of us to an odd philistinism. We tend to take Nature as a somewhat simpleminded, but altogether trustworthy guide. No riddles asked, no riddles to be answered. A kindly and altogether trustworthy Nature tells us what is right and proper–or so we think. Are we not married to one another? Our hopes and fears, and desires, are not all of them spontaneous? The rite of marriage has forever justified our natures. Custom and law have kissed and blessed what would otherwise be mere waywardness.

"But, you may ask, is Nature such a Philistine? Well, dear Stafford and Claudia, let sluggards go to the ant. Let us go to Samson's honeybee for our answer. Here, they dart in and out of myriad blossoms and, then, heavy with pollen, they return to the lion's carcass. And, what, exactly do they make out of that pollen? Why, naturally, they make honey.

"Anything else? Oh, yes! They make venom for their stings out of that same pollen, naturally. A riddle! And, that self-same desire and love that have brought you two together and led you to profess publicly your intention to remain together must not go unmediated by thought or self-examination. Never obey Nature as if she were a Philistine. See her as a riddle. Remember the wisest of the Greeks, Heracleitus: 'Nature likes to hide.' So, my friends let Nature bring forth her gifts from her dark, hidden depths, in unending profusion. Then, dear ones, you must prudently and thoughtfully choose from that profusion what appears good and acceptable to you. Being there in very great abundance marks it as natural; choosing it because it is good marks it as truly yours.

"Bless you both and may the light of God's entirely choice wisdom enlighten you all the days of your life. Amen."

Purcell's graceful airs had tuned two lovers up the aisle and now Mendelssohn swept a husband and wife out of the church with his urgent and joyful chords.

Somehow, the couple undressed and, then, redressed for their reception at the country club, where everyone had the best and most drunken of times.

After drinks and kisses had gone their rounds, Aunt Adele openly wondered at the happy chance that had led an economist and a dramatic poet to fall for one another. A somewhat grave Claudia pointed out that her own taste for abstract models and Stafford's talent for, first, taking the day-to-day events of life and, then, making something out of them, were complementary.

"Stafford has an astonishing talent for taking one or two everyday events or actions and immediately finding a plot as their context. They become interesting and important. If I could make hypotheses for economic events in the way he makes plots out of ordinary people, I'd already have a Nobel Prize."

Michelle asked, "So, marriage is a sort of plot?"

"What do you mean?" Claudia asked back.

"I take it for granted that, as a couple, you two are meaningful and important. Are you now also saying that at one time you lacked a context? I mean, before you were married?"

"Damned good, Michelle!" Stafford said, slapping his thigh hard and feeling no pain from it. "What a writer's dream! A single man and a single woman. Each is uninteresting...merely events. Then, bingo! They find each other. Then they sit together and they read a book of plots. There really is such a book, 'PLOTTO.' Well, these two souls, hitherto merely floating on the vagrant breezes of whatever..."

"Yeah, yeah. Get on with it," Rick piped up.

"Well," Stafford resumed, "they are reading this-here book and they come across the entry, 'The Marriage Plot,' right there on page two hundred and seventy-five and they decide that this is what will make them interesting. At last! Two characters coming into being in a plot!"

"Sounds to me like two corpses," Rick said, with an exaggerated shake of his head.

"Exactly wrong!" Stafford replied. "These are not grave plots. There, 'tis said, none do embrace'. But, in this here marriage plot, there's just no end of embracing. This here marriage plot is a life plot, not a grave plot."

"But, isn't the decision to get married a grave one?" Michelle asked, her face a blank. Then, when she saw that Stafford was too drunk and out of it to answer, she continued, "So, without a context, a plot, we are..."

"Not even a figment of a writer's imagination," Rick finished and then belched loudly.

Stafford sat up and, with a wide grin on his face, said, "Exactly! The poor souls, before they read page...what page was it, wife?" he asked, turning to Claudia.

"Search me, husband."

"Now, now, children. You'll have to do your mutual searching in a while," Rick said, with a smirk on his face.

"Well," Stafford continued, "the two unfortunates, before they have re-located page whatever-the-hell-page-number-it-was in 'PLOTTO,' are less than a figment of a writer's imagination."

"Yes," Pat interrupted, nudging John, his young, handsome companion, "the unplotted are more like third-trimester fetuses. They are there, but they can't make it on their own."

"If I might interrupt here," Bonapoggio said, "you people are all laboring under a third-trimester misconception."

"Medically speaking, a very unsound diagnosis. Quite impossible!" Michelle interjected, in a grave, official-sounding tone of voice.

"Be still," Stafford ordered, "and let's see what the marriage of Old Testament Exegesis," and, here, he bowed in Bonapoggio's direction, " and developmental biology produces," and, here, he nodded in Pat's direction.

"Easy!" Rick said, waving his arms. "The Virgin Birth!"

"Be quiet!" Pat responded, shooing him away like a fly.

"Well, then, Rabbi," Michelle asked, "what are we without a context?"

Bonapoggio answered gravely, "I know little, or no, biology, Michelle. But, I do have some little knowledge of plots, both burial and literary. I think Rick is not so far off. Two people without any context and, of course, I mean human context, are as much dead as alive. They are not quite either."

"Okay, Avram," Pat answered at once. "Suppose you're right. Exactly what is it they need each other for? Each one has a body and each one has a soul, as you call it, or a life force, as I call it. Or, whatever. All the rest is gravy."

Bonapoggio looked at Pat. His friend, John, standing next to him, was strikingly handsome and Pat was obviously very much taken with him. With a wave of his hand and a slow smile spreading over his face, Bonapoggio answered, "Really, Pat. Is your young and beautiful friend a gravy boat to you and nothing more?"

Pat was furious and turned scarlet. "For Christ's sake, Avram! You talk like a drunken sailor. John is my guest!"

"But, my dear Pat, You have your body and your life force. Your friend, John, has his body and his life force. *C'est tout*! I rest my case,"

Bonapoggio answered cheerily.

"'Say too,' or whatever you like, but say it in English!" Pat answered, smiling in spite of himself, at Bonapoggio's snappy comeback. (His friend, John, didn't seem to have a clue as to what was going on and stood by Pat's side, smiling charmingly at the guests, who were all looking at him and Pat.)

"Now, Pat," Bonapoggio insisted genially, "be fair. It was you who said all that the life force needs is a body and all that the body needs is life force. Okay?"

"Do people ever get raunchy at weddings!" Rick observed to no one in particular. "We sound like the witches in MacBeth, arguing over whether this delectable child's carcass should be boiled down for gravy or served as the main course. Well, by God, if he's the gravy, I'll take two slices of the roast. Pass the pepper please!" Rick sidled up to John and began to leer at him. Pat poured a dribble of champagne on his head and Rick ran off screeching that Pat had poured gravy on him and that "I don't want to provide the main course for a zombie-feast over at the local gravy-yard."

The banter continued for a few minutes and then Stafford announced they would go to the table where there were several wedding presents.

"We are friends here and I want you to enjoy these presents as much as we do."

"I hope someone gave you condoms!" Rick shouted.

"Oh, be quiet," Pat ordered, laughing in spite of himself. John was scandalized and blushed a becoming scarlet.

"Perhaps each of you can give a sort of good luck toast as you hand us your present," Stafford proposed.

"Yes, and then you can also tell us why you gave us these particular presents," Claudia added.

A few of the guests objected that they were too drunk or too tongue-tied to do this, but several agreed that they would like to try.

The presentation began with Mamman, who spoke in halting, but clear West-Indian English. The combination of her lilt and British was interesting to those of the guests who had never heard this accent before. Several of the guests said they preferred it to B.B.C. British.

Mamman came forward in a bright, lemon yellow linen dress. She wore a large, floppy hat that all but hid her tiny, wrinkled face. After gravely curtsying to Claudia, she picked out a small box from the presents on the table and, then, turning to Claudia again, she held out the box in both hands and said slowly, "Claudia, nature, in her most excellent wisdom, has arranged desire between men and women and this, both to make their lives more joyful and to leave the Earth populous upon their several deaths. Now, in the great heat of that peculiar desire that leads a man to clasp his wife in love, odd and, sometimes, exceedingly lovely things are formed in their souls, just as jewels are formed in the hot bowels of the Earth. But, one bit of this Earth of ours forms sapphires, and another forms diamonds, and yet another forms emeralds, and so forth, in a very great variety. Likewise, Claudia, deep in the bodies of the clasping couples, certain jewels are formed, each different, depending on the condition and degree of heat that exists between them. Thus, and take careful heed, Claudia, for I know what I am saying, thus, and not otherwise, Claudia, is a true marriage formed out of the blood around the heart, in the heat of mutual desire. Foolish priests, men of course, have taught a terrible folly concerning these matters, and they say that marriage is something given us by high heaven above. They are wrong, Claudia, very wrong, and very foolish to say this thing. A marriage is a jewel, and it is forged deep in the heart's blood. I know these things, and I tell you them. To help you remember this lesson, Claudia, here ...Take this present, and wear it to remind you of my teaching when your husband's eyes are glazed with the desire to hold you in his arms."

Claudia gravely accepted the box and bent down to let Mamman kiss her cheek. She unwrapped and opened the box. Inside was a pair of earrings with sapphires dangling off of thin gold chains anchored onto brilliants. This prompted a general gasp and an angry buzzing. No one else had anything to give which could begin to rival this present, either in worth, or elegance. Laura quickly stepped forward and, with a laugh, told the guests a story about the earrings.

"While Mamman still lived there, a terrible storm hit St. Lucia and some fishermen had brought her a nearly-drowned man who had come from a yacht that had foundered just off the shore in front of Mamman's little house. She had revived him. When he could speak, he told Mamman that he was a Brazilian and an exporter of precious gems. 'Tante! I am very rich. Name your price and you shall have it. You have saved my life.'

"Well, Mamman only laughed and told him that her fee for a visit was three dollars, for everyone and anyone, rich or poor. For fishing folk and for rich Brazilian jewel exporters alike, there was but one fee. Three dollars.

"The man was beside himself. 'Three dollars! For saving my life? Dear Tante. I am...' but, before he could continue, Mamman pointed out that he was once more in good health, but there were other folk waiting to see her.

'Three dollars, please. And, if you do not have so much with you, since you have been enjoying such a swim, then send it to me when you can. Go now. I am busy. I must tend to others.'

"Mamman made an impatient gesture and the rich Brazilian saw that he should leave at once. So, once he returned to Brazil, he sent these in payment and, dearest Claudia, Mamman never accepts more than three dollars for a visit. Not even for resurrecting a man from the brink of death."

Everyone laughed and came forward to congratulate the economist, Claudia, on her three-dollar pair of gold, sapphire, and diamond earrings.

Next, Laura went to the table and picked out a box. Turning around, she curtsied to Claudia and began her presentation.

"Claudia, I can neither make alligators purr nor words fly, as can Mamman. But, I must tell you about my own present. In our village, there were a number of fishermen who, from time to time, were fortunate enough to catch in their nets the great sea tortoise. When they had eaten its flesh, they took its shell to those men who bought it. Those men, in turn, sold it to other men in the cities and it was these who carved that shell into lovely things. Here is a gift of the deep sea, as Mamman's was a gift of the deep Earth. As your sapphires were formed in the hot, dark embraces of the Earth's depths, so this shell was formed in the cool, green depths of the seas that flow around our island."

Laura then handed Claudia a thin box. Claudia kissed her and unwrapped and opened the box. She took out a pair of intricately carved, matched, tortoise-shell combs.

"After you have brushed out the cares of the day, you can use these to hold your hair away from your ears, so that Stafford can see Mamman's gift and whisper his particular love into your ears."

Claudia looked at Stafford sitting next to her and he leaned forward and whispered into her ear. Everyone applauded and Bonapoggio came forward and picked up his box from the table. Going up to Claudia, he kissed her on both cheeks and began.

"Claudia. As we have seen, the Earth has yielded up the jewels of its hot depths for your ears and the sea has offered up its cool treasures for your hair. But, Claudia, as mere creatures, we humans have not been heated and hardened to that brilliant perfection of the sapphire, nor sculpted to that elaborate perfection of the tortoise-shell comb. Thus, we need combs to complete the imperfect beauty of our hair and we need carefully worked and brilliant pendants to ornament the elaborate magic of our earlobes."

Here, Pat and John cheered loudly, and Rick, who was nearly bald and whose enormous ears were each capped by an astonishing point, danced around, begging the group to run their fingers through his raven locks or, better yet, to nibble his tiny apricot earlobes. He was finally shushed into silence, and Bonapoggio continued.

"Dear Claudia, the wise Galen has, quite correctly, as I think, called the human hand, 'the tool of tools'."

Here, Rick made obscene gestures and Pat's friend, John, finally tipsy enough to enjoy himself around all these "intellectuals," gave Pat a broad stage-wink and said, in a very loud whisper, "My, my. That makes us 'handymen'."

Pat responded with a pretend dizzy-spell, as Bonapoggio looked on with his best uncomprehending-professor look. When things had calmed down a bit, he continued, in his most professorial voice, "So, the first intimation of any intimacy between the sexes in the created order of procreation or, for that matter, even in the human order of simple friendships, is a handclasp."

This broke up the clowns in the company and finally Claudia ordered, "Let Avram finish. I want to see my present."

With a haughty look at the clowns, he continued, "So, Claudia, since you have lovely rings for your fingers, I shall give you something for your nails."

A polite, puzzled titter greeted this statement. Claudia looked very sincere and opened the box, taking out a very good manicure set with carved ivory handles.

"Oh, thank you, Avram. As I run my fingers through Stafford's hair, my nails won't snag. Bless you."

Claudia kissed him on both cheeks and he returned to the group. Next, Rick hobbled up to the table with an exaggerated limp and, in a lisp said, "And, what shall Quathemotho give to the be-you-tiffle gypthy printhess? Thith poor vethal of clay ith but a wretched instrument of my thexthy thoul within."

Then, making a low bow, Rick handed Claudia a small package he had taken off the table earlier. She leaned over and made Rick present his cheek to be kissed. She opened the package and took out a miniature of herself he had painted on an ivory disk and then hung it on a thin gold chain. Everyone was amazed. The likeness was both exact and a little ethereal, very much what a lover might see in her face.

"Oh, Rick! This is lovely. I will think of you each morning as I look first at it and then at myself in the mirror."

"Think of me when the lights go out, Sweetie." He then continued, in a sober, deep voice, "Claudia, my artist's blessing on you and Stafford. Whenever you look at that likeness, remember its artist and think about art's perfection of Nature."

Claudia nodded gravely and swore that she would look at his gift daily and remember his blessing.

Rick bowed deeply and slowly walked back into the group. Since the presents had all been given to Claudia, the group broke up. Some of the guests went to dance in an adjacent room and others wandered onto the terrace. Rick, his face a study in mischief, stopped at the outer edge of a small group that had gathered around a table loaded with seafood hors d'oeuvres and looked around for something to do. A hand on his right shoulder made him whirl around with a startled look on his face. It was Michelle.

"Can we go and talk somewhere, Rick?" she asked, in a low voice.

Rick nodded and followed her out of the room. They entered a long hall with a number of doors along its length. Michelle tried each of them, until she came to one that was unlocked. She surprised Rick by opening it, ushering him in and, then, shutting it behind her.

The room was roomy and elegant. A large leather sofa faced a wide, deep fireplace and dominated a group of smaller chairs. A long coffee table was set in front of the fireplace, and small side tables were set at either end. The rug on the floor was thick and very good. A tall, glass-fronted cabinet exhibited row upon row of liquors, and a small, simulated wood refrigerator completed the invitation to drink. Michelle walked briskly over to the cabinet, made two strong drinks and handed one to Rick. She took the other and sat on the sofa, indicating a nearby chair for Rick.

"You know?" Michelle said, after she had taken a long drink from her glass, "I know what I look like. But, what's inside is not beautiful. Not even a little. I'm miserable. But, look at you! We're switched around. Your outside and my inside! Your paintings are yellows, and blues, and reds. You don't paint misery at all. Why not? What's inside you that's so different from what's outside, Rick? Tell me that."

Rick looked away from Michelle and at his own hands. He slowly ran the fingers of one hand down the back of the other, the thumb of the stroking hand running along the outside edge of the index finger. He almost seemed to be wringing his hands, but there was something about the motion that suggested a musician stroking his hands before starting to play. Slowly looking up at Michelle, he said, in a barely audible voice, "Michelle, why are you miserable? Just look at you and then, look at me! Yeah. Just look at you. A painter's dream. Tall. Your coloring. Your figure. Your Titian hair...stroking the immensity of your forehead...dark tongues of desire brushing the heart of a lover. You, miserable? Look at me, Michelle!"

He was silent for a long moment and, then, looking at his hands as he stroked them, he continued, "One eternity ago, I met a woman who was something of a saint, at least I suppose she's what a saint is. I don't know. But, she looked at my ugly, little, twisted body, and she saw what she said was my soul. She told me it looked like a beautiful shore bird that had been caught in an oil spill. With love, she told me, it could fly. But, now, she told me, it strutted in the stupid morass of my body, and so it couldn't fly. She loved me, Michelle. It wasn't pity. She really loved me."

Rick was silent for a while and, then, with a deep sigh, he continued. "One night, she unclothed me. She traced my crooked spine with her fingers...and she bit these asses' ears and she kissed me. Me!"

Rick stopped and shuddered. Then he placed his hands on his knees and went on, in a flat tone of voice. "Well, Michelle, nothing happened, and for the first time in my life, I was ashamed...please, let me finish. Don't interrupt."

But, Michelle interrupted. She slapped the arm of the sofa and made an impatient gesture with her head. She got up from the couch and, smacking her balled up fist into her hand over and over, she began to stride up and down in front of the sofa. "When I was seventeen, Rick, I got into bed with a guy. The first, and the last. I screamed the moment he touched me. He was scared out of his wits and he tried to put his hand over my mouth. I bit it until I tasted blood. Then he socked me in the face. I let go and he jumped up and ran out as soon as he was half-dressed. I committed myself to a hospital, but the shrinks were all crazier than I was. I left and began to think about what had happened. You know what I came to see, Rick? I saw that this body of mine is me! It's all there is to me. What you see is all there is, and sure as hell, Rick Vogel, no one else can have it. I love it," Michelle hissed through clenched teeth, still striding up and down and slapping her fist into the palm of her hand. She stopped, whirled around to face Rick, and continued, "You know? My girlfriends aren't shorthaired bruisers. They're all beautiful and very feminine. When I'm with them, they're mine! I take them. They don't take me. Oh, no, not me, Rick. They can't have my body. It's mine, because it's me. Rick, I eat those people alive!"

"Rick...?" she continued after a moment's pause for a drink from her glass, "you know, there's a sea slug that eats the Portuguese Man O'War sea nettle. It digests everything but the stinging cells. It keeps those in its own body and becomes as deadly as its food. What a joke on the Man O'War, huh? Well, I do that to them. I feed on my lovers' bodies and I keep their beauty. They sting with that, you know? That's their stinging cells and tentacles, both, and I'm both prey and predator. I sail the calm seas of cocktail parties, weddings, whatever, and I see one of those girls and they think they are the predators. Ha!"

She punctuated this with a final hard slap of her fist into her palm and went slowly back to the couch, looking as if she had just wakened from a dream.

"You sound very successful, dear Michelle. Why aren't you satisfied?"

"Rick, I'm in love with myself, sexually in love with myself. Satisfied? Me? Me satisfied?"

Michelle got up again and resumed her pacing, still hitting her palm with her fist. She asked, "How in God's name could I ever get enough of myself?"

"Can I say something?" Rick asked, but Michelle looked blankly at him and continued, "I take my lovers...literally, Rick. I mean, I possess them. Completely! It's only me there, Rick. Their breasts become my breasts. Their thighs, my thighs. Their lips, my lips. They are mine! They become me as I make love to them. I possess myself sexually then. Rick...? Oh, God, the more I take, the hungrier I get."

Michelle hit her palm hard with her fist again and was about to continue talking, when she was amazed to hear a deep rumbling in Rick's belly that worked its way up to explode into a howl of delighted laughter. Michelle stood rigid with fury until she saw that the expression on Rick's face was not contemptuous. It was delight. Her anger changed into complete perplexity. She sat down and took a long drink while Rick pulled himself together.

"Okay, Rick, let's have it. What the hell is up?"

"Well, Michelle, I had the most wonderful picture of you making love. It was an artist's sketchbook. You've seen them. Here a nose. There an earlobe. Here lips. There a breast. You know? Those sketches are nothing, only scattered parts of a model's body. So are you. No wholes. Of course, you're not satisfied. How could you be with that kaleidoscope of parts? Please, let me finish," Rick said, as Michelle began to interrupt. She settled back with a frown and he continued. "I don't know what sexual satisfaction is when it involves my body. I've never been with a woman all the way, as they say. But, I certainly don't want their breasts, mouths, ears, thighs, or whatever, one by one. I want them all. I mean all of it...together. I'm a crippled shadow of a man, and I may be talking nonsense, but I think greed is love's tragedy. Let me finish," he pleaded as Michelle snorted and began to say something. She subsided back into her chair and looked as though she was trying to look interested.

"Look, Michelle, love wants it all, the whole. But, greed makes love take it bit by bit. Now a breast. Then a thigh. Now an earlobe. So, that's what we do, even if love wants it altogether. Of course, it's never satisfied! It can't put them all together and that's what it wants. All the king's horses, and all the king's men, can't put Michelle back together again. That's the way I see it. What do you think?"

Michelle sat forward in her chair and looked at Rick through narrowed eyes. "You know, Rick? Your soul really doesn't fit your scrunched-up body. Don't ever think that. It isn't true."

Rick looked at her and then he shrugged. He continued talking as if he had not heard her. "Love's tragedy...It wants the whole thing, but all it gets is this part, that part. Do you know how many parts of the human body are, at this very moment, somewhere in this world, being used to make love with? Lord! If we could use them all at once...What a picture!"

Michelle looked at Rick and shook her head with a frown of disbelief on her face. This crumpled dwarf was one of the night creatures, who lived his life in the same cave she thought she lived in alone. Reaching out, she took his hand in hers and stroked it gently. She felt a hot, impatient stirring in her belly. Then she looked up and surveyed his small, twisted frame and dropped his hand as if it had burned her own. He repelled her.

Rick spat out, "That's what I mean, you silly idiot! Now you know what I mean!"

"I'm sorry. I just can't."

"Well, of course, you just can't. Of course, you just can't!" he mocked. "Now, you listen to me, Michelle; you couldn't anyway. No one can! I could be all the beautiful women of song and story, and, Michelle, you still just couldn't. You just couldn't."

"That's crazy!" Michelle shouted.

"Oh, piss!" Rick shot back. "You think you can make love piecemeal. It's the only way we can, but, Michelle, it doesn't work. Ah, but me, Ulrich Vogel, the painter...It's me and only me, who knows how to bring your breasts, and lips, and all the rest, together. I may be a sexual joke, Michelle, but I am a painter. I know how. Then my brush is my whole body. Only, with that brush, I can do things that no genitals teased into tumescence ever did."

Michelle sat back and looked at Rick for a long time. Finally, she sat forward again and gently took his wonderful hands from his knees. She shuddered at the grotesque heaviness of his eyes, just as she had sighed the moment before at the slender loveliness of his graceful hands. But, this time, she held them in hers.

"Will you paint me naked, Rick? And, don't leave anything out? Maybe that would satisfy me. I think I'd like to try it. Would it be too hard for you, Rick? Please. I'll try. Will you paint me? All of me? Entirely naked, Rick? All of me? Please?"

Rick nodded and murmured, "Sure, Michelle. That's what a painter does."

# PART III:
## PROPHETS OF THE LAW

# CHAPTER 10
## The Days of the Week

The rule of Justice seems to require that the arrival of bright day in one part of the globe require the onset of black night in another. And, so it was that, while Claudia and Stafford were celebrating the dawning of their new life together, a far different dawn was being planned for them in West Athens, Vermont, where Suleiman Sussi, Mustapha's uncle, was among the permanent guests at The Geneva Inn. The recent events in Iran and Iraq had tied up a large part of his vast fortune and some of J.J.'s business partners were key figures in delicate negotiations aimed at releasing that fortune. J.J. admired and feared Suleiman Sussi, a silent man whose business sense far outstripped his own and whose remaining fortune, reduced as it had been to merely a part of what it had been, was still legendary. On his part, Suleiman detested J.J. and, during his numerous daily devotions performed facing what he hoped was Mecca, he often prayed to merciful Heaven to forgive him those of his sins whose expiation was presently forcing him to associate with J.J. Rufus. During those prayers, he often beseeched that merciful Heaven to help his nephew, Mustapha, to mend his wicked and perverse ways. Only Suleiman's deep and unshakable conviction concerning his duty to his dead sister, Mustapha's mother, kept him from ordering the boy out of his sight forever.

J.J. felt far otherwise about Mustapha. He never tired of hearing his tales of strange sexual adventures in New York and, when he told J.J. about tearing up Stafford's library, J.J. laughed until tears came to his eyes.

"Ah, my boy. You are a one," was his stock response to Mustapha's tales of perversity and random, pointless, destruction. Since his uncle, Suleiman, was deeply offended by such stories, Mustapha never told them in his presence. He always waited until he and J.J. were alone. His story of his expulsion from college also amused J.J.

"A little time off never hurt anyone," he insisted. "Just be sure that you either make up with your writing-teacher, or find another as good as you say this one is. I insist that you learn screen writing. There is lot of very easy, dirty money in Hollywood and I want a good man out there, snooping for me. Then, dear boy, who knows? Perhaps I will some day adopt you for my own. Hmm?"

A few weeks after Mustapha returned to West Athens, Vermont, for the remainder of the fall semester, a rape-murder occurred in one of the motels along Route 53. A local girl, who worked there as a chambermaid, was the victim, and the community was up in arms. A suspect was apprehended almost at once. He turned out to be the twenty-two year-old son of a big New York City defense attorney. J.J. smacked his lips and sat glued to the TV set, listening to the coverage. After several days of a local media blitz concerning the case, J.J. bet the company assembled for dinner in his private dining room that the suspect, who was obviously guilty, would get off with at most a few years at a minimum security, country club prison.

"Of course!" J.J. scoffed, "he's guilty as hell, but his father is rich and knows the ins and outs of the law. Ha! The law. *Quelle merde*! The law is what the weak use to cry themselves to sleep. The strong use it to get rid of whatever they want to get rid of. Any bets that he will get off lightly?"

No one would bet. As the evening wore on, however, J.J. began a general conversation about law, a favorite topic of his. "Look. No one here will bet me that this guilty bastard gets a light sentence, or perhaps off altogether, with just a few months in a posh, private sanitarium. But, I'm in a sporting mood this evening and I will bet any of you, or even all of you, for that matter, big money that I can take a completely innocent man and frame him so that he is found guilty."

"On a capital charge?" Mustapha asked excitedly.

"Oh, no. In this country, a capital charge almost never sticks. It takes too long. No. But, I can frame him for attempted murder, so that the latest in scientific detection methods prove, beyond any shadow of a doubt, that he is guilty. Anyone want to bet?"

One of his associates, Mister Kio Yammamoto, took him up on the offer and bet him one hundred thousand dollars–with the proviso, however, that a professional detective, trained in the latest scientific methods of criminal investigation, would be the principal investigator. "Very good! Make that two hundred and fifty thousand dollars and you have made a bet."

"Done!" Yammamoto said and they shook on it in front of the others.

"Now, gentlemen. Does anyone here have any candidates in mind? He, or she, for that matter, cannot be too rich or influential. They would just buy off the law. No. What I want to prove is that a smart man like me, with my knowledge of human beings, can make fools of both man-made law and the so called natural laws these pygmies use to make life less frightful. Laws of nature. Garbage! Whatever nature is, it is not lawful. It is lawless and unpredictable. Whatever I want, that's law!"

His guests rolled their eyes and looked at one another. J.J. was on another one of his law-jags.

"So, give me a respectable middle-class male and I'll frame him. Any nominations for this important position, my friends?"

"Damned right!" Mustapha blurted out. "That sonavabitch who got me thrown out of college. Just because I had a little fun with his crummy books."

"Are you sure there are other teachers in the area who you can study with, if you go to another college after our escapade has put this man in prison?"

"They're a dime a dozen."

J.J. beamed at him and soon dismissed all the other guests, so that he and Mustapha could discuss this particular candidate further. "Too many people spoil a good frame-up."

They were together for several hours. At the end of that time, Mustapha came out with a long list of things needed to prepare the ground for the frame-up.

"If we succeed, I'll give you half the money. How about that, eh, my boy?" He reached over and pinched Mustapha's cheek. "Well," he continued, "business before pleasure. Always. Now, then. Let us check out the list."

It listed:
1. Married? Single?
2. Sexual tastes?
3. What is wife like?

4. What is home like and how easily penetrated?

And, as a heavily underlined note, J.J. wrote: Call Fliebig in White Plains and get another copy of the Wyatt-poet's book at once! Cost no object. Mustapha ordered the book at once. As luck would have it, Fliebig had a very good copy, for $700. He ordered it and, when it arrived, wrote a letter of abject apology and included it with the book, which he mailed to Stafford at Chaldes College, "c/o 'Creative Writing Department'."

His letter was a masterpiece. It begged forgiveness on the grounds that his mother had been shot by a revolutionary firing squad in Iran and he had only received news of this the day before he was to meet with Stafford. He was thus beside himself with grief during their "most unfortunate meeting," and, "could Professor Wyatt perhaps find it in his heart to give him another chance?"

J.J. read this and, looking puzzled, asked Mustapha when his mother had died.

"Oh, about six years ago. A taxi hit her when she was crossing a street in Paris. She left me a great deal of insurance money. So, aside from my uncle's occasional gifts, I have my own, very substantial income."

"My boy. You will go far! Yes, far!"

Mustapha had sent the book with the letter a week after Stafford and Claudia returned from their wedding trip. They were in high spirits and were very touched by the letter. Stafford was further delighted to have a replacement copy of his beloved namesake's poems. He opened the book at random and intoned to Claudia:

"'They flee from me who sometime did me seek, With naked foot stalking in my chamber.' What a poem! What a man! It's you, Claudia, you. Listen:

'Once, in special, In thin array after a pleasant guise, When her loose gown from her shoulders did fall and, she caught me in her arms long and small...' What a line! It's you and me."

Claudia pretended distress, took off her shoes and, with naked foot, caught him in her arms, which were long and small.

Later that day, Stafford wrote Mustapha a warm letter of thanks for the book and ended with his and Claudia's condolences for the recent, tragic death of his mother. Mustapha read it out loud to J.J. and they enjoyed a good laugh over it.

"Now, my lad. Stage two. Write a thank you note and ask Mister Wyatt if you can resume studies with him in February."

Mustapha wrote the letter that day and J.J. looked it over and approved it with only minor changes and it was sent out at once. Several days later, Mustapha received another warm letter from Stafford, saying that he looked forward to working with Mustapha that spring semester and could he come down to Chaldes a little early, so they could make the necessary arrangements. Mustapha wrote a card saying he would very much welcome the opportunity to visit early and mentioned a date in December. Stafford wrote that this was fine. Before he went, however, J.J. made him take off all his heavy gold jewelry and replace his Rolex Oyster with a battered Timex. The clothes he wore to his meeting with Stafford were rumpled and not altogether clean.

They met again in Stafford's office and, seeing Mustapha's somewhat bedraggled clothing, Stafford asked him, "Do you need any scholarship aid? I understand that several slots are reserved for me."

Mustapha sighed deeply and confessed that, with his mother's death, he did, in fact, have only a pittance to live on. But, not wishing Stafford to nose around in the business office and thus learn the true state of his finances, Mustapha said that he had saved up and had already paid that semester's fees.

"But, Sir," Mustapha said, with a forlorn look on his face and a voice full of shame and trepidation, "although my tuition is paid for this semester, I really need a place to stay. I do yard work and general housework. I am not in the least ashamed of honest labor."

"I think I can help there," Stafford said, slapping the top of his desk. "Doctor Harris and I live in a large house a little ways out in the country and we would like someone to live in a little guest cottage on the grounds and to help with the yard and a little housework. Not much. Just a little. Would you be interested?"

"Oh, Sir. Thank you. Thank you so very much."

When Mustapha returned to the Inn with this report, J.J. was beside himself with excitement.

"Good, my lad. Very, very good. Now we will get the bastard. Okay. Now, you must go through all your clothes and jewelry and be sure to take out everything that seems expensive, unless you have something lying around that is old and a little worn. He will feel that much sorrier for you. Now listen to me, very carefully, my lad. You are now to see the inner workings of J.J. Rufus' mind. When you go down there, pretend to yourself that you are already a screen writer and that you are using them and their house as a setting for a screenplay you are writing. Notice all the little things. Where do they get any extra money? What mail do they get? Does she play around? What sort of reputation do they have in the community, at the college? What do they eat? What sort of candy? Coffee? What sort of deodorant do they use? The same kind for both of them? Toothpaste? Is there any particular area of disagreement between them? Pretend, my lad that they do not as yet exist and you are writing them into existence. Notice everything! All the details. Am I clear?"

"Yes, sir. You'll get a screenplay inside of two months. What an idea! I am learning screenwriting from this very Mister Wyatt!"

They laughed until they had tears running down their cheeks.

"Trust me, sir."

"Oh. I trust you, lad," J.J. said, pinching him on the cheek.

Mustapha drove back down to Chaldes in an ancient Ford he had bought at a used car dealer on Route 35 and he moved in with Stafford and Claudia soon after New Year's. He was a dream around the house and grounds. He was everywhere at once, doing everything. No job seemed too small for his intense concentration. Little by little, Stafford and Claudia came to depend on him. When they went away for a weekend, they felt very comfortable about leaving the house keys with him. Mustapha used that time to inspect every drawer, medicine cabinet and box, both in the house and in the cellar. He knew where they kept the keys to all the locked drawers and he used them. Nothing spectacular, he thought, but still...He noted everything down on a large, legal size pad of yellow, lined paper and his inventory was an insurance-adjuster's dream. He even flipped through their books and anything that seemed noteworthy, or even possibly so, was noted down on his pad.

By the beginning of his fifth week there, Mustapha had a sheaf of sixteen legal sized sheets, which, in case they were somehow found, he had written in Persian. Just as the eighth and last, week began, while

*Naturally Bad Manners*

Stafford was away overnight at a conference, Claudia received a telephone call from Celeste in New York. Mustapha happened to be in the living room with her when the call came. It seemed that Mike was very ill. He had a pathological degeneration of the kidneys, brought on by his inherited high blood pressure and his love of drinking and smoking. The disease, called Kindstiel-Wilson's Disease, sometimes killed its victims in as little as six to ten weeks after it made its presence known clinically.

Claudia was in a panic. "Of course I'll come right down. Mt. Sinai Hospital? It will take me, oh say, five hours. See you then."

Claudia hung up and then turned around to Mustapha, who was carefully listening to all of this new information about the family. "Oh, damned! Stafford knows Manhattan well. I always get lost. I don't know how to get to Mt. Sinai Hospital!"

"If I may be permitted, Professor Wyatt, I know Manhattan very well and I know exactly where Mt. Sinai Hospital is located and how to get there most easily from here. May I offer to drive you, Misses...ah, Professor Wyatt? Please. It would be a pleasure."

Claudia automatically said "Harris," by way of correction to Mustapha's "Professor Wyatt," and smiled gratefully at him, nodded her assent and ran upstairs to pack a few things. Mustapha was delighted by the prospect of a four-hour drive with a semi-hysterical woman. What a chance to mine some real information for J.J.! He had paid no attention to Claudia's correction concerning the fact that she was Professor Harris and not Professor Wyatt.

After an hour on the road, Mustapha sighed deeply and audibly and, then, he began to talk about his own mother, whose recent death had been such a blow to him both emotionally and financially. "My own parents were the ideal couple, Professor Wyatt. Simply ideal! They ate the same food, smoked the same cigarettes"–his mother had never smoked a cigarette in her life and did not allow them in the house–and, would you believe it, they even used the same deodorant! And toothpaste," he added, for good measure.

A thoughtful, quiet Claudia was struck by this confession of such an intimate character by a recently bereft student, so far from home. She volunteered, in response, that she and Stafford also used the same deodorant, but that they most certainly did not use the same toothpaste!

She had very sensitive teeth, which required her to use evil-tasting toothpaste that gagged Stafford.

"Hmm," Mustapha said to himself, as he noted all of this down mentally.

At the hospital, Claudia and Celeste kissed one another outside the door to Mike's room and Claudia hurriedly introduced Mustapha. She asked him if he would mind waiting on a bench just outside the door, while she went inside for a while. Mustapha said he would not mind at all. They left Mustapha in the hall and tiptoed into the room, leaving the door open a crack. Mustapha's bench was right next to it and he could hear nearly every word spoken inside. Nothing much of interest to him was said, other than Mike's insistence that he was not going to swallow up his family's money by going on the dialysis machine. He wanted to die as he had lived and he had not lived as a cripple.

"God, I'm in such pain," Mike groaned out and the buzzer sounded down the hall, bringing a nurse with a tray that, Mustapha saw at once, had various sedatives and painkillers on it.

"Hmm," he thought to himself, "On the street, that little tray would bring several thousand dollars."

As the nurse came out again, Mustapha heard Celeste say, "He's sleeping now."

The talk rambled on until Claudia asked how the other children were set up financially, pointing out that she, Claudia, was tenured and made ends meet more than adequately, given Stafford's contribution. Celeste launched into a long list of financial details. Mustapha, as interested and even excited, as he was by this conversation, realized, at just that moment, that he had not been to the bathroom since he had left Chaldes and that he had to go. Right then. He dashed down the hall, nearly knocking down Mike's nurse and returned within four or five minutes, just in time to hear Celeste say, "So, when your father dies, you will come into a million dollars of insurance money."

"Oh! This is too wonderful. What a set-up. What a frame-up," he thought to himself, never wondering if, by chance, he had missed any important information while he was obeying nature's call.

After a long wait, Claudia came out with a stricken look on her face and she asked Mustapha if he could drive the car back without her. She gave him fifty dollars and said she would be back in a day or two and would he be so kind as to sleep in the house. He had the key.

"Of course, Professor Wyatt. I hope that things are not too, too difficult. I feel sure all will turn out for the best."

Mustapha was beside himself with that odd combination of rage and joy that gets hold of weak and fearful people when they think they have someone completely in their power.

"Fifty dollars? Christ. I have ten times that much in my wallet. But, the car is a nice touch."

And, so, Mustapha spent the greater part of that night cruising the less savory sections of lower Manhattan in search of what he considered friends. He woke the next morning without a cent, but could not have cared less. These pick-ups always picked their "friend" of the evening clean and Mustapha had, long-before learned never to carry much money in his wallet or wear much jewelry on his hands and neck. He had taken the precaution of hiding both money and jewelry under the hood of the car, in the air filter.

The next morning, he recovered his money and jewelry and then drove back to Chaldes. He called J.J.

"Well, sir, I have all you need...ah, we need, I mean. It's too much. Really. You will find it difficult to believe, Sir. I swear it to you, Sir. You will find it hard to believe."

Mike died a week later and Claudia and Stafford spent some time with Claudia's family. After they had returned to Chaldes, Mustapha, after offering his deepest and most heartfelt sympathy for their recent loss, took his leave and returned for a long weekend to The Geneva Inn. After the usual greetings, he and J.J. went into a private conference-room, which had been electronically washed and cleaned of any possible bugging-devices. J.J. used this room for conferences involving millions and when that sort of money is concerned, one can take no chances.

Mustapha spread out his lists he had written down on his yellow, legal sized pads. After all the information had been sifted through several times, then numbered, weighed and measured, for usefulness, only one or two points were highlighted for further consideration.

Item: Stafford used one sort of toothpaste and Claudia, because of some problem with her teeth, used another, very strong-tasting dentifrice.

Item: Claudia and Stafford habitually overspent on luxuries, which were almost always Stafford's idea. (Claudia was, in fact, rather modest in her needs and tastes. Stafford, the only son of two physicians, was not.)

Item: Mike Harris, Claudia's father, was a successful contractor, who had just died, leaving Claudia one million dollars.

When this abstract had been prepared, J.J. looked up from it with a sort of gurgling gasp of delight. He pinched Mustapha's cheek until it hurt, but neither of them said a word. The rest was simplicity itself. It is not hard to frame a trusting man who overspends his and his wife's income when that wife has just inherited a million dollars from her father.

Mustapha returned to Chaldes and was in constant evidence around the house. Claudia and Stafford were still deeply distressed by Mike's death and they relied on Mustapha's constant help more than ever.

One morning, several days after he had returned, Mustapha was emptying trash baskets in the living room, idly looking at the contents for potentially useful bits of information to make his easy task even easier. Just then, Stafford walked in and listlessly began to help him.

"Your father was a physician, was he not, Mister Wyatt?"

"Yes. He was," Stafford answered absently.

"I have always thought that the tools of that profession were uniquely beautiful in the way their form expressed their function."

"Really?" Stafford said, interested in spite of his generally gloomy mood.

"Oh, yes, Mister Wyatt. I once went to a medical museum and I guessed nearly all the uses of the instruments on display. I was very pleased."

This interested Stafford, who answered, "Well, come upstairs to the attic with me. Let's see."

They went up to the attic and Stafford went to an enormous cabinet, and, on opening it, Mustapha saw rows of gleaming medical instruments. He also saw a small black, leather case.

"What is that, Mister Wyatt?"

"That's my father's set of hypodermic syringes."

"Oh."

This is what Mustapha had been waiting and watching for. Stafford showed him a number of instruments and Mustapha guessed exactly what they were. He had no trouble recognizing them because his interest in drugs had led him, one summer, to volunteer as a paramedical helper.

"Now," he thought to himself after he returned to campus later that day, "a little rumor-mongering and everything is set."

After lunch, Mustapha sauntered into the video game room of the student union and, standing at one game, he said out loud to no one in particular, "Tom Martin told me Professor Wyatt's wife inherited a million dollars. How about that?"

Several nearby players looked up for a second, whistled and then bent back over the controls of their games. By dinnertime, everyone on campus was whistling over Tom Martin's gossip.

\* \* \*

The next morning, soon after she had cleaned her teeth, Claudia became violently ill. She vomited and sweated profusely and Stafford called an ambulance. She was rushed to the hospital, but the usual tests revealed nothing and, since she soon felt very much better, she returned home the next morning, after a quiet night's sleep at the hospital. The first thing she did when she returned home was to brush her sensitive teeth with her old toothpaste. Within a few minutes, she was ill again and Stafford called the ambulance again. The doctor looked very worried. He had her stomach pumped out and the contents analyzed. As he suspected, Claudia was being poisoned with arsenic.

It was Jim Dixon's unpleasant task to tell Stafford that he was under suspicion as the poisoner of Claudia Harris and that he was not to leave Chaldes. He was to be either at the college, at home, or visiting his wife at the hospital.

When he heard this, Stafford told Dixon he would be either at the hospital or with Bonapoggio. Jim Dixon agreed, since he wanted the house clear so that he could go over it for any clues in the case. Stafford had denied the charge, of course, so it was up to Jim to prove it. More stunned and amazed than fearful, Stafford told his friend what had happened and, when he began to protest his innocence, was somewhat sharply cut off by Bonapoggio. "Stafford Wyatt. Please. I am not a fool. Of course you did not do this terrible thing. I know that. You know that, and, when she hears about it, Claudia will know it. Be patient. We will find out what happened."

Jim went over the house with his crew and was becoming more and more frustrated when one of his men told him someone was hanging around outside.

"Bring him in. I want to know who it is and why he's here."

It was Mustapha.

"Oh, sir, this is terrible! First, her father dies and then Professor Wyatt gets so sick. And, where is Mister Wyatt?"

Jim evaded the last question and began gently to grill Mustapha, who pretended complete ignorance of what was going on. Jim finally gave up and told Mustapha about the poison found in Claudia's stomach. Mustapha was shocked and horrified.

"Oh, sir. I don't...that is, I won't believe it. Who could have done such a dastardly thing? How...oh, my God!"

"What is it, Mister Sussi?"

Mustapha told him about the conversation in the car on the way down to New York and wondered out loud if that could have anything to do with this truly terrible business.

"But, no, Mister Dixon. It is quite impossible. Why would Mister Wyatt wish to injure his wife? After all, they could barely get along on their combined salaries as it is...with his extravagances. It used to worry Professor Wyatt a great deal, I am sorry to have to say. Such a fine woman, too. And, always worried."

"Was she?" was all that the detective replied as he entered into the master bathroom and, taking out his handkerchief, picked up the tube of special dentifrice that Mustapha had told him Claudia always used.

"Yes. That is it!"

"Very well, Mister Sussi. We'll take over from here. Thank you very much, but don't leave town for a while. I will almost certainly need you for a material witness."

"Oh, no, sir. But, sir, please. I just cannot believe that Professor Wyatt did this thing. I confess that I just cannot believe it."

With a song in his heart, Mustapha left.

When the crime unit investigators received the tube of toothpaste, they soon detected small scratches on the lip of the tube–just as

*Naturally Bad Manners*

Mustapha had meant them to. They took a small sample of the contents and found enough arsenic in it to kill a horse. One of the men called Jim and told him, adding, "It's a good thing that stuff tastes so bad. One good swallow would've killed her. As it is, just enough remained in her mouth, after she had rinsed her mouth out, for her to swallow a little. And, even that made her sick as hell."

Jim knew he now had to charge Stafford formally. "What a clever bastard this guy is. But, why?"

He found out the moment he got on campus. Everyone was buzzing about the odd coincidence of Prof. Wyatt's wife's sickness–twice in a week–and her million-dollar insurance money. When he returned to the lab, the staff in forensic told him that the scratches on the lip of the tube were made by a hypodermic needle.

"Of course! He got in there with a needle. What a bastard!"

Jim then returned to Stafford's house and collared Mustapha. "Did you ever see anyone here with a hypodermic needle, Mustapha?"

"Hypodermic? Oh. You mean one of those things the physician uses to give shots with? No, Sir. Was Professor Wyatt on drugs, too, Sir? That is expensive. But, no. That is impossible!"

"We'll have to look for it," Jim said angrily. "He probably threw it away. Damned!"

"But, if he was not on drugs, sir, why would he want to buy...but wait. Of course! What an ass I am! There is a whole cabinet in the attic, simply bursting with medical supplies."

The detective went with him to the attic and, opening the cabinet door, was shown the leather case.

"Is this it, sir?"

Jim took the case and carefully opened it. He shut it immediately, looked very grim and told Mustapha to keep out of the house and not to say a word to anyone. If he did, he would be charged with obstructing justice.

"Oh, no, sir. Not I. Not a word. I still just cannot believe..." He fell into a mournful silence and followed Jim out of the house.

A simple inspection at the lab showed that one of the syringes had traces of arsenic on it and a perfect set of Stafford's fingerprints.

"That does it. He's as guilty as hell," Jim said, shaking his head in disbelief. "This is going to finish his wife off. What a bastard!"

Jim Dixon was a kind man. He could not bring himself to tell Claudia that her husband of a few months was trying to murder her for her money. He called Bonapoggio and asked him to tell Claudia. Bonapoggio asked him to come over.

"There is something I might be able to help you with, Captain Dixon. And," he added, "I would like to include Doctor Simms and Ms. Miller, too. Is that agreeable to you? Stafford is with his wife at the hospital. He is not going anywhere. Claudia is coming here a little later with him and we'll see them here."

"Of course, Professor Bonapoggio. Whatever you think appropriate. But, it looks as if I will have to charge Wyatt formally. I will put a guard on duty outside Mrs. Wyatt's hospital room for now."

They all met in Bonapoggio's living room. Laura was in shock and could not speak without tears welling up in her eyes. Ted looked very grim. Only Bonapoggio looked at and spoke about the whole mess quite cheerfully.

"Hello, Jim," Ted said to Dixon when he arrived.

"I'm sorry, Ted. It's my job. You know?"

"Sure, Jim. But..."

"There are no buts here, Ted. I am a trained professional investigator and this is a textbook, open-and-shut case if I ever saw one. I am sorry, Ted. That's the way it is."

"My dear Captain Dixon," Bonapoggio broke in. "Do sit down, please. There. Now. I have something here that Stafford wrote as a post-wedding present for Claudia several days ago. I have had copies made. Here is one for each of you. Will you please read it?"

Bonapoggio passed around a single sheet of paper with a poem on it. It read:

> *"To Claudia: Now and Then"*
> *Before light was, it was your eyes that set the style*
> *for Heaven's stars;*
> *And, Then, when all light is died out from the world,*
> *Your face will save an image in that dreadful*
> *barrenness.*
>
> *Before sound was, your mirth demanded music;*

*And so, when sound is silenced,*
*And the soft immensity of Nothingness is stilled in*
*all its parts,*
*Then your merriment will measure still...*
*Why, some airs, some tunes, some melodies.*

*Before Time was, you quickened listless, languid,*
*idle love with life;*
*And, when Time runs dry through all its long and*
*tortured courses,*
*Your thrilling Now, never grounded in the killed*
*stalls and stills*
*of Time's once roiling rivulets, streams and rills,*
*Will end Time's old end, and resurrect it in the*
*meter of your stirring heart.*

Ted looked up slowly and said, "It's so generous to her."

Jim looked up angrily and said, "Well, Ted. What he wrote to her isn't the problem; it's what he did to her that was neither fine nor generous. It was stingy and hateful, Ted. But, we are not discussing a breach of good manners here. This is attempted murder."

"The man who wrote this a few days ago wouldn't do that, Jim," Ted answered in a quiet voice.

"Exactly," Bonapoggio thundered. "That kind of stingy, hateful deed is precisely what a poet hates most–I mean, a real poet. And, Captain Dixon, Stafford is a poet – a real poet. And, Captain Dixon, if I may be forgiven for running the risk of appearing to be condescending, one of the epithets the medieval Christian theologians applied to God was 'suave.' Their God was not primarily Calvin's furious avenger. He was sweet, and the greatest scholar of early Christendom, Jerome, was known as 'urbanus studiosque,' 'studious and urbane.' Jerome's manners were flawless."

"He's right, Jim," Ted broke in. "Damn all your evidence to Hell! He's right!"

"He is not right, dammit!" Jim shouted back, "because, my learned friends, if Professor Bonapoggio is correct, the sciences of logic and forensic medicine are wrong. They are not wrong, Ted, and God did not create this world to be a mad house where evidence points to nothing and where, in the face of all the evidence in the world, good manners prevent men from attempting very terrible crimes."

He fell silent and looked embarrassed. He then shook his head as if to clear it of any possible doubts and continued in a low, precise voice. "Look. I am both a trained scientific investigator and a Christian. I have been taught and I believe it, that the things my creed enjoins me to believe really happened are, in point of fact, part of the same divine Creation I study as a police investigator. The law given on Mt. Sinai and, as I believe, reconfirmed in the Sermon on the Mount, is part-and-parcel of the law that governs this world. The word of the same Creator, I believe, guides my faith and my sciences. I am a scientifically trained law enforcement officer, even though my family is very rich. I do not have to earn my daily bread. But, I became a law enforcement officer, Ted, because I truly believe that the body of the law is now the repository for the spirit of divine truth. But, now, my friends, I am told by my good friend, Ted Simms and by a distinguished scholar and Rabbi, Professor Avram Bonapoggio, that I am to believe that the soul, friends, the soul of one Stafford Wyatt is not able to permit him to do what everything the laws of nature–the laws of logic and forensic science–say conclusively that he did. What am I to believe? What do you believe, Professor Bonapoggio?"

Bonapoggio was obviously distressed by Jim Dixon's quandary. "What do I believe, Captain Dixon? I believe that it was very wise to group theology, law and philosophy together, as the three leading faculties in the medieval universities. That much, I am sure I believe. But, Captain Dixon, which of those three should have absolute precedence over the other two...? I do not know, at all, what to believe about that."

Jim answered, "The laws of deduction and the laws of analytical chemistry, which, together, guide forensic medicine, are not merely conventions, I think. They are the laws of nature as laid down by nature's God. My science points exactly to Stafford Wyatt's guilt, without any conceivable qualification. My science contradicts your psychology and, if you are right, is not my God merely a malicious deceiver? And, if He is merely a malicious deceiver, then no contrary evidence–soul, poem, whatever–is worth a hill of beans. Is it?"

# CHAPTER 11

## The Sixth Day of the Week

"That's it!" Ted shouted, jumping up and waving his arms. "Lord! What fools we are! A malicious deceiver! Of course!"

Laura and Bonapoggio shouted in unison, "A frame-up!"

"My God. What fools we are," Bonapoggio continued, his eyes raised to heaven. "Captain Dixon. Your laws of nature and nature's God are safe. Only, my friend, someone else knows about them, too, eh?"

For the first time, Jim was unsure of himself. "Well...okay...maybe. It could be. But, who? And, why?"

"Don't know," Ted said slowly, "But, let's assure Stafford that he is very much less under suspicion. Then let's find out. I'll borrow money from David for bail."

"You will do no such thing! I have not bounced a check for many years," Laura said.

Ted turned to Jim and said quietly, "But, we were not really prepared for the deception that, whatever malicious genie it was who framed Stafford, was pulled on us. Don't berate yourself. Okay?"

Jim was numb with indecision. "I'll try to be open-minded, Ted. And, whatever happens, thank you for being so decent. I'm still not sure, but I do see that it could be a frame-up."

After Ted and Laura had left to get Stafford and Claudia at the hospital and Jim had called the officer watching over Stafford in Claudia's hospital room to tell him to let them go, Jim asked Bonapoggio if he could use the phone.

"Of course, Captain Dixon. And, please. As a fellow traveler, of sorts, if not an altogether acceptable co-believer, perhaps you would accept my invitation to stay for dinner?"

"Thank you, Rabbi Bonapoggio. I would like that."

Dixon called the judge and told him that new evidence had just been unearthed that persuaded him that Stafford Wyatt was, perhaps, the victim of some very complex frame-up. Could Wyatt be released on bail?

Since Jim Dixon had the reputation of being a very cautious man, the judge granted his request, only setting the bail figure very high in order to salve his own conscience – and to help mollify the press when they heard Stafford was out on bail. This done, Jim turned around and faced his host and, looking him in the eye, said, "Rabbi Bonapoggio, I think you can understand what I am about to say. I am rich and I am highly respected in this town. My fellow law enforcement officers say they regard my work highly. I am a happy man, Rabbi. I have what I want and what I need, to be happy. But, Rabbi Bonapoggio, my very name, Dixon, is the name of a man who legally owned my great-great-grandparents. That man, named 'Dixon,' could kill or sell my great-great-grandparents. He also had unrestricted sexual access to all the women in my family and no one, either priest or sheriff, would provide any relief from their degradation. Their master and owner, Dixon, would not permit himself to couple with the females of any other species, but he permitted himself to couple freely with the women of my family. They were lower–oh, so much lower–than humans, but, somehow, higher than the beasts...at least, sufficiently higher that it was permitted by his church and his community to couple with them as he wished. And, Rabbi Bonapoggio, no priest or sheriff would grant them any relief from their degradation. And, I, Detective Captain James Dixon, the great-great grandson of one of these wretched people, I am a happy, rich and highly respected man of the law. And, so, Rabbi Bonapoggio, although I am rich, I work. That work is not always pleasant and sometimes it is dangerous. And, I do this," and here Jim looked up and sighed deeply, "yes, I do this, Rabbi, because I believe that I have truly seen the mercy of the Lord in the land of the living, a very great mercy that led my ancestors out of their wretched enslavement. The Lord has been exceedingly merciful to me and to mine, Rabbi...and God's mercy, I believe, is the principal ornament to His handsome justice. And, so it seemed to me as a young man and it still does now, Rabbi Bonapoggio, that a life of service furthering both justice and the causes of justice is a good life. It is, however, a life that uses as its tools the laws of logic and the laws of chemistry and all those curious techniques that we officers of the law use nowadays."

Jim was silent for a moment and then, looking out of the window, continued. "Officer of the law. What a title! Ah...well...So, Rabbi Bonapoggio, those laws of logic and forensic medicine pointed to Stafford Wyatt as guilty of a very terrible and ugly injustice. And, justice, both divine and human, requires that the perpetrators of such crimes and injustices suffer for them. And, in this case, that Claudia Harris be protected from further mischief."

Jim was silent for a long time. Bonapoggio sat opposite him, motionless and watched him with a perfectly blank face. Then, seeing that compassion required him to break the silence, he said, "Good, I think. But, and I here inquire of you, as a fellow traveler, Captain Dixon, whether the laws of the human soul are the same laws governing the stars, or even the laws governing those organic molecules that forensic medicine uses?"

"Rabbi, my own religion teaches and I for one believe it implicitly, that the very word of God given on Mt. Sinai was later made flesh and dwelt among us here on Earth. For, as I believe, my Christ is God, the same God whose creative word earlier made the Heavens and the Earth. That same Christ is the living law and that very same medicine that studies the bicuspid valves of the human heart also studies our redeemed flesh...as I believe."

Bonapoggio smiled a slight smile and answered, in a soft voice, "My own people, Captain Dixon, say that there is a very ancient city, which was first taken from the Jebusites and then sanctified by King David by his dancing naked before the Lord. And, that Jerusalem, as we now call that old Jebusite city, a place of stone and of wood, is particularly favored, my people believe, by the spirit of the Creator of Heaven and Earth who is also the giver of the Law at Mt. Sinai. Our two religions, Captain Dixon, have a certain deep and not unsubtle, affinity. No?"

Jim was silent for a long time. He then answered slowly, "The soul of Stafford Wyatt is part of the evidence, you say. 'Stafford Wyatt's soul!' Oh, yes! And, those lines on the mass spectrograph that identify metallic poisons, such as arsenic...These are all equally part of the evidence. What an idea!"

"Ah, but Captain Dixon, our common heritage tells us that Deity created mankind on a day distinct from the creations of the Earth, with its metallic poisons. Somehow or other, we human souls are in the very week of creation, but not on the same day of that week as the metallic poisons. Be of good cheer, Captain. God has been good to us...to you and to me. Be of good cheer."

Just then, they heard a car pull up and Ted's jubilant voice ring out, "Kill the fatted calf! The prodigal son is returned with his foreign woman!"

Bonapoggio and Jim opened the door to Stafford, Claudia, Laura and Ted and to Mamman, who had been persuaded by Laura to accompany her, by pointing out the danger Stafford was in. After they had settled down, Claudia asked Jim in a puzzled voice, with a deep frown on her face, "What's all this about, this tale of Stafford and toothpaste? I hate the damned stuff and it tastes like a quarterback's post-game sock. But, it doesn't kill you."

"Well," Dixon answered, "the story is that your husband tried to poison you because you are an heiress."

"An 'heiress'? Me? An heiress? What are you talking about?"

"Well," Jim explained, "the news around campus is that when your father died, you inherited a million dollars."

Claudia looked at Stafford and the two of them hooted in derision.

"'A million dollars?' My wife an heiress? Not a chance! But, Captain Dixon, Claudia's father is not, as far as we know, even sick, let alone dead."

"What do you mean? Wasn't Mike Harris your father?"

"No. He was my uncle. He adopted me. I don't know my natural father, beyond a name."

"Good God! Are you sure?" Jim asked, shaking his head in disbelief.

"Of course I'm sure," Claudia answered, shaking her head in disbelief at Jim's disbelief.

"Then who in hell tried to frame you?" Jim asked Stafford.

"Let's do this step by step," Ted interjected. "Sorry, Jim. But, I think I can be of help here."

"Now," Ted continued, turning to Claudia and Stafford, "who knew that you had that set of needles and that Claudia used that toothpaste and that you didn't, Stafford?"

"Sussi!" they chimed together.

"And..." Stafford began and then stopped. He frowned and continued, "Of course. I should have known. That little bastard. Claudia? Could he have heard Celeste tell you about Mike?"

"Yes. But, we had rung for a nurse to give Mike a sedative and the door was ajar. I thought I would also check on Mustapha to tell him I would be some time, but he had left for a minute to go to the bathroom."

"But that means that he could have missed just the piece of information to the effect that Mike was not your real father. And, then he could have come back, just as Celeste told you that you would inherit a million dollars when your father died."

"He had to," Jim interjected. "Otherwise, he would not have tried to frame you after your Uncle Mike had died."

Shaking her head, Claudia began to recount the trip to New York with Mustapha.

"So. What a sterling character that one is! On the way down to New York, he gave me a long song-and-dance about how close his mother and father had been and that they had used the same deodorant and even the same toothpaste. I told him I used special toothpaste for sensitive teeth and that it had a strong taste that you couldn't stand. A nice guy, this pupil of yours, Stafford."

Stafford then told the group about Mustapha's interest in medical implements and his bet that, if Stafford could show them to him, he could guess their uses. This last story finally overcame any lingering doubts in Detective Captain James Dixon's mind. He said, screwing his mouth up in his effort to see how he was going to pull it off, "I have a pretty good relationship with the press here in Chaldes. I can try to stall them for a month. We must build up a case against this Mustapha guy. They're going to want somebody's head."

Ted asked, "Who the hell is this guy? Avram, do you know?"

Shaking his head, Bonapoggio scowled and then smiled and then called the bursar's office. He learned that Mustapha's legal guardian was an uncle named Suleimon Sussi. His present address in America was listed as The Geneva Inn, West Athens, Vermont.

"What is this man doing living at an inn?" Bonapoggio asked out loud to himself.

"Well, Dixon answered, "I know Tom Peterson the police chief there. He and I hunt together. Let me call him and ask him what he knows about the place."

A few minutes of operators and information supplied by the ghostly voices of computers that, for reasons not known to ordinary men, seemed very concerned that the caller have a pencil and paper handy–were there such things as lazy computers who, (or should that be which?), do not like to repeat information? And Jim had the number.

After the usual greetings and a promise to come deer hunting as soon as things in Chaldes permitted, Jim asked Tom what he knew about The Geneva Inn.

"Lily White? Eh? Why not coal black, you bigot? No breath of scandal? Who runs the place? Okay. I have it," Jim said, writing a name down on a piece of elegant notepaper Bonapoggio had by the phone. He continued, "And, Tom, please. This is a very delicate matter. Not a word to anyone. Not even to Doris. Thanks. Oh, and give her and the kids my best. Thank you. Goodbye."

"Well? Any news?" Bonapoggio asked.

"No. The place is as clean as a whistle. Some guy runs it named, ah, let's see...J.J. Rufus. Odd name..."

"My God!" Laura cried out at the same moment Claudia quietly said, becoming very white, "Stafford, I feel a little faint."

Everyone ran over to Claudia and Bonapoggio gave her a little brandy. She was soon her usual color and, although frowning, looked well. She looked around her for a long time, saying nothing.

Stafford knelt down at her side and, gently stroking her hair, said, "Whatever it is, it'll be alright. Tell us, if you can."

Taking another sip of brandy, she explained, "Celeste told me at the hospital that Mike was only my adoptive father and that my so-called 'natural' father's name was J.J. Rufus. I'd never even heard it before."

"Claudia's middle name is Rufus," Stafford pointed out.

"It seems that, after all, it was not your husband who tried to poison you, Claudia," Jim said quietly, "but it might be your father."

"No, Jim," Laura interrupted. "I know this J.J. Rufus from a long time ago. My husband, Lotario, was working for him before he was killed in an automobile accident. J.J. is a coward. He's no murderer. He might want to be in on some sort of frame-up of someone to prove one of his theories about this or that. He was full of theories! But, actual murder...? No. Not J.J. Rufus. I do not know and I cannot even begin to imagine, why he might want to frame Stafford, but, then, no one, not even J.J. Rufus, knows why he does some of the things he does. That Mustapha pig probably referred to her as Mrs. Wyatt. And, of course she would get money only if J.J. died, not if Mike died. And, Stafford would not get anything if she died–except, if J.J. died first. Follow?"

"I think so," Jim said. "But, we do know something about this mysterious man. We are pretty well certain that Stafford was framed. We certainly know the guy who did the actual dirty work. We have some grounds for thinking that this J.J. Rufus is mixed up in this business somehow. What we don't know is how...or even why."

Everyone agreed with Jim's assessment.

"You know," Bonapoggio said, "let me find out something more about Uncle Suleimon Sussi. Excuse me."

He went to the phone and dialed a long distance number with a string of digits that seemed to go on forever and was soon talking in a guttural language that Stafford immediately recognized as Hebrew. After a short time, he hung up.

"Yes," he said to the group, with a puzzled frown on his face. "Ibrahim Sussi. That name is a great one in the Middle East. It is a family that boasts of great financiers, statesmen and scholars. Suleimon is a financier and Ibrahim is a scholar. This Suleimon is a half-brother to Ibrahim, who is older and the patriarch of the family. Mustapha...?" Bonapoggio shrugged dramatically. "And, now," he continued, "Stafford and Claudia would stay here with me, Mustapha will be lulled into a false sense of security and no alarm will be given in West Athens. I shall excuse myself now. I must make some phone calls in order to penetrate the security of The Geneva Inn."

They saw that Claudia was looking tired and glum and they said their goodbyes, after Laura had added a short note on her own adventure with J.J.

"Not much is ugly to that man," Jim said, looking contritely at Stafford.

"No," Laura agreed. "He positively likes the ugly, the mean and the low. That, Captain Dixon, is why I think he did it."

"Laura," Jim answered, "just between us and entirely off the record,

I shall enter your observations under the hard evidence column in my book concerning scientifically admissible evidence."

After he and his housekeeper had seen to it that Stafford and Claudia were settled in comfortably, Bonapoggio made further phone calls. In the space of a few minutes, he had found that Ibrahim Sussi was then pursuing his researches at the Institut Oriental just outside Paris. Since it was then nine-thirty in Chaldes, Paris time would be two-thirty in the morning, Greenwich Mean Time and Professor Ibrahim Sussi was not likely to be at the Institute.

Bonapoggio called the next morning at ten Paris time and was soon talking in Arabic to his scholarly *confrere*. They first exchanged the prescribed flowery compliments, which included the congratulations of each speaker to the other on the nobility of his line of ancestors and on the felicity of being, presently, the distinguished holder of such a noble name. Bonapoggio then told Sussi the story about Father Ryan telling him that Holy Water is thicker than blood and, keeping silent for a moment, while Ibrahim Sussi chuckled out loud at the picture of a Father Ryan lecturing Rabbi Avram Bonapoggio on blood and Holy Water, Bonapoggio continued. "But, between us, I am persuaded that it is ink that is thicker than blood. Eh?"

This story, ending with the great Semitic, "Eh," met with a noticeably guarded enthusiasm on the subtle Ibrahim Sussi's part. "But, what," he asked himself, "could Rabbi Avram Bonapoggio, in New York, be doing telling such anecdotes to me, here, in Paris?"

Bonapoggio waited long enough to let that entirely inevitable question become thoroughly alive in Ibrahim Sussi's active mind and then he told him the story of Mustapha Sussi. When he had finished the story, he continued, "And, so, my esteemed colleague and confrere in ink, since, as I think, ink is truly thicker than blood, I wished to call and to ask you what we might do. For blood is still thick."

"But, what can I do?" Ibrahim Sussi asked in a voice that revealed its distress, even in trans-Atlantic transmission.

"Ah. I am sure that this young scion of your ancient and noble house is only a tool in the hands of a very wicked and depraved older man. My thought, esteemed and noble colleague, is this, that, if we could catch the puppeteer, the puppet need not accompany him to the scaffold. Eh?"

Ibrahim Sussi realized the full extent of Avram Bonapoggio's wiliness. He answered, after a long moment's pause, "Ah! Avram Bonapoggio, subtlest child of Shem, himself the eldest child of Noah, truly, yours is a deep and fertile mind. What, then, may I do to assist?"

Bonapoggio pointed out to Ibrahim Sussi that his near relative, Suleimon Sussi, was presently Mustapha's only American contact with the ancient, noble and very prolific Sussi family and could he, Ibrahim Sussi, relay pertinent information concerning his nephew to this worthy relative, Suleimon Sussi? And, then perhaps, just perhaps, this would help him, Avram Bonapoggio, to redress the terrible wrongs done to a junior member of the noble and ancient Sussi family by a wicked and depraved older man? Perhaps, just perhaps, he, Ibrahim Sussi, along with Suleimon Sussi and him, Avram Bonapoggio, might meet to discuss possible ways to avert this very great disaster which threatened the previously spotless, exceedingly old and honorable name of Sussi.

"And, then, my dear Ibrahim Sussi, we shall see what we shall see. Eh? For, both the reader of Torah and the reader of Holy Koran are equally children of our commonly-shared namesake, Abraham, from whom, I have no doubt, we derived our remarkably precise sense of propriety..."

And, here Ibrahim broke in to finish that sentiment by saying, "Surely, we are equally children of that wiliest of Shem's children, the patriarch of patriarchs, Father Abraham. Good, my learned, virtuous, and, if I may be permitted to seem to run the risk of condescension, my most generous and thoughtful, friend. Give me your telephone listing and I shall call you soon."

Bonapoggio did so and the two scholars bade one another a long and complex farewell.

Just as he was finishing his personal prayers that evening, Suleimon Sussi received a collect call from Paris. He accepted it and was astounded to receive a very strongly worded summons to Paris from his elder half-brother, the great scholar, Ibrahim Sussi. Three days later, while he and his revered elder half-brother sat sipping black coffee in a small Moroccan restaurant in one of the Oriental quarters of Paris, he was told the whole story of his nephew, Mustapha. Ibrahim unfolded the story with a clarity that hid little of his contempt for an adult Sussi who would permit his young nephew to stray so.

"Ass's dung! You seek profit as the bitch greyhound seeks a dog, any dog, to breed with when she is in heat. And, so your charge, that stinking caul of an aborted leprous jackal, Mustapha Sussi, has committed crimes both felonious and dishonorable in the extreme. Shall you both be formally excluded from the family worship? Speak! You who seek gold in the market place as a cock seek corn in the dungheaps of the barnyards of Basrah. Speak!"

Suleimon Sussi huskily asked what he could do to rescue the family's honor. He was told that Rabbi Avram Bonapoggio, the victim's teacher, friend, councilor and patron–"none of which you have been to your own flesh and blood!"–was a great scholar and that Rabbi Avram Bonapoggio's victimized friend, also a notable man of letters, must be cleared of the terrible charge of trying to murder his new wife for her money. "What is more, this wise and merciful man, he whose friend Mustapha Sussi tried to snare, does not wish to sully the Sussi name. He will rest entirely content and forever silent if, but only if, Praise be to Allah the Compassionate, the designer of this very terrible plot against his student, friend, protégé and client, is brought utterly low and the name of the gifted and promising young man of letters, Mister Stafford Wyatt, be totally and forever exonerated, beyond any shadow of doubt. It is thus, and thus only, dung beetle, that I shall rest nights. I shall presently fly to New York. Reserve a place on the Concorde for me and a commodious suite at the Waldorf Towers...both to be paid for by you. Call my secretary and let him know the arrangements. Until then, Suleimon Sussi, live carefully under the merciful, but just hand of Heaven. For you are a Sussi."

\* \* \*

Suleimon Sussi did exactly what he had been told to do. When Ibrahim Sussi had heard from him, he called Bonapoggio, who soon caught a commuter flight to Manhattan. The three met in a spacious Tower suite and they plotted. The conclusion of their machinations was that Suleimon Sussi must observe this J.J. with an eye to separating him from his cronies at The Geneva Inn. Bonapoggio could arrange a séance for them, if Suleimon could fabricate a pretext to get J.J. down to New York as his guest.

His elder half-brother abruptly dismissed Suleimon Sussi, and the next few days were happily spent by the two scholars, talking, arguing, comparing and never concluding. On parting to go back to Paris, Ibrahim Sussi presented Bonapoggio with an early thirteenth century Arabic treatise on Earth Daimones. The Metropolitan Museum, along with the Harvard Divinity School, had been trying to buy this manuscript from the Sussi family for years.

"Here, Avram Bonapoggio. I beg you to be pleased to accept this small, but, as I think, choice gift. Your generous care for my honor and our profession has turned the ink of scholarship into the blood of true friendship. From this day on, dear Avram Bonapoggio, be as a brother to me and to all my family. My descendants, to the uttermost limits of time, shall be brethren to yours. May Heaven bless your mercy...and, Rabbi Avram Bonapoggio, your good manners."

The scholars exchanged a kiss of peace and each bowed deeply to the other.

\* \* \*

Time was now all important. Everyone in town knew that Captain Jim Dixon was friends with many of the Chaldes faculty and there were always individuals around who would ask, in the columns of the local newspapers, why Stafford Wyatt was not being actively prosecuted for attempting to poison his wife. On the other hand, it was agreed by those of the Chaldes crowd who were in on the counter-plot against Mustapha that J.J. must be brought down and that this could be done only with Suleimon Sussi's help.

"Otherwise, ladies and gentlemen," Bonapoggio reminded them, when they had all reassembled at his house, "all motive evaporates. Why would Mustapha Sussi wish to poison Claudia and frame Stafford Wyatt for it? Cui bono?"

Stafford and his friends waited by their phones, from minute to minute, for a call from Bonapoggio, telling them he had heard from West Athens. It came after three endless days, late on Thursday night. It seemed that J.J. had a birthday coming up and that he, Suleimon Sussi, had insisted that J.J. be his honored guest in New York City at the Waldorf Towers, for a small celebration with some of his financier friends from the mid-East.

It was that simple. J.J. accepted at once. Had not Suleimon Sussi been both his richest partner and least ardent admirer? Bonapoggio told him to call back late the next evening. By then, he would have had the time to plot with Claudia, Stafford, Laura and Ted and, if she would agree to it, Mamman.

The editor of the Chaldes Times was persuaded to minimize the number of letters to the editor inquiring about the Wyatt affair and it seemed that the group had nearly three weeks in which to expose J.J. Rufus–but no longer. And, since his birthday party was in two weeks, they all saw his party as their one chance to get him. But, how?

Meeting again at Bonapoggio's, the group saw that he was anything if not cheerful. The shortness of time vexed him, but it did not depress him, as it tended to do with his friends, especially Jim Dixon, who felt with some truth, that this whole mess was in large part his fault.

"I am a scientifically trained detective and I went about this case like a hick!" No one in the room had the slightest inclination to correct his assessment of his own behavior. On the other hand, all was forgiven and they told him to let the past go and to begin to address the problem at hand.

After dinner, Bonapoggio received the call from Suleimon Sussi. Everyone was stone still and looked at Bonapoggio's lips as if they could lip-read Arabic, even if they could not understand a word of it when spoken out loud. After what seemed a long time to the listeners, Bonapoggio put the receiver back into its cradle and turned around. "Good. It is all set. Now it is up to us. The suite is reserved for seven on Thursday, until noon the next day."

"There is not the slightest doubt we could get a conviction on Mustapha Sussi, you know," Jim said. "But, if this attempt to get Rufus fails, then I am not so sure. Entrapment and so on. Slander even. God knows what-all."

Bonapoggio nodded assent, shrugged and continued, "Now then. This frame-up was obviously prepared very carefully. Rufus must have planted Mustapha in your house. If he can frame you, we can net him! And, he knows no more about our suspicions than you suspected him earlier. So...to start. What do we know about this man?"

"That he is terrified of seagulls," Laura volunteered at once, to the amazement of everyone. Then, Laura told the group the outlines of the story of her encounter with J.J. aboard the yacht, The Enlightenment–*La Lumieres*–only leaving out some of the details that might particularly hurt Claudia.

"Good," Jim said, as he began to write on his pad of legal paper. "Let me take that down. I don't as yet see how that might come in handy, but it might. Shall I put down: Item: Terrified of seagulls named Larry?"

"Yes. And, add that he would probably be somewhat upset to see me again," Laura answered.

"Okay. What else?" Jim asked, after he had duly written down these suggestions on his pad.

Claudia added, in a quiet, strained voice, "That I am his daughter. He might be somewhat unnerved to find out he nearly had me poisoned. He certainly did not know who I was."

"Hmm. Perhaps I'll say: Item: Claudia, as unknown daughter, whom Rufus nearly poisoned," Jim said. Then, looking around again, he asked, "What else?"

Mamman surprised everyone by breaking her usual, self-imposed rule of silence. "As a physician, I have known patients very like this man. They are frightened in the extreme of any illness and at once lose their wits when they think they are seriously ill. I once saved an innocent man from the gallows by, shall we say, persuading, the real criminal that he suffered from a very serious malady. It was indigestion. But, I said to him that I could keep him from dying from his ailment if he confessed. He confessed and straightway died by the hangman's noose. He did not die from indigestion."

"Could you help us do this again, with the Rufus man, Mamman?" Ted asked.

She nodded a slight, "Yes."

Stafford slapped his thigh and called out in glee, "My God! The pot! Remember poor Hurlock and the marijuana brownies?"

"Good. Very good," Bonapoggio said. "We give him a good dose of marijuana and he will think what Hurlock thought. This is justice indeed."

Laura whispered something in Mamman's ear and she nodded assent in response. Laura said to the group, "And, we will play bird catchers and animal trainers. Leave it up to us. And, no marijuana. We will supply some choice mushrooms of our acquaintance."

"And, I can make my entrance truly awe-inspiring. I did theater right up through graduate school and I was, so I am told, rather thrilling in the role of Cassandra in the Oresteia," Claudia trilled.

"And, I will replay parts of the rape scene, if need be. Sorry, Claudia. I don't like this either. But, Stafford..."

"Thank you, Laura. The whole damned thing stinks, doesn't it?" Claudia answered.

With Jim Dixon acting as Major General, the group began its preparations for the final scene. The next morning, Laura and Mamman, with Ted along for good luck, drove to Port Washington, on Long Island Sound. The yacht club there had numbers of tame seagulls and, using her peculiar clucking and whistling, Mamman soon had a huge male captured, captivated and, in a short while, totally charmed. They brought it back to Chaldes under cover of darkness and put it, unfed, into a shower stall until it was ravenous with hunger. They then presented it with a number of small fish swimming in a twenty-gallon glass tank. It soon learned to catch its dinner. Then, they moved the tank so that it barely showed from behind a large sofa. The bird that, of course, was named Larry, soon learned to scan the room when he was brought into it. As he caught sight of the tank, he squawked loudly and ran across the room, displaying his full six-foot wing-spread. After four days of this, they hid the tank completely under a tablecloth, and, when he could not find it, Larry uttered piercing shrieks of fury until they uncovered it. In a short time, those piercing shrieks came to be Larry's polite request for his dinner. The stage was now set.

The day of J.J.'s birthday arrived and Suleimon Sussi's Rolls pulled into the circular entrance of the Waldorf Astoria. J.J. was very mellow as he sat in the back seat listening to 1960's golden oldies and drinking rum and coke.

"Finally," he thought to himself, "I'm beginning to make an impression on this man. God knows it took long enough." He mused for a moment over the oddness of the fact that Suleimon seemed to have changed in his feelings for him almost overnight, but, the prospect of a high level, intimate little gathering with some of Suleiman's New York financial colleagues was more than sufficient to erase all unpleasant thoughts from his head.

"The group I work with will be here at nine, tomorrow morning. I have some friends whom I have asked to drop by this evening. I hope this is agreeable to you?"

"Friends? I don't think you mentioned them earlier?"

"Oh, it is nothing. Just a little extra treat for the day of your birth. I have told them something of your astonishing machinations and they are anxious, in the extreme, to meet such a clever manipulator of human destinies, if I may be permitted such liberties of praise."

"Why, thank you. It will be my pleasure," J.J. said, beside himself with his contented joy.

The suite was already set up for their private supper when they arrived. They were both hungry and sat down at the table soon after they arrived. Jim Dixon, in a five hundred dollar tuxedo that he usually wore to homecomings at Harvard, acted as butler. The irony of the idea appealed to him and made him feel less of a fool.

He began by serving cold vichyssoise. Jim then made considerable haste to clear off the soup and serve the main course. J.J. was in a splendid humor.

"The bastard's in some sort of jam! Before this, he has never even given me the time of day, if he didn't have to. He'll have to dance a merry tune for any favors from me!"

The main course consisted of cold oysters, squab in its own consommé, and tiny new peas with mushrooms. The evening's wine was a strong *Chateau-Neuf-du-Pape, St. Michelle*. J.J. wondered for a moment at Suleiman's choice of wines with such a delicate fare, but then shrugged it off as Islamic ignorance of alcohol.

"I'm not feeling quite well," J.J. said, after his third glass of wine.

"Oh, please. Do sit in this chair. It is very comfortable. I am sure that it is merely a passing indisposition," Suleimon said, leading him to a small Queen Anne armchair placed next to a large tubular plastic fish-tank with a number of racing, shiny silver fish. There was a light at the bottom of the tank, but it was not switched on. As he sank back into the chair, J.J. closed his eyes and, then, opening them again, said, in a thick voice, "How distant and still, each object in the room seems. But, the room is blurry at the same time. Oh! I feel terrible!"

"Oh, my! Tell me, Mr. Rufus...is there any history of heart attacks in your family?" Suleimon asked, rushing over to the terrified J.J. and loosening his shirt collar, his face a study in panicked concern.

"Oh, my God! No. I mean...I don't know. Oh, God. Call a doctor. Am I dying?"

Then, right on cue, the door to the suite opened and in walked Laura, with the generically named "Larry" under her arm. His beak was held shut by a large rubber band. J.J. saw her and the bird and he squealed in terror, "What are you doing here?"

He tried to get up out of his chair, but his legs simply would not support the effort. His arms were as heavy as lead and he felt a terrible desire to giggle, even though he was beside himself with genuine fear for his life.

"At the moment of death, J.J. Rufus, our past comes back to us. Claudia Harris, daughter of Mary Harris and John-Jacques Rufus, enter!" Laura said in her deepest, most commanding, voice. Claudia entered.

"I am your daughter. My dead mother was Mary Harris. Good evening, Father. But, just why did you wish to poison me?"

"Oh, God. Oh, God. Stop. What is this?" J.J. said, in a gurgling, strangled voice.

The light at the bottom of the tank next to J.J. came on. The rubber band that held Larry's beak was slipped off. The indignity of having its beak snapped shut had made the huge bird beside itself with fury and so its screech, when it also caught sight of its dinner swimming in the fish tank by J.J., was ear-splitting. Laura dropped the bird and, skimming over the carpet with its six foot out-spread wings, it headed, still screeching, right for J.J.'s legs.

At that moment, Mamman came in. She had dressed in her full costume as La Videnta. Brilliant parrot-feathers sprouted from her tufted hair. Her dress was a loose gown of green, red and silver sequins and, to particularly impress the superstitious J.J., it was festooned with chicken feet and fish heads. She was in her glory, but J.J. was not disposed to find her glorious.

"What, exactly, is killing you, my son?" Mamman asked in her most spine-tingling cackle.

"It's my heart. Please. Call a doctor."

"I am a great healer, my son. But, what crime of yours has called

## Naturally Bad Manners

forth this bird?"

J.J. struggled to get up, but the mushrooms were too much for him. The bird was dancing in fury around his feet and J.J. felt that if his heart did not stop beating first, having this bird castrate him would surely kill him.

"But, tell me this, my son. Why did you want to kill your daughter, Claudia Harris?" As she asked this, Mamman came so close to the immobilized J.J. that the fish heads and chicken feet brushed against his face. And, out of the corner of his eye, J.J. had a very blurred vision of the terrible bird. Its cries of triumph and rage went through his skull like hot needles.

"Why did you do it, my son? Tell us all about it," Mamman asked, in her most sing-song voice, taking hold of a chicken foot and poking one of its long nails into J.J.'s mouth.

"It was only a mistake. A frame-up. I didn't know. I swear. I didn't know who...Oh, God! Stop it! Please!"

Detective Captain Jim Dixon moved in. This is what he had been waiting for. "A frame-up, you said?"

"No. Yes. I don't..." J.J. began to realize dimly what he had said, but Mamman did not much care for the rules of valid evidence and decided that J.J. was not to get off the hook so easily.

"You must die, my son. I cannot, alas, help...well...my religion will not permit it...to cure you in your state of wickedness. You framed Stafford Wyatt and your agents tried to poison his wife, your own flesh and blood. Tell this kind black man the truth and I promise you that you will feel much better, soon. But, if you don't...I cannot say what might happen."

J.J. was beginning to hesitate, but, just then, Larry leaped up on the edge of the tank to get at the remaining fish, which had sought refuge at its bottom. His great wings brushed J.J.'s face as it shrieked its furious delight at having its prey so near.

J.J. broke.

"I'll tell. Just make me well. Get that damned thing away from me. Please!"

\* \* \*

And, so, by an oddly logical quirk of fate, Claudia Harris became a millionaire because her real father did not die when her adopted father did. The financial world was shocked, both to hear that J.J. had confessed to the attempted poisoning of some obscure economist and that he died shortly thereafter. But, his death was as fraudulent as his life. Once the triple effects of the mushrooms, the wine and the fright had worn off, J.J. realized the seriousness of the situation; that is, he realized that Suleimon Sussi, could and was perfectly willing to, ruin him and that, even without him, this bunch of academics seemed to know all the details of the story.

Stafford, Bonapoggio and Ted had come in to be witnesses to J.J.'s confession. Ted listened carefully and, at the end, pointed out to the exhausted J.J. that the "Roman" way was the only way out.

"Look," Ted pointed out, "you have tried to kill your own daughter for a lark and then pin it on your son-in-law. Now, you surely have a series of numbered bank accounts scattered all over the world. It might be a good idea for you to arrange that J.J. Rufus die in something like a tragic boating accident. No bodies recovered. Claudia will get her money and you will not spend the rest of your life behind bars. The food in prison is terrible!" Ted added matter-of-factly, "And, they would probably murder you within a month anyhow. Americans have this thing about fathers trying to poison their daughters."

J.J. caved in. He was last seen by several unimpeachable witnesses, who swore up and down that they saw him fall off a slippery rock into a raging mountain stream in northern New Hampshire–not far from the Canadian border. He had been spending a week with his dear friend and confidant, Suleimon Sussi, while he awaited his trial. His body was never found and the treasuries of a dozen countries greedily sliced most of his empire up. An insurance policy matured at his death and a million dollars was given to Claudia Rufus Harris-Wyatt, who began her joyful dissipation of that fortune by throwing the most magnificent party anyone in Chaldes, including the very cosmopolitan Avram Bonapoggio, or his friend from Paris, Ibrahim Sussi, had ever seen. Jim Dixon expressed regrets, during a local talk show, that J.J. Rufus had escaped justice, but he said he felt certain that Justice seeks out the wicked and that it always finds what it seeks.

# CHAPTER 12

## "One thing only do I require of Thee."

So it was that Claudia prematurely collected her inheritance. Since her bogus father, whom she had loved dearly, had died, her real father began to experience a bogus death which was brought on by his own ignorance that he was Claudia Harris-Wyatt's natural father. As Claudia's father, Mike Harris had lived J.J.'s life and J.J., in dying, died Mike's death, to give his own daughter her premature inheritance.

And, then it came time for the very old Mamman to die. Her life as a healer had been spent in concocting and then applying, her natural medicines to counter what she saw as death's premature claims on her patients. She had made these by factoring simples, specifics and general tonics from the blood, entrails, feathers and skins of the host of living creatures she had killed to cure others. She had borrowed sound and healthy lives from these creatures' bodies and she had loaned these lives to the ailing bodies of her patients.

Mamman awakened one morning several months after J.J.'s bogus death and she felt the presence of her own death. "Angelina, will you and Ted take me back to the volcanic fields of Soufriére? The Earth breathes there and that will revive me, perhaps."

"Of course. We will gladly go with you. You will be well, once the sulfur airs have restored you. Be of good cheer, dear Mamman."

"Oh, Angelina, I am dying."

The Castries airport on St. Lucia had a runway that could accommodate Lear jets. Laura rented one and, as they circled to land, Mamman sat up.

"Why should I die, Angelina?" she asked Laura, in a small, childlike and whining voice. "I have never taken life, except to give it to another, or to nourish myself as a healer. Who shall be the stronger for my death?"

"No one, Mamman, no one."

Mamman lay back and, with a slight smile on her lips, began to doze. When the plane had landed and the door was opened, the ardent light reflected off the snow-white coral sand blinded them. As their eyes became accustomed to the brilliant glare, Ted and Laura could see a crowd of thirty or so islanders surrounding a huge tilt-cart drawn by two red oxen. They had assembled in response to Laura's message that she was coming down with Mamman. The crowd cried out its greetings and love to Mamman and a number of women held their children up for her to bless. By now, Ted could understand a good deal of the island patois and he figured out that many of these children had been made her godchildren in her absence.

Two enormous women stepped out of the crowd and demanded to carry Mamman's stretcher off the plane. They wore long, blue, cotton robes that reached to the Earth and, on their heads, they wore tall turbans the color of ripening bananas–neither altogether green nor yellow. Framing their dark, glistening skin in the brilliant light, their turbans seemed to change color from a deep canary yellow to a bright green yellow. They wore large gold hoops in their ears and necklaces of shark's teeth. The yellow tones of their carved ivory bracelets picked out the subtle yellow tones in their dark skins.

These two women took the stretcher with Mamman on it. Tenderly crooning, they lifted it off the plane and onto the floor of the tilt-cart and, as a child puts its favorite doll to bed at night, they laid Mamman down on the bed of palm fronds, which they had spread thickly on the bottom of the cart. One motioned for Laura to get in with Mamman, while the other gently guided Ted to the rear of the cart.

The red oxen started up. At each step, the brilliant sun glanced off their huge bodies with a different tone of red. Their hooves raised little puffs of snow-white dust and their great mouths foamed pearlite clouds of thirst. The heat beat down on the procession and everyone in it glistened with sweat. Laura held an enormous palm- frond over herself and Mamman, while the two women, one on either side of the cart, slowly fanned the pair in it with other giant, blue-green fronds. The men and women in the procession sang slow, deep songs, and, as they proceeded along on the road to the volcanic fields at Soufriére, each little village added one or two newcomers to the procession. This went on for several hours.

The sun was slowly sinking on the left of the procession. As it turned evermore red, the dark skins of the islanders became more and more copper colored and their cotton robes began to appear washed in a light red dye. Just as the sun was about to touch the sea, which was now blood red, the first hint of sulfur in the air told everyone that the volcanic fields were near. Mamman even sat up and chattered excitedly. The two women gave her raw eggs to eat, along with a little coconut milk by way of drink and, from time to time, Laura washed her face with a white cloth. Mamman lay back on her bed of palm fronds with a contented smile on her face. Then, the procession stopped to eat.

The crowd following the cart had reached over a hundred persons. Somehow, chickens and goats materialized. These were slaughtered amid loud squawks and pitiful bleating, while fires were being built. While everyone ate, the true tropical darkness set in and a myriad of fireflies set up a ballet mocking the tropic skies with its wash of stars. Ted fed Laura bits and pieces of meat through the uprights on the cart and Laura gave Mamman little sips of coconut milk to drink.

After everyone had eaten, the procession started up again and Ted noticed, for the first time, that the oxen had no driver. The two women were walking at the mid-section of the cart and no one was in front of them. After half an hour or so, the procession came to a very sharp twist in the road. The sea was hundreds of feet at the base of the cliff on their left, at the flank of the mountain they saw dimly towering over them. As they rounded this flank, hugging it to keep away from the sheer drop into the booming sea far below them, they entered Soufriére's volcanic fields.

Ted had seen the huge, boiling volcanic fields in Iceland and Yellowstone. But, he had seen and smelled these in the daylight, as a tourist. Here, he saw an enormous tropical moon rise over the sea and illuminate the plumes of vapor rising into the sky, as stinking bubbles of mud collapsed on themselves like diseased organs. The whole place smelled like the guts of a newly butchered goat.

As each of Mamman's well wishers in the long procession rounded the mountain's flank and these fields came into moonlit view, he or she fell silent. After a few minutes, they had all entered the fields and all were still. The only sounds were from the snorting of the oxen, occasioned by a particularly strong whiff of sulfur tickling the lining of their nostrils, together with the faintly hissing sounds of the mud bubbles, as they broke and plopped back into their semi-liquid matrix.

Occasionally, a deep fissure lunged its way to the surface of the earth and a geyser of steam and hot water shot skyward. As the huge yellow moon caught this shower, each droplet celebrated its release from the gloomy depths of the Earth by sparkling its golden, moon lent thanks to the eyes of the procession.

The fumes revived Mamman. She called out to be picked up and placed on the ground, "where I belong." Fronds were taken from the bottom of the cart and Mamman was carefully laid down on them. Several of the nearby women unwound their outer garments to make a large roll of cotton cloth to prop up her head.

A deep silence fell over the crowd. Over the sounds of the cooking mud and the small convulsions of its breaking bubbles, Ted could hear the rumblings coming from the great bellies of the oxen and their deep, serene breathing. But, then, Mamman's cry tore through those ancient golden mists, "Give me breath, Angelina. You know how."

A woman, carrying an enormous red rooster with the most magnificent wattles Ted had ever seen, stepped out of the crowd. She handed it to Laura. Holding its murderous spurs with one hand, Laura then took its head in her other hand and held its beak between her thumb and index finger. Forcing all the air out of her lungs, she took the beak of the bird into her mouth and sucked in. The bird's lungs collapsed, and, wildly flapping its wings in its death-throes, it was thrown to the ground, while Laura put her mouth to Mamman's and breathed the newly taken life of the fearless, hot-blooded rooster into Mamman's old, sick body.

"Oh, Laura. For God's sake!" Ted breathed to himself, as he looked at his beautiful friend and lover kneeling over the old woman, cupping her tiny, gasping head in those lovely hands that had held his own head so often.

"Oh, God, let Mamman go, to save Laura's heart!" Ted prayed to high heaven, with its great, golden moon.

Mamman seemed to feel that prayer. She sat up and cried wildly, "Oh. It's my blood. Give me fresh blood, Angelina. Mine is too old. Too cold. Fresh, young blood. Oh Angelina, please!"

A tiny newborn goat, whose mother had been slaughtered for supper, was brought forward, wheezing in terror. Laura held its muzzle up and it bleated its fear to the lovely heavens as a knife cut its throat. The bleating gurgled into silence and one of the two fat women took a handful of its spurting blood and dipped her fingers into it. Then, she gently applied her bloody fingertips to Mamman's lips, but the old woman and the newborn goat had died together. Ted went to Laura and lifted her into his arms. Desolated by grief, she clung to him as he whispered to her, "Be comforted, dearest of hearts. Now, Laura, I am your flesh of flesh and your blood of blood. Mamman died your life and, now, we shall live her death. It is only just."

\* \* \*

A great priest of Obeah came to the island from Brazil to perform the rites of interment that were due such a great doctor and seer as La Videnta had been. Laura felt it was her duty to go to the interment. Ted begged her not to subject herself to more grief or to the strange and dark rites of this religion, but she was unbending.

"Then I shall come with you," Ted insisted.

"But, you cannot, Ted. You are neither her patient, her blood, nor her colleague. And, we are not married, you remember?"

"Then we shall be married by the priest," Ted answered.

"You would do this for me?"

"Oh, yes. That and much more. You know? I'm just a little glad to have a chance to earn...well, to...yes! To earn...

"You will."

And, so it was that this Roman Catholic orphan, the adopted son of the celibate Father Feeney, subjected himself to a ritual that was both exceedingly unsanitary and extremely distasteful. But, it earned him what he had gotten all too easily before this and Lotario Ursina's widow gave him the whole of her generous heart in exchange, and her pity for Ted was entirely replaced by her delight in his own generosity and courage.

"Your sacrifice touches my heart of hearts, Ted," Laura whispered, as the priest's assistants smeared a mixture of goat's blood and bull-excrement on Ted's genitals. "If I had known..." Laura began to apologize, but Ted's involuntary erection made her forget what she was going to say.

"It's okay. I'm most catholic," Ted answered, somewhat bleakly.

The marriage service ended with a meal, whose main ingredients seemed to be the generative organs and gonads of every animal on the island.

When the meal was over, Ted was a true son of Mamman and he could not be excluded from any celebration that did not exclude all men. The interment itself, which took place immediately after their Obeah wedding, was oddly lacking in drama. Neither Ted nor Laura understood any of the priest's language as the ceremony proceeded, but it reminded Ted of the whistle-click speech of Southern Africa. The simple ritual was soon over. Mamman's body had been anointed with oils and wrapped in a white shroud. She was lowered into a shallow grave, which was then nearly filled with a compost of plants, flowers, bones and the thoroughly rotted flesh of a number of the different kinds of animals and fish eaten on the island. As Laura later told Ted, a local priest would come to the grave at each full moon that year and, as the compost sank, he would fill the grave to ground level with more compost. In years to come, the contents of this exceedingly holy grave could be used to fight off blight, plant-rust and even cancer.

\* \* \*

The whole year following this was difficult for Laura. She threw herself back into her travel consultant work, and, although she did not need it, made a great deal of money. Her nights with Ted were infrequent, but, when they occurred, they were passionate and full of grief. Laura now had no one but Ted. Little by little, however, Laura came to accept Mamman's death and Ted's life. Then, one morning, soon after they had observed the first anniversary of Mamman's death, Laura looked speculatively at Ted over breakfast. Since Marie had not wished to leave after Mamman's death, the house was still full of laughter, children and good food.

"Ted. I am nearly thirty-five. I want a child, but if we have one it will, you know, maybe...that is, it may be very dark. Like Mamman."

"Well. If it's a girl, we can name it Sheba."

"And, a boy?"

"Solomon. He also loved black queens."

Once she had decided to have children with Ted, Laura next began to wonder about its religion. She had been brought up with Mamman, but she had also gone to a British parochial school on the island and she had very pleasant memories of its kind and patient nuns.

"What religion would our child be, Ted?" she asked him one morning. "We cannot raise up a university brat who practices Obeah." She paused and continued in a low voice, "We have to get married in a Roman Catholic Church."

"Why? I like your idea of Obeah. Our daughter. Doctor Sheba Simms, Professor of Biochemistry. She arrives in Stockholm for an international congress on molecular biology, with her briefcase and a crate of chickens. And, she would have a dual appointment as the campus witch doctor. No one would dare vote against her tenure!"

Laura was not paying any attention to Ted's japes.

"I know, Ted. Why not have an enormous conversion and wedding party at the orphanage church...or would that distress you too much?"

Ted was silent for a long time. "That's not bad, Laura. We could invite all of our best friends and make this a real celebration. And, I will take a wife to be..."

Ted could not finish. He clenched his jaws and looked glum. "I will choose my bride of my life...I mean..." he stammered, "I mean, Laura, my life's bride."

"Tell me what you mean, Ted, please. I want to understand you."

"Well, my heart has been given out too many times. I keep losing the people it settled on. When I was ten or so, I dreamed I knew my parents and that they had loved me and then they had died. I made up a picture of them. I could see them absolutely clearly when I shut my eyes before I went to sleep. You know, it's almost like those birth defects, where the baby is born with its heart on the outside. I sometimes look at myself that way. First, this one and, then, that one comes by and takes Ted Simms' heart and massages it for a while. My blood pumps faster and I love the person for a while and then they leave...go away, or die, or...whatever. I want you to make a body with me, Laura...And, Laura, by God, that body will have my heart and your heart, making its blood race in it. I want a body with you and my heart will be inside it."

Laura stopped his mouth with a long kiss. His breathing became slower, but not his heartbeat. After long moments, held together by the binding power of their shared love, they moved apart and Ted finished speaking. "What I am trying to say, Laura, is this. If we get married, let's stay married. No more open-heart surgery for Ted Simms. Do you know what I am trying to say? I'm not being brave and adult, perhaps, but this is the best I can do."

Laura answered by biting his ear, hard.

The wedding was held on Thanksgiving Day. Ted and Laura had visited Cicero in August and spent a week at St. Paul's. At totally unpredictable times during their visit, Laura's eyes would begin to fill with tears and, without speaking she would lean over and kiss Ted's neck.

The new rector was named, "Father Giovanni Rosso." He was a big, fat, ruddy man, with an enormous red beard. It was love at first sight between the three of them. They drank, ate, talked, wept and laughed, from morning 'til night. Ted told his story and Laura told hers. They told him of their marriage by the Obeah priest and Father Rosso was reduced to a state of helpless laughter by the idea of Professor Sheba Simms arriving at Stockholm Airport, with models of organic compounds in one hand and a crate of chickens in the other.

"Yes, yes, *mes enfants*! We must church you both. And, this time, Ted Simms, you can keep your pants on until after the service. Ah yes, you are now living in bliss, to be sure, but you must and you will be, churched! Yes, yes...long practice," and here Father Rosso raised an admonishing finger, "has taught me to deliberate drunkenly and then to judge soberly, or," and here he waved his hands over his head to indicate a complete change of scenery, "to deliberate soberly and then to judge in my cups. Which will it be, my beloved in Christ and in His very suave and joyful dispensation? Only choose and so shall it be. Shall we design your churching soberly and marry drunkenly, or, shall we, this instant, repair to a fine pub of my acquaintance – and, in this immediate vicinity! – And get looped without delay, so that we can reflect over the service?"

They decided, at once, to go and get looped.

On the way to the pub, Father Rosso said, "Ted, you must not at all think that your marriage to Laura is not sanctified in my eyes. Pure sacrifice is always sanctified. I find it a privilege to be here with you.

Your generous love for one another enlivens the love that led me to be a priest. And, for that I thank you both. Thank you, dear friends, thank you. And, now, let's enter and drink!"

They entered, they ordered, they drank and they became drunk. Then, they were "wiseguys," in the way that only drink opens up to humans.

"How wise our Blessed Lord at Canaan," Father Rosso blurted out, after three Stouts. "Consider water, which He so prudently changed into wine. Water! One shaves with it," he snickered, pointing to his enormous red beard, "if, that is, one is so disposed. One cooks vile food, like oatmeal and other such horrors, in it. Sometimes, even, to give the devil his due – and it was the devil that gave water to men, mes enfants, the Creator, in His infinite wisdom, separating water from dry land on which the grape is cultivated...Ah, where was I?"

"You were, surprisingly enough, giving the devil his due, although why that is ever necessary is beyond me. That seems to me to be humans' life-long occupation – giving the devil his due!" Laura observed, herself none too steady after several screwdrivers.

"Ah, yes, thank you. Yes, one also steams artichokes and fine fish, employing this element. Indeed," and here he rolled his eyes to Heaven and patted his enormous paunch, "one must constantly wonder at the wisdom of the Creator. Water, the devil's solvent! And, yet, when used to steam strictly fresh fish and young artichokes... Ah, the devil is a coarse buffoon and the Deity's own fool. Steamed artichokes! The Creator's laugh at Satan's element. Ha!"

"*Mais, Mon Pére,*" Ted answered, "do but reflect! Charged by $CO_2$, we have soda water and that same element, thereby enlivened and, then, in tinctured liberally with a good sour mash sipping whisky, say George Dickel, it becomes a mighty and noble adversary to stupid depression born of excessive sobriety."

Father Rosso was about to answer, but Ted shushed him into silence.

"No, *Pére*, hear me out. I am no celibate and so, I know things concerning water that you do not, Reverend Father. Did you know...but, of course, you don't...At any rate, it is not usually known that the reason men who drink too much are unable to perform the act of love is because they mix too much water with their whiskey! Did you know that? Shush! Both of you. We men then want loving as never before, but we can't perform. The reason for this great misery on the part of men folk and the source of much amusement on the part of our womenfolk is this...take note, for this is not generally known... The whiskey doesn't make us impotent. Indeed, not! The whiskey makes us lecherous. It is the water that does us in!"

"No! Really?" Father Rosso responded, with a look of utter astonishment on his face.

"Yes!" Ted answered, with a sober, smug expression on his face.

"Then, why, Ted," Laura asked, "does a drink with a little whisky and a lot of water enable a man to perform, but not strong drinks? Answer me that!"

"Easy! A little bit of whiskey, in a lot of water, doesn't mix much. It's when there is a lot of water that it mixes and dilutes the...no, the other way 'round. When there is a lot of whiskey and a lot of water, there is the devil, himself, at work. He mixes the water and the whiskey...Oh, hell! Let's have another drink."

And so the days sped by, full of drink and the details of their three lives. Mamman's death and of Ted's part in it, were particularly moving to Father Rosso. "Ah, Laura, you great Sheba of a wise dark, beauty, this Ted is a fine man. Clasp his head often and kiss him into life when he needs it. I love the blue-eyed Visigoth as if he were my very own."

They all drank to this.

\* \* \*

Thanksgiving Day was perfect for the wedding. Cicero had been scrubbed clean, from top to bottom, by the tail end of a hurricane which had been born in the waters off St. Lucia. The guests all stayed at The Friendly Inn, Cicero and, since a friend-of- a-friend of Bonapoggio's was a very major stockholder in the corporation that owned this chain, their meals were all catered and no one, before or since, ever ate at a Quality Inn as did Bonapoggio's friends.

If Mamman's ghost personally delivered a storm that made Cicero clean and smog-free that day, the orphanage church was at its utmost beauty, dressed in its Thanksgiving harvest robes and finery. Piles of pumpkins lined the chancel steps and stacks of cans and fruits framed boxes of clothes and toys piled high on the chancel floor.

Father Rosso had listened very closely to Ted and Laura's account of their Obeah wedding and of Mamman's death and funeral. He started the nuptial Mass dressed in his most splendid vestments, with a number of assistants comprised of young novitiates in attendance. These young men were glowing with love for their mother, the church, and each ritual act they performed in the course of the service was done with a finely-tuned precision that only youthful ardor could lend to these high acts of love and devotion.

Father Rosso began the nuptial Mass by intoning, "All things come of Thee and of Thine own hath we given Thee," a formula usually said only halfway through the service, at the time the collection is to be offered, before the Mass, proper, began. But, Father Rosso had wished to make it clear to the congregation that this wedding service was especially intended by the couple as an act of chosen sacrifice. This had been Father Rosso's idea, seconded by Ted and Laura, to announce that they now chose to sacrifice thereafter in a way that excluded slaughter and the smearing of blood and excrement on what should be private between a man and his wife, between a woman and her chosen husband.

"A sanctified love is our wine. Your conjugal warmth is its sweetness. Never part that mighty and charming bond," Father Rosso continued.

"Amen," the lovers' friends chanted in response.

After the Mass had been performed, Father Rosso preached a short sermon. He called the couple to the chancel steps and spoke to them.

"Dear friends. The wisdom of a celibate priest's nuptial-sermons is always somewhat suspect. The love that passes all understanding, which the wise Greeks called Eros, has never, no, not once, touched my body to make me clasp a woman. But, I think, that self-same Eros has touched me as a celibate priest. It has taken up my vowed, chosen barrenness and it has made it fruitful in my love for my flock."

Ted looked up at the priest and thought that these mysteries were no less dark and impenetrable than those he had experienced on the island.

"My barren life, Laura and Ted, is a creature of my choice. My priestly choice, vocation, if you will, is a human creation fed and nourished by divine love and grace. I am a priest and my love renews old things. Your love, Ted and Laura, shall begin new things. And, dear Laura, your Mamman also renewed old things with the breath of new things. She, too, was a priest, but not of us."

Bonapoggio said a quite audible "Amen to that!" under his breath. He stood in the congregation, looking enormous in his brilliantly colored medieval robes from the University of Salamanca. Father Rosso beckoned him to come forward to the chancel steps and he did so. Then, the priest began to sing a duet with Bonapoggio, after his quiet observation to Laura and Ted, "Your Mamman was a priest of Obeah. Now hear Israel's song of mountains, goats and life. Psalm 114."

Father Rosso began to sing and Rabbi Bonapoggio, in a voice of such richness and timbre as no one had imagined could well up out of his slender El Greco body sang back to him over the heads of the couple. The antiphony roared up to the rafters high above them and then streaked its blessings back down onto the bride and groom.

Raising his great beard to the vaults high above them and, in a bass that buzzed the church's rosette, incensed sunlight into a torrent of crystal-clear comprehension, Father Rosso sang,

*"Hallelujah! When Israel came out of Egypt, the house of Jacob from a people of strange speech,"*

Here, Bonapoggio sang his response,

*"Judah became God's sanctuary and Israel His dominion."*

Turning to Laura, the priest sang his mighty answer,

*"The very sea beheld it and fled. Jordan turned and went back."*

Bonapoggio's lighthearted alto relaxed the seriousness of this miracle, as he turned to Ted and sang,

*"The mountains skipped like rams and the little hills like young sheep."*

Laura turned to Ted and leaned her head on his shoulder for a moment. Then the priest boomed out his response,

*"What ailed you, Oh sea, that you fled? Oh Jordan, that you turned back?"*

Bonapoggio's joyful response rang out again,

*"You mountains that you skipped like rams? You little hills, like young sheep?"*

Drawing himself up and, extending his enormous bulk to its utmost, the priest sang out his counsel,

*"Tremble, Oh Earth, at the presence of the Lord, at the presence of the God of Jacob,"*

The song ended with a sweet, quiet reflection, incarnate in Bonapoggio's clear, sunlit voice,

*"The God of Jacob who turned the hard rock into a pool of water and the flint stone into a flowing spring."*

This ended the service.

Laura Miller and Ted Simms had freely chosen a way of worship for their unborn children. The lives that would someday leap in answer to Ted's embraces, defined as they were by his love for his wife, Laura would have more than a loving mother and father to welcome them into the world of human beings. They would also have a God waiting to welcome them when they left their mother's womb and entered into the light of day.